MAI

P

Trucking and the Public Interest

Trucking
and the Public Interest
The Emergence of
Federal Regulation 1914-1940

William R. Childs

The University of Tennessee Press

The extract from John Steinbeck's *The Grapes of Wrath* is reprinted by
permission of Viking Penguin, Inc. and by permission of William
Heinemann Limited.

The paper in this book meets the guidelines for permanence
and durability of the Committee on Production Guidelines
for Book Longevity of the Council on Library Resources.
Binding materials have been chosen for durability.

Library of Congress Cataloging in Publication Data

Childs, William R., 1951-
   Trucking and the public interest.

   Bibliography: p.
   Includes index.
   1. Trucking—United States—History.   2. Trucking—
Government policy—United States—History.   3. Trucking—
Law and legislation—United States—History.   I. Title.
HE5633.C42   1986   388.3'24'0973   85-5315
ISBN 0-87049-473-2 (alk. paper)

This book is dedicated
to my father,
RALPH CHILDS, JR.
(Capt. USN-ret.)
1918-1984

Contents

Preface

A huge red transport truck stood in front of the little roadside
restaurant. The vertical exhaust pipe muttered softly, and an almost
invisible haze of steel-blue smoke hovered over its end. It was a new
truck, shining red, and in twelve-inch letters on its sides—
OKLAHOMA CITY TRANSPORT COMPANY. Its double tires were new,
and a brass padlock stood straight out from the hasp on the big
black doors. . . .
. . . .

. . . There's the backbone of the joint. Where the trucks stop, that's
where the customers come. Can't fool the truck drivers, they know.
They bring the customer. They know. Give 'em a stale cup of coffee
an' they're off the joint. Treat 'em right an' they come back. . . .
. . . .

The transport truck, a driver and relief. How 'bout stoppin' for a
cup of Java? I know this dump.
How's the schedule?
Oh, we're ahead.
Pull up, then. They's a ol' war horse in here that's a kick. Good
Java, too.
The truck pulls up. Two men in khaki riding trousers, boots, short
jackets, and shiny-visored military caps. Screen door—slam.
Hi'ya, Mae?
Well, if it ain't Big Bill the Rat! When'd you get back on this
run?
Week ago.
. . . .

. . . Truck drivers, that's the stuff. Gonna leave a quarter each for

Mae. Fifteen cents for pie an' coffee an' a dime for Mae. An' they
ain't tryin' to make her, neither.

. . . .

. . . The motor roared up for a moment, the gears clicked in, and
the great truck moved away, first gear, second gear, third gear, and
then a high whining pick-up and fourth gear. . . . The truck tires
sang on the road.[1]

1939. Twenty-five years before, no American author could have described the life of a trucker in such detail. Twenty-five years before,
when John Steinbeck was only twelve, there were no diesel trucks with
steel-blue smoke; there were no uniformed company drivers overly
concerned with time; there was no Route 66; there were no truck stop
cafés; and there were no federal truck regulations.

In this book I use an interdisciplinary approach to describe the rapid
emergence of motor trucking and the imposition of federal controls. In
1935—less than twenty years after the truck had proven its commercial
worth and before the industry had had a chance to mature—Congress
enacted the Motor Carrier Act, the statute that extended regulation to
interstate trucking. My twofold purpose is to describe the business
history of trucking (its economic structure, why and when it appeared)
and to analyze why the federal government began to control the new
business before it had had a chance to develop fully.

The story takes place within the larger drama depicting an evolving
political economy in the United States. From an essentially market
economy in the 1790s, in which there was some but not much government direction, a more and more symbiotic relationship developed
between business and government interests as industrialism drastically
altered the set in the nineteenth and early twentieth centuries. Business
and government wrote a new script that retained the old characters
(private property, wealth and accumulation, and competition) and that
expanded the role of government regulation. The changes did not
proceed smoothly, for neither government nor business really understood how much the state should interfere. Consequently, even though
each desired the same goal—a stable-growth economy—each often
viewed the other as an adversary. And this adversarial relationship
intensified in the 1930s when government and business attempted to
deal with the Depression. From the ambitious yet abortive National
Industrial Recovery Act to the Justice Department crackdown on trusts
late in the decade and from banking and securities regulations to

financial aid for farmers, business and government experimented with new institutions that carried forward the story of capitalism. Thus, the extension of regulation to interstate trucking in the 1930s was not revolutionary, or even anticapitalistic, but instead was part of the evolving tradition of a political economy part private and part public in nature.[2]

As a leading historian of regulation has written, "The major dividend available from the study of regulation [is] the illumination of that shadowy zone where public and private endeavors met and merged, where regulator and regulated experienced a confusion of identity and assumed each other's roles." This shadowy zone is the essence of the political economy, for it is there that the inherent tensions of capitalism, the conflict between the spirit of individual enterprise and the needs of the common good, are most pronounced, most debated, and most obscured.[3] It is within this zone that interest groups compete one against another for governmental policies favorable to them. Motor trucking, with its numerous small-scale firms and the widespread consequences of its operations, reflected these tensions in the 1920s; and when the Depression intensified the conflicts, the movement toward federal regulation gained strength.

Examination of the shadowy zone demands an interdisciplinary approach. An economic analysis alone is misleading, for it tells us what might have occurred, but not what happened or why. Similarly, to concentrate only on the legal trends or political conflicts obscures the relevance of economic realities.[4] The human element also contributes, for competing ideologies and political abilities of the regulated and the regulators help define the winners and losers in public policy. People, moreover, operate within institutions. Business associations and government agencies often assume personalities of their own; some are dynamic, others sluggish in acting upon regulatory issues.[5] What emerges in the narrative that follows is a complex story of shifting relations between men and institutions, played upon a background of economic and legal change and political power struggles.

The book is divided into three parts, in an overlapping chronological order. In Part One, we discover how the business of trucking grew during times of prosperity and depression. Included are vignettes of the people who founded trucking and a description of how their business derived from and promoted the consumer culture. Given the new technology's flexibility, competition with the railways was vigorous. By 1932 nearly 90 percent of trucking firms consisted of only one or two vehicles whose routes covered relatively short distances (compared with the railways then and trucks today). A few consolidations were taking place, but the Depression bred more chaotic competition, as the large-scale railway and trucking firms faced the rate cutting of small-scale independents. Rates charged often failed to equal operating costs. Uncertainty plagued the business and the markets it touched.

Part Two surveys the early private and public attempts to stabilize the effects of the new and competitive technology. Economic responses (consolidation and rate cutting) did not bring stability, so businessmen turned to political responses (state laws and business associations). State regulators, railway officials, manufacturers, and large-scale truckers responded at different times and in different ways to protect their interests. None was successful in the 1920s in bringing stability, but each laid groundwork for action in the 1930s. Meanwhile, the U.S. Supreme Court and the Interstate Commerce Commission also dealt with trucking. The Supreme Court cases heard between 1925 and 1932 clarified the legal issues of truck regulation, reflected the rapid emergence of motor trucks, and contributed to the high tribunal's shift from a restrictive to a permissive view of government control of business. The ICC's early responses to trucking present an interesting case study of regulatory administration. Drawing from secondary and manuscript sources, I suggest that it was within a pragmatic method developed over several decades of railway regulation that the ICC discovered trucking and then designed and promoted a structure to regulate it. The pragmatic method, however, always seems to have lagged behind the changes in the economy; the ICC was the last major interest to recognize the regulatory issues the truck had created.

Parts One and Two, then, establish the background and the issues for the political and bureaucratic story presented in Part Three. The narrative diverges into two paths in the spring of 1933, only to merge again early in 1935. One path leads to the New Deal experiment in industry self-regulation during which the National Recovery Administration forced all trucking interests to join into one national trade association. Although the experiment failed to bring stability (rate cutting continued), it did produce the American Trucking Associations, Inc. (ATA), which in a brief fifteen months matured to the point that its leaders could influence national legislation. The other path led to federal regulation. In 1933 Congress ordered the Federal Coordinator of Transportation to find a solution to the transportation problem that plagued the economy. Under the leadership of Joseph B. Eastman, a member of the ICC, the coordinator's office investigated the issues and concluded, in part, that extension of regulation to trucking would be in the public's interest. With help from the ATA, Eastman persuaded Congress to enact the Motor Carrier Act in August, 1935. In the closing chapter, we will look at the early years of regulation and note the relationship between the regulated and the regulators who attempted to administer the controls Congress had authorized. The partnership was a close-knit one and the narrative will show why this was necessarily so.

In one sense, this story focuses on the notion of "the public interest." Most participants used the term; the Motor Carrier Act included it; but it was an elusive concept that changed over time, following the rhythms of the political economy. The debate between those who favored competition for trucking and those who supported regulation was really a debate over the nature of the public interest: would society be better served if trucking matured free of government controls with all the uncertainty that entailed, or would society benefit more from the imposition of regulations that by their nature would restrain private initiative and technological innovation? Given the complexity and breadth of the industry, an important issue was whether it was even possible to construct a system of controls. A third option, government ownership, was never seriously raised. Government ownership of the railroads and telephones had been considered, but those two industries fit the concept of a public utility and trucking did not.

In another sense, this story focuses on special interests and the cartelization of trucking. From the early 1920s on, many groups advanced schemes to control competition in motor trucking. Generally, truckers themselves preferred self-regulation; others, such as railways and state commissioners, desired government regulation. Self-regulation involved educational programs sponsored by truck associations that were designed to improve business practices and eliminate unscrupulous truckers. Government regulations, on the other hand, involved deciding who could be a trucker, what rates he could charge, and what size vehicle he could use; these controls were designed to restrict the growth of trucking and to protect older forms of transportation. Whether educational or restrictive in nature, these regulatory programs reflected a key theme in this story: for the most part, unfettered competition was not a guiding hand. Instead, cartelization, the use of economic controls to eliminate competition, shaped the growth of trucking.

Those who desired cartelization of trucking had to deal with other themes in the political economy. Too often studies of regulation ignore the role of legal issues. Whether the states or the national government or some combination of the two could implement economic controls was a constitutional question. Even after the courts defined the boundaries of regulation in 1932, the growing body of administrative law continued to influence the story. Regulatory procedures evolved from practices begun in the early years of the ICC, but novel ones emerged also as the commisioners responded to the peculiar features of trucking. Related to the public interest and to legal themes are the structure of the industry and of the bureaucracies involved. The industry structure—its atomistic and local characteristics and its central nature in the economy as a transportation mode—may have presupposed and, indeed, accelerated the requests for regulation and then dictated the forms that regulation assumed.[6] The nature of the bureaucracies that played prominent roles and of their interactions also affected the development of public policies.

Apparent throughout this story is the importance of personality. The management and administrative abilities and the ideologies and desires of competitors and regulators alike sometimes fell victim to and sometimes altered the laws and institutions with which they dealt. Of the several hundred thousand anonymous truckers who composed the industry and the many bureaucrats who regulated it, one in particular, Joseph Eastman, rose above the din of competing voices and conflicting issues to forge a system of controls.

The story that follows, then, is a complex one, demanding excursions from the central narrative to establish economic, legal, bureaucratic, and biographical perspectives. Thus, although it is focused on trucking, it reflects the inherent conflicts of the American political economy. In addition, the empirical evidence presented calls into question those modern theories that suggest trucking should not have been regulated.

Although interstate bus lines were regulated along with interstate trucking firms, I have omitted that portion of the story. The two businesses were quite different, even if they both used the highways, for buses hauled people on identifiable systems while trucks hauled freight wherever and whenever business dictated.

Introduction
Genesis

The term "truck" has been associated with small-scale trade and everyday human intercourse. Assuming various spellings (trucke, truke, troke, trock, troc), the concept appeared in the English language as early as the fourteenth century. Perhaps the earliest use of "truck" to connote a physical form of conveyance appeared in the seventeenth century: "a little wheele used under sleds. Gunners call it a trucke." In transport language, the term included wheeled vehicles sturdy enough to haul large stones as well as hand-propelled, wheelbarrowlike carts used to move small pieces of freight and luggage around railroad depots. By the late eighteenth century in America, "truck" also signified market garden produce or vegetable farming: "A large Room . . . for his Customers to lodge in, and deposit their Market-truck" (1784); "I was drivin / my two-mule waggin, With a lot of truck for sale" (1890).[1]

Although the advent of motor power in the late nineteenth century altered the physical nature of trucking, the term has retained many of its earlier meanings. In fact, the modern truck was born from several historical continuities; it did not appear in a vacuum but rather from the progression of transport and technological developments. Much as the steel rail and steam locomotive had solved the problem of hauling heavy loads over long distances, so too did the internal combustion engine offer a solution to moving small shipments more quickly and efficiently than horses, railways, or steam wagons could do it. While electric motors caught the fancy of some (in 1894 *Scientific American* predicted that it would supplant all other motors), it was the internal combustion engine that carriage makers and bicycle engineers used to produce prototype automobiles and trucks. Much of the early motor vehicle development in America materialized in the Midwest, for the hardwood forests of Michigan and Indiana had been the backbone of the carriage industry, the immediate ancestor of trucking. Meanwhile, experimentation proceeded in Germany, France, and England.[2]

In the United States in the 1890s, the relatively fragile motor conveyances required smooth road surfaces for efficient operation. Few such roads existed. As popular culture embraced the cycling craze and the national economy demanded more markets, numerous groups began demanding better highways. Cyclists, farmers, and ironically, railroad executives marshaled their forces and created the Good Roads Movement. Articles in newspapers and magazines extolled the virtues of hard-surfaced roads. Weatherproof arteries to the major railway depots would benefit farmer and railroad alike; good roads would furnish quicker access to rural areas for traveling doctors; and they would encourage people to buy autos, which in turn would eliminate the central cause of disease in the cities, the horse. These appeals, however, produced scant results. The states did not have the money, and it was not until 1916 that Congress enacted the first (not very comprehensive) national road-building program.[3]

Despite the lack of good roads, inventors and engineers improved the capabilities of motor-driven vehicles. In 1902 the invention of the steering knuckle (the coupling between the front axle and the steering wheel) increased the versatility of autos and trucks, for it allowed the front wheels to turn without moving the entire axle. The Burton cracking process produced cheaper and more efficient fuel mixes. By 1915 new rubber fabrics and pneumatic tires increased load capacities beyond three thousand pounds. Charles F. Kettering and Vincent Bendix in 1912–13 replaced the crank with an electric starter that saved time and prevented injuries.[4]

These improvements notwithstanding, the modern truck was not an everyday sight in America on the eve of the First World War. Historian James J. Flink has suggested that public acceptance of the truck lagged behind that of the automobile because large-scale examples of its abilities were needed to persuade manufacturers to produce them. A few privately funded road tests (in 1896, 1903, 1904, and 1916) failed to raise commercial consciousness. Although the trade journals *Power Wagon* and *The Commercial Vehicle* appeared in 1905, widespread acceptance of the truck would not occur until the u.s. Army motorized its cavalry ten years later.[5]

The nature of trucking was basically individualistic—one driver, one truck. As with so many elements in the modern political economy, however, trucking could not avoid collective activity. Organized actions began early in the twentieth century when the Society of Automotive Engineers (SAE), founded in 1905, promoted the standardization of parts in motors and of viscosities in lubricants.[6] As we will observe through the narrative that follows, collective activity at once defined and harnessed the new technology and affected the people who used it. Motor trucking would continue to embrace the trading of small-scale items, but the method and extent of trucking commerce would change drastically from the earlier periods.

PART ONE

A New Business Appears, 1914–1932

One is struck by the fact that the truck is exhibiting a good deal of independence. Its place in the economic scheme does not seem to be entirely that of a passive agent subject to human planning and direction. People begin using it, for one reason or another, and soon find it is taking them somewhere—possibly somewhere of which they had no notion in the first instance.

—*The Traffic World*
April 12, 1930

I

War, Commerce,
and the Motor Truck

In 1914 Henry C. Kelting stripped the rear seat from a Ford roadster to convert it into a motorized van and began carting light freight between loading docks and shops within Louisville, Kentucky. More efficient than horse-and-wagon firms, his business grew the following year to embrace a 180-mile route on which he delivered city goods to country stores and farm produce to urban markets. Then, taking advantage of the wartime economy, he hauled foodstuffs to three nearby army camps. Kelting added new vehicles only after he had secured new contracts during this initial phase of his motor-trucking career.

Promise of greater success after the war motivated Kelting to join others in exploiting the new business of trucking. In 1919-20 shippers and chambers of commerce encouraged the new corporation, railroads furnished start-up capital, and the Union Transportation Lines was established. The joint venture began with a terminal, sales facilities, and nearly twenty trucks; as business boomed, Kelting and his partners added a repair shop and still more vehicles. Union Transportation at its height daily handled 150,000 pounds of freight, mostly milk and livestock. The use of tractor-trailer rigs helped to sort the shipments and to streamline operations. Like wagons from which the horses could be unhitched, trailers could be dropped off at docks or stores in the morning and picked up in the afternoon. Fewer power units were required since one tractor could manage several trailers per day. Despite such economies, Kelting watched operating costs soar: tires cost $100 each; some bolts, $1.75; and axles, which broke often on the unimproved Kentucky roads, $45. Costs soon exceeded revenue and Union Transportation declared bankruptcy only a year or so after its founding.

Kelting tried again. He furnished a new terminal, the Central Truck Depot, to truckers who had purchased the old Union equipment at auction. One of Kelting's first customers was a desk and chair factory in Jasper, Indiana. Thereafter, an enameled kitchenware manufacturer, a meat-packer, a baker, and a hardware wholesaler signed delivery agreements. In 1928 Kelting reinvested his profits to build larger facilities.

Central Depot embodied a mixture of nineteenth- and twentieth-century business practices. It consolidated numerous functions under one roof and yet retained a flexibility attractive to shippers. Clerks processed waybills and settled claims for losses and damages, and dispatchers coordinated shipments, trucks, and drivers. As a result, the four-day delivery time of the railways was reduced to one. Such speedy and regular service enabled manufacturers to lower inventory costs and retailers to respond quickly to consumer demand. Central Depot, moreover, included a personal touch: initial business dealings always occurred in person, either in the terminal or at the country store or on the farm. After a contract was signed, customers informed the drivers or used the telephone to place new orders. These efficient truck services supplanted the sluggish railway system, which had not reached many of the small towns anyway.[1]

This story of failure and success reflects many elements in the new transport business of the 1920s. Kelting was not alone in taking advantage of the wartime economy. World War I thrust motor trucking from an initial period of experimentation, adaptation, and growth into an era of rapid expansion. After the war, individual initiative, large-scale manufacturing, technological advances, and highway construction and other government actions interacted with the burgeoning consumer economy, and modern motor trucking was born. Within a decade, trucking affected such diverse areas as plant location, market distribution, and eating habits. The major difference between the truck revolution and those of the steamboat and railroad of earlier times lay in the short time required to complete the changes.[2] Before the revolution could begin, however, the commercial society had to be convinced that the new technology was adaptable to its needs.

I

The first full-scale test of the motor truck's capabilities occurred during the second decade of the twentieth century. The U.S. Army first realized the advantages the truck provided, thus continuing its role, begun in the early years of the Republic, of supporting sound transportation.[3] Initial ventures met with skepticism, but individual efforts, army-sponsored field trials, and actual combat experience silenced the doubters by 1919.

General Nelson A. Miles, the famous Civil War and Indian Campaign veteran, first perceived the need for motor vehicles in the modern army. In 1903 in his last report before his retirement, Miles suggested that five truck units replace an equal number of cavalry units. The wisdom of the retiring officer was ignored for eight years until Captain William F. Williams of North Carolina took up the cause. Although manufacturers and officers scoffed at his ideas, Williams persisted in his crusade and in 1912 received official permission to conduct two field trials. The first one covered fifteen hundred miles between Washington, D.C., and Fort Benjamin Harrison, Indiana; the second, shorter one followed a march from Dubuque, Iowa, to Aparta, Wisconsin. Numerous setbacks marred both journeys. The army overloaded vehicles, straining chassis and driveshafts; engines overheated as trucks moved at foot-soldier pace; and the ever-present mud of dilapidated roadways slowed the convoy advance. Overall, however, the trials proved successful. Despite the protests of traditionalists harnessed to the cavalry, the tests clearly showed the potential adaptability of the truck to army needs.[4]

American armed forces employed motor vehicles during the Mexican Campaign of 1916, but several problems still forestalled efficient application. Insufficient numbers of trucks and of drivers and mechanics to man and maintain them delayed General John J. Pershing's quest of the elusive Pancho Villa. Spare parts were difficult to locate, for the campaign's motor pool, reflecting the infancy of and intense competition in truck manufacturing, comprised 128 makes and models. Nonetheless, truck convoys supplied troops more than two hundred miles from the U.S. border.[5]

The Mexican experience proved fortuitous. When General Pershing led the American Expeditionary Force into the First World War, he requested fifty thousand motorized vehicles to aid him. Such numbers did not exist. Despite the success of 1916 and that of the Europeans since 1914, American military and manufacturing planners had not foreseen the value of the truck in wartime, and the AEF had to borrow vehicles from France and Italy. Ironically, trucks that were produced in the United States were slow to arrive in Europe because a massive railroad jam on the American East Coast blocked deliveries. By the time assembly lines were in full swing, hostilities had ceased.[6]

The war experience nevertheless thrust the truck into the American consciousness. For example, at the direction of the Highway Transport Committee of the Council for National Defense, some of the 227,250 vehicles produced in 1918 were loaded with valuable war goods and driven from the Midwest to East Coast docks, clearly demonstrating the utility of the new technology. Wartime demands, moreover, stimulated advances in manufacturing, most significantly in the cooperative movement toward standardization of parts. Lighter, stronger materials and sturdier pneumatic tires appeared in response to the rigors of combat. A new device, the fifth wheel, contributed to efficient allocation of resources during the war effort. Attached to the rear of a tractor, it permitted easy coupling and uncoupling of trailers. Doughboys returning from Europe transferred working knowledge of the truck to the commercial society; their experience and the excess supply of trucks that were never shipped helped set the stage for the expansive growth of the motor trucking business.[7]

2

The war experience and a generally prosperous economy encouraged manufacturers to build more vehicles. Between 1918 and 1925, yearly truck production totals increased from 227,250 to 557,056. As in the railroad experience of the 1880s and 1890s, big business practices and technological innovation created a period of intense competition that resulted in an oligopoly of truck manufacturers. At least 314 different truck firms appeared at one time or another before 1925, but most of these had disappeared by the end of the decade when two firms controlled nearly 75 percent of the market. Like most large-scale enterprises, Ford and Chevrolet (General Motors Corporation) followed specific strategies to gain substantial market shares of 42.4 percent and 30.5 percent respectively. Typically, each utilized mass production to cut costs, created distribution systems to sell its products, and secured financial and legal expertise to sustain its dominance.[8]

Despite the market shares held by Ford and Chevrolet, the inherent one-man-one-truck nature of trucking presented opportunities for smaller firms unable to undertake large-scale production. By 1929, about nineteen manufacturers still remained in business. The success of several of the small firms—Mack with 1.2 percent of the market; Kenworth, whose share at that time is unknown; and International Harvester with 6 percent of the market—shows that attention to special features in the final product could sustain small-scale manufacturers in this early period. A couple of independents entered the competition with the advantage of name recognition. Mack's Bulldog and eighteen thousand White trucks had performed well during the war in Europe.[9] For the most part, however, the independents who survived the 1920s did so because they used technology to reduce costs and to offer variety in their products.

Mack Trucks, Incorporated (known as International Motor Company until 1922, when it changed its name to distinguish itself from International Harvester), used technological research to emerge as one of the successful independents. Between 1919 and 1928, Mack filed 270 patents; between 1928 and 1935, the firm added 576 more. These innovations boosted sales well into the 1930s. One of the most important discoveries occurred in shock-absorbing materials. Beginning in 1920, engineers tested suspension systems constructed with live rubber. Better than others, the Mack Rubber Shock Insulator (1921) cushioned the vehicle from hard jolts suffered on rough roads. Throughout the decade, the company experimented with rubber in mounting engines, transmissions, and radiators. The results not only softened the ride for the driver but also prolonged the life of the entire truck.[10]

Another independent, Kenworth Motor Truck Corporation (1922), emphasized important characteristics of trucking, adaptation and specialization. The basic frame and four-wheel motor vehicle proved readily adaptable to diverse job requirements. Road builders, freight haulers, oil well drillers, and produce farmers each required special equipment. From the beginning in 1915 (as Gersix), Kenworth workers consulted individuals and engineered customized trucks to perform special tasks. For example, clients in the Pacific Northwest (where Kenworth was located) wanted trucks capable of hauling heavy logs over rough terrain; Kenworth produced a better, stronger axle for such work. Specialization did not necessarily slow the firm's production totals, for while only 99 Kenworths were finished in 1926, 159 rolled out the following year.[11] Kenworth thus reflected the complex relationship between manufacturer, customer, and technology in the emerging business of trucking.

The International Harvester Company, which had produced over nine thousand trucks for the war, was another independent that successfully adapted to the competition. Located in the Midwest where motor trucking first proliferated, the firm met the desires of commercial truckers for strong, light-weight, and speedy vehicles. In the early 1920s, International presented its Model S design. A few years later, the Red Baby cabs with softer seats and more conveniently arranged instrument panels answered drivers' demands for comfort. International's managers realized, however, that these innovative designs would be bought only if an effective sales system existed. The newer products, moreover, contained more complicated machinery, which required trained mechanics. International accordingly established service stations staffed with skilled workers and tied these to the sales branches positioned across the country, a response that followed the legacy of the founder of the firm nearly a century before. Creative managerial organization, then, allowed International to retain a profitable share of the market.[12]

Technological innovation, specialized production, and aggressive marketing created a vibrant manufacturing industry that produced more and more motor vehicles that in turn encouraged the expansion of trucking. Of these factors, technology remained central. Advancements in refrigeration, for example, extended in distance and volume the distribution of perishable goods. From grass and sawdust insulation and barrels of water and ice, the technology of refrigeration improved to embrace dry ice and eventually mechanical devices. As nighttime driving increased during the 1920s in response to market demands and the desire to avoid the growing number of daytime pleasure drivers, lighting became important. Early in the decade, electric headlights and side and tail lamps replaced oil and acetylene lamps. Electric stoplights appeared ten years later. As driving in darkness became sufficiently safe, truckers established overnight delivery schedules, an advancement railways could not duplicate.[13]

The pneumatic tire, in conjunction with smoother roads, stimulated the growth of trucking more than any other innovation. At once it allowed longer hauls with heavier loads and transportation of breakable goods without the expensive packing crates common in railway service. Connected to improved tires was the progress achieved in brake systems. On the earliest trucks, external devices similar to those on wagons (where a half-moon-shaped metal shoe directly contacted the wheel to create friction) constituted the sole means of stopping the vehicles. Since drivers often overloaded trailers, these systems failed to provide sufficient stopping power. As loads grew still heavier, truckers required more efficient and longer-lasting brakes. By 1930 engineers had developed hydraulic brakes applicable to all wheels of the truck.[14]

New truck styles and innovations in the 1920s reflected not only drivers' needs but also reaction to state laws. The cab-over tractor in which the driver's seat, steering wheel, clutch, gearshift, and dashboard rested directly over the engine, was a direct response to regulations restricting vehicle length. The design reduced the length of the tractor unit, allowing longer trailers to be used and aiding the growing number of interstate trucking firms that, because of different state laws governing trailer lengths, had been forced to transfer loads from one trailer to another at state lines. Trailer manufacturers were less fortunate. Different state laws respecting length, width, and height played havoc with standardization of vans. Application of lighter materials such as aluminum and magnesium remained the only response to these laws, short of changing them.[15]

Manufacturing statistics for the 1920s indicate the improvements achieved in overall carrying capacities. Nearly 85 percent of trucks manufactured early in the decade were lightweight, with a carrying capacity of 3/4 to 1 1/2 tons. Near the end of the decade and during the early years of the Depression, medium-size vehicles dominated. By 1931, 1 1/2- to 3 1/2-ton trucks made up 70 percent of production.[16]

Truck manufacturing affected the economy in significant ways other than producing larger transportation units. At mid-decade the motor vehicle industry (including autos and trucks) topped the list of the ten largest wholesale producing industries, outdistancing meat-packing, gasoline, rubber, and plate glass. It also supplied, directly and indirectly, jobs for over five million workers. In the financial sector, capital investment increased from $1.015 billion in 1919 to $2.089 billion in 1926. These totals fell somewhat after 1926, but still totaled $1.880 billion in 1930.[17]

Truck manufacturing, then, held a complex relationship to the economy. Even though two firms controlled a majority of the market, smaller independents occupied important specialized roles. As a whole, the industry stimulated technological innovation, utilized raw materials and finished products, and provided jobs. Manufacturing, moreover, buttressed another business, that of highway construction.

3

Although war surplus vehicles and more and more new autos and trucks crowded America's roads in the 1920s, no national highway system existed. Indeed, the majority of roads and bridges could not support the increased traffic. The prewar Good Roads Movement, historically tied as it was to local and state support, had failed to provide for the demands of the consumer society. Farming and railway lobbies, among others, had successfully pressured President Woodrow Wilson to sign the 1916 Federal Road Aid Act, but that statute fell short of forging a national highway system. Federal monies would be used to construct only 7 percent of the proposed state roads.[18]

Government promotion of highways expanded during and immediately after the First World War, with several agencies contributing to the upswing. The U.S. Army publicized a transcontinental convoy that once again proved the truck's commercial value. Postal service, national defense, forest development, and promotion of general commerce were the central reasons offered for federal aid to road construction. Congress established the Bureau of Public Roads in 1918, and by 1919 every state had a highway department. A reflection of the progressive belief in institutions and trained experts, state highway department officials designed and directed the construction of road systems. To hasten the task, Congress in the Federal Highway Act of 1921 distributed twenty-five thousand surplus war vehicles to the states. Despite this infusion, however, a conservative road-building program emerged.[19]

The trend in road-building, according to a Brookings Institution study, was to "maintain a decreasing total mileage at a somewhat higher standard of serviceability and to pay off previously incurred debt." Total mileage in the United States in 1921 was 2,924,505, of which 202,915 miles represented intercity highways. Of the intercity roads, only 41.6 percent were "surfaced" and the majority of those were of inferior quality. During the decade, the quantity of road mileage increased only slightly, but the quality improved dramatically. Of the 3,034,893 miles in 1930, 329,000 represented intercity roads and 73.8 percent of these were surfaced. Fifty percent of the surfaced roads were now of good quality.[20]

Financing for quality improvement programs presented a problem, for the federal government was less than fully committed, state and local coffers were usually lean, private road construction was not feasible, and the land grant solution used for nineteenth-century rail-roads was not seriously considered. Thus, a new form of finance had to be devised. What appeared was perhaps the only popular tax ever enacted in the U.S., the gasoline tax.

In 1919 Oregon, Colorado, and New Mexico simultaneously and spontaneously adopted the gasoline tax. Because this tax automatically measured vehicle use of the roadways, it was seen as a legitimate and equitable means to pay for construction and maintenance. Highway department officials supported the concept, and by 1925 forty-four states financed road construction through gasoline taxes; by 1929 all states did so. The new tax aroused scant popular objection, for it was paid in small amounts over long periods. Moreover, highway conditions were so bad—mud in winter, dust in summer—that road users willingly contributed to improve the roads. A petroleum glut on the market also conditioned public acceptance. The price of gasoline declined, from an average of 29.38 cents in 1920 to 16.98 cents in 1931. Thus, as legislators raised the tax, consumers did not object because the price appeared to remain the same. The oil industry opposed the concept early on, but came to believe that the better roads the tax made possible would create more motorists to buy petroleum products. Since improved highways meant improved service, bus and truck groups supported the tax. As the assessments increased, however, and as legislators found nonhighway programs to fund with such an easily collectible levy, road user groups opposed any more increases.[21]

The gasoline tax modified highway financing. In 1921, gasoline receipts paid only 0.8 percent of state roads; by 1931 this had risen to 35.3 percent. Adding motor vehicle fees, those who used the highways paid 58.5 percent of the costs. Federal aid, meanwhile, increased to 20 percent. One study reported that while motorists had not paid a fair share of the costs in the early 1920s, by the end of the decade, they "as far as state highways are concerned, not only [pay enough taxes] to cover the maintenance and interests costs and current depreciation, but also to make up a substantial part of the deficiency of collections in the early years."[22] The gasoline tax, then, furnished an equitable source for road construction funds.

4

The war, motor vehicle manufacturing, technological innovations, and better highways were the underlying conditions of the truck revolution. To understand the complete picture, we must look also at the people who built the new service business. During the 1920s, personal contact between motor carrier and shipper remained a central reality of trucking. Not only did truckers supply better and quicker service than did the railways, but they also furnished a human element that big business did not.

As Henry Kelting's story indicated, trucking provided a fertile field for individual initiative. Truckers succeeded or failed on the basis of individual savvy within a relatively protected environment, for the government supplied the roads and controlled the major competitor, the railroad. As more truckers appeared, however, each met forces seemingly beyond his control: rate cutters and incompetent businessmen among themselves, railroad-sponsored restrictive state laws, increasing taxes, and a growing oversupply of transportation. One of the central paradoxes in the story is that those who succeeded in the 1920s on the basis of individual ability found themselves in the 1930s acting in concert to protect the business they had built.

In Norwalk, Ohio, in 1913 John F. Ernsthausen and his partner modified the back of a 1909 Overland auto purchased for six hundred dollars and used it to deliver eggs. By 1921 their produce company had grown to the point that they hired independent truckers to haul their yield to Cleveland. Two years later, Ernsthausen bought out the independents for a thousand dollars, receiving three trucks, delivery contracts, and the truckers' good will. The new Norwalk Truck Line now included general freight hauling. Unfortunately, the firm's expansion slowed when Ernsthausen overextended himself playing the stock market. He lost investment capital and profit. Thus, the company "sort of tumbled upward rather than rationally growing."[23]

Before the Great War, A.J. Harrell sold buggies, horses, and mules. In 1921 he and his brother established the Yellow Cab Company in Oklahoma City. Diversification ensued; a bus line appeared in 1924 and, shortly thereafter, a system of retail gasoline stations. The latter not only reduced operating expenses for the buses and taxicabs but also created additional revenue. Harrell then sold the bus company and, with the money from the sale, developed a consolidated trucking terminal, the Yellow Freight System. The service stations once again proved convenient. An astute businessman, Harrell purchased cattle and petroleum interests and, naturally, his trucks hauled beef and oil field equipment.[24]

Maurice Tucker's life unfolded along the lines of an Horatio Alger novel. A Polish immigrant who arrived in America in 1902 at age eleven, Tucker worked first for the railroads, then attended business school where he learned accounting and sales techniques. Then he sold jewelry, later cigars, and eventually settled in South Bend, Indiana, where he managed a stationery supply office. These diverse jobs taught Tucker the high value customers placed on service. Early in 1927, he joined Pierce-Arrow truck manufacturers and designed an effective accounting system for the firm. Later that year, with only $645, he and his brother-in-law leased three trucks and formed the Ziffen-Tucker Freight Company. In 1929 the two split the company and Tucker received rights to the South Bend area. The Crash caught Tucker with $55,000 in debts; in the Alger tradition of moral responsibility, he focused his energies solely on trucking and paid back the full amount in less than two years.[25]

Carl Ozee, a descendant of French immigrants, entered trucking through his in-laws. In 1911 he left a railway job to work for Hayes Transfer Company, a local cartage firm in Mattoon, Illinois, owned by his wife's father. In the mid-1920s, because it offered faster service for small shipments than did the railroads, Hayes Transfer secured its first long-distance contract with the Loose-Wiles Biscuit Company. Later, for similar reasons, Procter and Gamble shipped with Hayes. Ozee diversified operations early in the 1930s to include larger terminal facilities that could handle greater amounts of small-scale shipments. By mid-decade, Ozee's 2,200 trucks and trailers served points in Kentucky, Missouri, Indiana, Illinois, Michigan, and Wisconsin.[26]

Still another enterprise grew from a marriage. In 1928, Mr. and Mrs. Willard E. Drennan, of Hempstead, Texas, acquired a Model T Ford on credit with no money down and entered the oil field hauling business. The Drennan Truck Line soon earned $1,500 to $2,000 per month. Mr. Drennan died in 1929, but his wife, Lillie, assumed the management. She continued driving trucks and made a reputation for herself not only because she was a woman managing a trucking firm but also because she carried a six-shooter when she drove alone. Lillie Drennan was the first state-certified female truck driver in Texas and perhaps in the entire country.[27]

The Ernsthausen, Harrell, Tucker, Ozee, and Drennan firms represented legitimate enterprises. Illegitimate trucking operations also arose in the Prohibition decade, but for obvious reasons, few records remain available. A former truck driver for one of these business, identified only as Mr. X, remembered that Johnny Torrio, an associate of Al Capone in Chicago, bought war surplus vehicles and used them to transport illegal liquor into the U.S. from Canada. In substantial five- to eight-ton loads, trucks hauled whiskey from points on the Great Lakes to the Midwest for domestic consumption.[28]

These brief sketches suggest several important themes about the emergence of the new business of motor trucking. No special qualifications seem to have been necessary. The variety of previous business experience and the low capital requirements show entry into the motor carrier business was rather simple. Each trucker responded to specific geographical opportunities. The Drennans took advantage of the oil boom in southeast Texas; Tucker capitalized on the consumer-oriented short-haul trade to South Bend; Ernsthausen drew upon the experience of independent operators; and Torrio tapped nearby Canadian distilleries. Expansion occurred in a variety of ways. To serve larger areas, some entrepreneurs built more terminals to integrate horizontally, while others bought additional vehicles to expand internally. Others integrated vertically through gasoline stations. The business of trucking, then, reflected a wide-open field in the 1920s in which only the limitations of the individual appeared to matter.

Aiding the ambitious was the economic structure of trucking, which presented advantages over the older forms of transport. Fixed costs were only 10 percent of the total, consisting chiefly of the truck itself; and attractive downpayment and note requirements reduced the financial risks considerably. Since capital investment was small, so too were interest rates and property taxes. Gasoline, oil, food, and sometimes labor (when a helper was required) constituted the bulk of variable costs, though these fluctuated with the length, weight, and geographic area of the haul. Thus, low fixed costs, gradually improving highways, general economic growth, and the flexibility of the truck encouraged individuals to try the business.[29]

Yet, two related factors—the backhaul and deadheading—raised serious management problems for all truckers. The backhaul is the return trip home; deadheading is the time spent driving an empty truck to the next load. Each incurred costs for oil, gasoline, and the driver's time. Many truckers did not understand the nature of these problems, and some went broke because of them. When contracting for a shipment, a driver often considered only the costs of transporting that particular load; he did not account for the possibilities of returning home empty or of having to drive to the next town for cargo. Empty backhauls and too much deadheading resulted in a high number of failures in trucking. When more people entered the business during the Depression, these problems intensified and that in part brought demands for government controls.[30]

5

The trucking firms that Kelting, Harrell, Ozee, and the others established joined a general trend of expansion in transportation during the 1920s. The Panama Canal trade, pipe and power lines, improved rail facilities, and the new airplanes and trucks served the expanding consumer-oriented society. As advertising fueled American fantasies and factories mass-produced the objects of desire, more transport firms appeared to deliver them. Trucking probably affected the economy more than did the other transport industries, but in analyzing the part, we should not ignore the whole.

The truck revolution would not have occurred without the presence of other elements. For example, the opening of the Delaware River Bridge in 1926, connecting Wilmington to New Jersey, and the completion of the Holland Tunnel from Jersey City to New York less than two years later provided the means for an expanded interstate truck trade in those urban areas. The general practice among merchants of keeping low inventories that would allow them to respond to the latest fads, provide variety, and yet reduce costs also favored trucking. Low inventories necessitated the regular small shipments for which trucks were especially well suited. And government actions affected transport, too, for in addition to road building and railroad regulation, the government was responsible, through Supreme Court decisions, for opening state lines to interstate truck traffic. Motor trucking accommodated the commercial society, but such diverse factors as technology, highway and bridge construction, mass production, consumer demands, business needs, and government policies conditioned the adaptation.[31]

Contributing to the multicausal nature of the truck revolution was the variety of businesses that used the truck. By 1930 at least sixty-two industries relied on motor vehicles. Those using the most were the Post Office, grocery and food producers, general contractors, autos (accessories and supplies), freight transfer companies, bakeries, and oil and gasoline, lumber, general merchandise, and meat-packing firms. Most of the vehicles in these industries were lightweight, 1- to 1 1/2-ton trucks, which indicates small loads and short hauls formed the backbone of the new transport business.[32] Heavier models were being produced but their impact was minimal in 1930.

The list above indicates the truck touched most sectors of the economy. In the beginning, trucking tapped mostly those markets bypassed by barges and railroads during the nineteenth century. Very quickly, however, motor trucks began to compete in regional and national markets; they changed distribution patterns, upset established markets, and opened new ones. One study suggested that trucking brought 10 percent of the population, which had been isolated from major railroad arteries, into contact with the economy. Trucking of newspapers, to give another example, introduced more people to news and advertising services.[33]

Although the truck affected many parts of the economy, it altered agricultural hauling the most. In a sense, motor trucking of farm products represented a return to the "truck selling" of colonial times, when a peddler simply bought a wagonload of produce from the farmer and hauled it to the town market. The new technology presented farmers and ranchers with a viable option to what they had viewed as an onerous monopoly by the railways since the Civil War. No longer tied to fixed schedules and rates, they used motor vehicles (either driving themselves or contracting with truckers) to send produce and stock to market and to haul supplies on the return trip.[34]

Before truckers like Kelting and Ernsthausen began to haul farm produce, the railroads did so. The usual procedure included grading the crop at the farm or at a co-op near a rail station, loading it into carload lots, and shipping it to market. The railways offered numerous extra services: diverting a shipment while in transit (when a commodity buyer resold it), icing the produce, and carting small shipments to retail stores. Extra services commanded additional charges.[35] With the advent of trucking, this complex system became simpler and cheaper, but it was not without its problems.

A trucker, whether the farmer himself or an independent, loaded the crop at the farm itself and hauled it to market. If it went directly to a retail outlet, no extra unloading or loading was required. The driver simply drove his rig from the market directly to the store to make what was known as a store-door delivery. Such a process saved time, cut labor costs, and prevented the damage that inevitably occurred during several handlings of a load. Truck rates were flat rates. Drivers did not add extra charges for loading and unloading or for refrigerating the cargo. For example, the rail rate in the early 1930s from Rochester to

New York City was forty-five cents per barrel of apples for a full carload. To deliver the apples to retail stores, the railroad charged an extra thirty-five cents, which brought the total to eighty cents per barrel. A motor carrier charged less than sixty cents for the same service, and he was faster and more efficient and would willingly haul less than a full carload of apples.[36] Not all trucking was cheaper than rail service, but the savings in time often offset higher rates, especially if the goods were perishable.

Despite these positive aspects of trucking, some disadvantages emerged. By the late 1920s, the undisciplined actions of independent truckers began to disrupt market activities. Railroad deliveries, as expensive as they were, had been coordinated; advance notice of quantity and quality and regular deliveries had sustained stable distribution patterns. When numerous truckers began hauling produce, brokers and retailers faced irregular supplies—too much one day, not enough the next—and loads of mixed grades that made it difficult to price transport charges for individual items. Most such problems were caused by those truckers who bought produce at the farm; farmers and retailers engaged in trucking tended to grade produce correctly. Adding to the chaos, some truckers, many of whom were ignorant of basic business knowledge, accepted rates that did not pay the costs of the haul and many itinerant truckers solicited nonagricultural goods for the backhaul. Still other factors contributed to chaotic marketing. Many motor carriers were underinsured, if insured at all. Thus, a shipper using trucks might have to bear the loss if breakdowns or inclement weather delayed a shipment and the cargo was lost or spoiled. These were costs for which the railroads would reimburse shippers using the rails. All of these problems added up, in some areas, to a situation in which many suffered from what otherwise appeared to be a remarkably free and competitive system.[37]

Some markets overcame some of this confusion by establishing systems in which trucker and producer dealt directly with each other in a central place. Such markets appeared in New Jersey, New York, Maryland, and Utah. One of the earliest regional truck distribution centers was a major fruit and vegetable facility located at Benton Harbor, Michigan. At this east shore Lake Michigan port, the comparative volume of rail and truck tonnages reversed in seven years. In 1925 the rails hauled 90 percent of the produce, but by 1932 the trucks hauled 90 percent, and the rails only 10 percent. Motor carriers based in Benton Harbor operated within an increasingly large area, forging a

750-mile radius that included, for example, Minneapolis and Duluth, Minnesota. In turn, farmers expanded production and Benton Harbor became a regional distribution point for produce.[38]

Benton Harbor was not an isolated example. Throughout the United States, trucking of produce increased while rail shipments decreased. Geography played no small role in the shift. In the East, motor carriers expanded operations to New York and Philadelphia because each was close to farm production areas. Los Angeles, located near a year-round farm region, also developed an extensive trucking service. Boston, however, did not. Not close enough to large farming areas to take advantage of trucks, Boston remained tied to the railroads for delivery of fruits and vegetables.[39]

Geography and technology also contributed to increased trucking of milk and cotton during the period. The introduction of refrigerated tanks made trucks so adaptable to milk hauling that distribution shifted from the rails to motor vehicles throughout most of the nation, though, again, areas such as Boston remained untouched. Cotton distribution shifted drastically in the South during the later years of the decade, in part because of increased rail rates and in part because of new interior cotton presses located far from railway depots. As road surface conditions improved in the Northeast, trucking of cotton supplanted rail services there.[40]

Trucking changed the nature of livestock hauling as well, and again, several factors conditioned the shift. New independent meat-packing plants arose and challenged the established ones. At first, hogs made up the largest percentage of animals trucked, mainly because they were fattened on farms in the corn belt within trucking distance of major markets. Cattle, raised mostly in the plains and mountain states, were too far away for efficient truck hauling until later in the 1930s when depression conditions and the advent of heavier trucks made the trucking of cattle to distant markets profitable. As competition increased, both the older and newer firms moved closer to livestock-raising regions. Concurrently, technology aided the ranchers. The radio furnished up-to-the-minute prices, and the truck provided the means for a quick response to upsurges. Between 1916 and 1931, the percentage of livestock trucked to sixteen major markets rose from 1.6 to 31.9. Only Chicago did not reflect this general trend, and again, geography played a vital role. The Windy City was simply too far away from livestock-producing regions to take advantage of truck transportation.[41]

The truck's convergence with geographic, technological, and competitive forces in the 1920s altered the way Americans lived. Urban dwellers now had access to more healthful foods year round. In conjunction with the automobile, the truck caused a great deal of shifting about in the United States. It created new markets for consumer goods as it reached out to areas between major rail distribution points. Manufacturers and retailers, of course, followed the movement to the suburbs and rural areas. Simultaneously, the automobile furnished rural inhabitants the means to travel to the cities to sample the markets there. As country residents motored to the cities and farmers hauled produce to the urban markets, they met cars and trucks going the opposite direction toward new markets. This movement in both directions, from country to city and from city to country, suggests Americans could not quite decide how best to use the new cars and trucks. It was a generally topsy-turvy transition period in the economy. A predominantly durable goods, producer economy was giving way to a consumer-oriented one, and in transportation specifically, a slow, rigid, and coordinated system was changing into a fast, flexible, and chaotic one. The motor truck was at the forefront of this transition.[42]

6

By the end of the 1920s trucking was an exciting new addition to the American economy, though how it would finally integrate into the transportation system remained unclear. For trucking in 1930 was not yet an industry; that is, it did not represent a distinct grouping of productive enterprises occupying a definable niche in the economic scheme. The boundaries had not been drawn; the revolution was still in process.

The motor truck had replaced the horse as the beast of burden for the cities; it had reduced congestion at transport terminals and had lowered costs of distribution. In serving customers never before touched by the national economic network, it had filled in the gaps the railroads had left. As trucking grew through more and better vehicles, expanded and improved roads, and more consolidated firms, it began to be recognized as a viable method of transportation.[43]

Even so, certain tensions clouded the immediate future. A small trend toward consolidation was perceptible, but the major tendency was toward numerous entries into and exits out of the business.

Another change also proved ominous: more and more trucking firms became less content with playing adjunct to the rails. They began competing directly with the older transport forms, particularly in the lucrative high-value freight markets (high-priced, small-volume articles). The growth in trucking, moreover, occurred at the same time that the airlines, railways, and canals were expanding their operations. In effect, economic and technological forces were converging in the 1920s to create an oversupply of transportation. If the consumer economy ceased growing, then competition in transportation would become acute. Given the atomistic and competitive qualities of trucking, the future for that business was uncertain indeed.

2

Railroads, Truck Terminals, and Gypsies:
Competition and the Transportation Problem

The Great Depression jolted the transportation industry as it did most of the American economy. Reduced commercial activity brought less freight hauling, an oversupply of transport facilities, and acute competition. This transportation problem loomed as a central one for businessmen and public policy makers because a sound transportation system would facilitate recovery.

By the early 1930s, the truck was no longer a simple, convenient substitute for the horse and wagon, but rather a direct competitor of the railroad. The revolution begun in the 1920s continued, for unlike most businesses, trucking crossed the 1929 watershed still young, vibrant, and innovative. Thus, there existed a paradox in transportation in the 1930s. While other transport forms, especially the railways, faced retrenchment, trucking expanded. The explanation of the paradox lies in the analysis of depression conditions and how the economic structures of railroading and trucking fit those circumstances.

When faced with depressed commercial activity, businessmen, whether engaged in mining, production, or retailing, have to cut costs. Expansion is curtailed, output reduced, wages cut, and workers laid off. Additionally, businessmen seek cheaper transport service. In the early 1930s, more shippers turned to the truck because it furnished faster, more flexible and lower-cost hauling for small quantities than did the railroads. The changeover did not come without risks to shippers. Only the larger trucking firms maintained regular schedules; many truckers were inadequately insured for loss and damage; and others failed to deliver, having bankrupted themselves through poor business practices. Large-scale shippers could buy their own trucks; small-scale shippers could not afford to do so.

To better understand the choices shippers made requires an appreciation of transport competition as it evolved in the 1920s and 1930s. The story is a complicated one. No clear demarcation between the two decades exists in the story of trucking, for trends begun in the postwar period only intensified during the Depression. The explanation, moreover, involves not only economics but also politics: state laws regulating the different kinds of transport affected the nature of the competition. Broken into its constituent parts, the story includes the structure of railroading, the attempts by transportation executives to coordinate rail-truck operations, the trend toward consolidated trucking firms, the legal constraints, and the emergence of independent truckers. All combined to bolster trucking and to create the transportation problem. In general, the railways and consolidated trucking firms lost business to gypsy independents because conditions favored the latter. Understanding the nature of the competition will clarify not only why more shippers chose the truck, but also why governments decided to interfere in the marketplace.

I

The railroad arrived in the first third of the nineteenth century as a product of economic necessity and technological innovation. To break away from the mercantile economy of the eighteenth century, commerce in the western world needed a form of transport that could carry huge volumes of raw materials and finished products over long distances. Development of the steam engine in the 1780s led to steam-propelled wagons by the early 1800s, but extreme friction between wheels and ground prevented efficient movement of large and heavy shipments any great distance. With the creation of iron rails, over which a steam engine could pull a string of loaded wagon-cars, the friction problem was conquered and the railroad was born. The iron horse ruled the transportation network that made possible the industrial revolution. [1]

The invention had drawbacks. In exchange for reduced friction, the railway remained rigid: the train was tied to the rails, restricted to moving only forward and backward. Tracks and terminals, moreover, could not be shifted easily when commercial patterns changed. The sheer size of the operation required large initial capital investments to construct the locomotives, boxcars and flatcars, stations, roadbeds, and rails. Additional fixed costs enlarged the capital burden, for

interest rates, property taxes, dividends, and administrative and maintenance costs persisted whether the train moved or not. Consequently,
each train had to haul a certain minimum amount of freight just to pay
initial capital investments and fixed costs.

Despite the drawbacks, the railroad included substantial advantages
over barge and horse transportation. With the increased power of the
steam engine and the friction-reducing rails, executives now had the
opportunity to utilize scale economies. The more goods a train hauled
over long distances, the cheaper was the unit price. For example, the
costs of hauling a hundred tons in a two-thousand-ton shipment 150
miles were less per ton-mile than hauling a hundred tons in a fifteen-
hundred-ton shipment only 100 miles. Stated another way, it was much
cheaper to haul a thousand wagonloads of wheat by rail than by a
thousand horse-drawn wagons.

Scale economies operate best in a monopoly or near monopoly
situation. The more control a railroad exerted in a market, the more
could scale economies be used. Railway managers, however, found
competition intense and monopolies difficult to establish after the
Civil War. Railroad construction stimulated growth in agriculture,
mining, and manufacturing, which in turn spurred even more railway
mileage. By the 1890s the private railways had knitted a haphazard but
fairly comprehensive national transport system of 200,000 track miles.
The majority of freight consisted of bulk products—iron ore, coal, and
agricultural goods—that furnished the means for industrial expansion.[2]

Just as the iron horse had altered the economic scheme in the
nineteenth century, so too did new forces in the twentieth century
change the status of the once-proud railroads. Their usefulness was
slipping, giving way to more flexible transport methods that used the
internal combustion engine—the airplane and the truck. As more
people moved from the country to the city, congestion in urban areas
made rail hauling less and less attractive; shipments were delayed and
even lost in the crowded switching yards. The inherent rigidity of the
industry prevented managers from responding quickly to change.
Government regulation also hindered innovation. Given the American
fear of monopoly, regulators and rail leaders alike remained hesitant to
integrate the new motor truck into the established systems. Instead, the
decision makers ordered more rail facilities built and old ones up-
graded.[3]

The Depression, of course, only made the railroad problem worse.

In 1930, for the first time in the history of railroading in the United States, total freight hauled dropped—so drastically that it slipped to the ton-mile figure of ten years before. The intense competition for this diminished tonnage squeezed the rail companies' operating ratios. Profits declined sharply. Lower profits, in turn, meant smaller dividends, less expansion, and curtailed maintenance. Such depressed operations shook the financial supporters, the securities investors, and many withdrew funds.[4] The great symbol of America's industrial revolution, the iron horse, like much of capitalism in the 1930s, faced a crisis.

2

While the rails faltered, the new business of trucking, which is based on different economic and technological factors, was emerging. Changes in distribution patterns and advances in motor technology during the preceding twenty years enabled the truck to take advantage of the railways' decline. The general outlines of trucking in the 1920s—the trend toward larger firms and numerous business start-ups and failures—became more evident during the early years of the Depression. In the process, trucking grew from a business essentially local in nature and tied to the railroads to one that included long-distance transport.

At first, motor trucks replaced the horse and wagon in pickup and delivery service for the railroads. In transportation, terminals present inherent bottlenecks in the process; in railroading especially, the goods have to be collected and sorted at the depot before a train can be formed and scale economies utilized. Prior to the advent of motor vehicles, a man drove a horse-drawn wagon to the manufacturer's door, loaded an outgoing shipment, and carted it to the dock where he unloaded it. He then loaded an incoming shipment and delivered it in the city. Meanwhile, dock workers organized the various outgoing lots into freight cars. Goods were transferred in the same way between barge docks and railway depots or between different rail terminals. Just before World War I, this system—known as local cartage—broke down. The new and noisy pleasure autos, darting in and out of traffic, scared the horses; at the same time, increased commerce clogged the terminals. After the war, local cartage improved. Not only could motor trucks haul more goods, but the rail managers also more efficiently organized the operations.[5]

The history of local cartage in St. Louis provides an example of the transition from horse to truck. Ferries interchanged freight between the east and west banks before the Mississippi River was bridged there in 1876. Horse-drawn vehicles then took over off-track deliveries and transfers, and by 1910 four local companies dominated the market. Through consolidation, one firm, the Columbia Terminals Company, attempted to gain control of all the transfer business. Columbia first used motor vehicles in 1919 but without immediate success, for until the costs of trucks came down and traffic increased, the horse and wagon remained more economical. By the mid-1920s, tractor-trailer combinations performed cartage functions more quickly and cheaply than the horse-drawn wagon. Modern business techniques also contributed to the efficiency of the firm. Columbia executives divided the St. Louis area into three districts. In each, a dispatcher guided the movement of trucks and trailers. Every afternoon, the dispatchers telephoned principal shippers, collected information on the next day's orders, and then coordinated the placement of equipment. By 1930 97 tractors and 439 trailers were transferring seven million pounds of freight daily and Columbia Terminals controlled 90 percent of the local cartage business in St. Louis.[6]

The Railway Express Company, a national small-parcel transport firm, followed similar strategies at its terminals in numerous cities. Having introduced motor vehicle service in Detroit before the war, the corporation by 1923 employed trucks in 43 percent of its operations. By 1930 tractor-trailer rigs operated throughout the entire Railway Express central district (Pittsburgh to Cheyenne, Wyoming). Railway Express managers took advantage of technological innovations to further improve service, using specially designed lightweight aluminum trailers, insulated vans for perishable products, and as in St. Louis, coordinated tractor-trailers to reduce congestion in terminals.[7]

Despite such success, only a few railroads instituted rail-truck operations during the 1920s. Although the Pennsylvania Railroad was apparently the first (in 1923), the St. Louis Southwestern—better known as the Cotton Belt—was the most advanced system by the early 1930s. Following the usual strategy for such operations, the Cotton Belt organized in 1928 a subsidiary firm, the Southwestern Transportation Company. Its high speed trains furnished overnight service to points between St. Louis and Shreveport, Louisiana. Trucks hauled goods from seven intermediate stops along the line over the road to Memphis, Little Rock, Texarkana, and smaller towns nearby. Cotton

Belt managers initiated a joint venture of the two technologies: loaded
trailers were secured to flatbed rail cars for high-speed runs to key
depots. At destination, the trailers were removed from the train,
hooked up to motor trucks, and delivered direct to retail outlets for
unloading. (Today, this is known as piggy-back.) In the East, the New
Haven Railroad inaugurated truck operations early in 1931 and report-
edly saved $300,000 per year. The Southern Pacific Railroad intro-
duced similar services along its tracks from Portland, Oregon, to the
Mexican border.[8]

These rail-truck activities represented the exception, not the rule, in
truck terminal services. In 1930 sixty railways used only seven thousand trucks; Railway Express owned an additional ten thousand but the
total number of trucks in the country at the time stood at over three
million. Although rail use of trucks was increasing and although other
trucks served the railroads, it is obvious that the vast majority of trucks
were not tied directly to the railroads.[9] From the perspective of efficiency, this did not make sense. As the examples above indicate, rail-
truck coordination reflected the revolutionary transition from horse to
truck, the efficient use of railroad scale economies, and the extension
of truck flexibility. The operations represented, moreover, creative use
of twentieth-century business techniques that made the cartage business more efficient. Why did so few coordinated terminals exist?

In part, rail managers responded too conservatively to the new
technology because of uncertainty over the application of antitrust and
regulatory laws. More important, however, was the sheer speed with
which the truck appeared on the economic scene. Rapid changes in
technology and distribution patterns allowed trucking to take on a life
of its own, separate from the established transport systems. The expanding highway network shifted lines of commerce away from rail
terminals, and as more and more vehicles jammed urban streets,
freight transfer at city docks became a process of perseverance amid
chaos. Thus, new terminals were built in less congested areas near the
newer commercial centers. The flexibility of the truck conditioned
such movement.

That same flexibility, moreover, rapidly challenged the railways
using the truck. Both Columbia Terminals and Railway Express,
initially established for off-track pickup and delivery, extended operations into over-the-road hauling. Columbia leased motor vehicles and
drivers to shippers, and Railway Express contracted directly to transport freight by truck. Similarly, the high-speed service of the Cotton

Belt subsidiary expanded into direct competition with the parent corporation.[10] The new technology, then, quickly outdistanced its cousin, the horse-drawn wagon, and challenged the iron horse.

3

Independent, one-truck firms represented one of the ways in which trucking competed directly against the railways, and large-scale trucking firms represented the other. Like the paucity of rail-truck operations, the truck terminals illustrated a growing but still minor trend in the new trucking business. They were important, nonetheless, for they reflected the competitive nature of trucking, the use of scale economies, and big-business strategies similar to those the railways had pioneered many years before.

Just as competition gave rise to the business mergers of the late nineteenth century, so too did competition lead to the consolidation of trucking firms. In the 1920s and 1930s many local cartage operators switched from the horse to the truck to serve longtime customers more efficiently. Nonetheless, the city transfer companies still lost customers to independent truckers who entered the market areas, offered lower rates, and lured away customers. To meet the competition, consolidation was necessary. United Motor Lines, Incorporated, for example, was established in Texas in the late 1920s in order to cut off the independents. One hundred trucks and ten warehouses were integrated into a twelve-hundred-mile system; stability, efficiency, and lower costs regained lost customers.[11]

Consolidated motor truck operations also addressed the backhaul problem. A single trucker remained at a disadvantage in finding backhauls, for he was too busy loading, driving, and unloading the truck to think ahead about the return load. An agent whose sole job was to secure freight for drivers would greatly improve the chances for homeward-bound shipments. In the late 1920s, the National Delivery Association established a Return Load Bureau comprising eight centers operating as clearinghouses for the truckers. A three-dollar fee assured the driver when he left on a haul that an agent at his destination would secure a return shipment for him. The problem and response was not unlike the experience of the railways in the nineteenth century when coordinated systems appeared to deal with the problem of empty and idle freight cars.[12]

Allied Van Lines, Incorporated, represented another organized reaction to the problems of competition and the backhaul in a specialized area of trucking, household goods movers. Through discussion at annual meetings, the furniture warehousemen recognized that a coordinated operation was the only response to independents who roamed into long-held market areas and contracted with shippers to move their furniture and belongings. Allied's Return Load Bureau, established in 1924, became efficient only in 1928 when the territory east of the Rocky Mountains was divided into five regions and forty sections. Twelve dispatchers coordinated the movements of the truckers with the contracts that sales representatives had made with the shippers. Drivers received 70 to 80 percent of the revenue per load and the remainder was divided between the parent corporation and the local agents. Uniform procedures, which the corporate officers designed and monitored, attracted shippers to the operation. Adequate insurance covered each shipment, receipts for shipments appeared on standardized waybill forms, and local agents familiar with local customers processed all claims on damage and loss. [13]

Other consolidated firms exploited the motor vehicle's flexibility and successfully competed against the rails for the growing trade in less-than-carload (lcl) freight. As the name suggests, lcl cargo (also known as high-value freight) consisted of goods such as foodstuffs, drugs, paints, clothing, and pipe fittings that did not completely fill a railway car. These items did not utilize railroad scale economies as efficiently as did bulk items, such as iron ore and coal. Lcl freight required sorting at the depots, numerous switchings en route, and resorting and loading into delivery trucks at the destination. The process was expensive and time-consuming. [14]

The Keeshin Motor Express Company of Chicago successfully competed against the railroads for the lcl business. Founded by Jack L. Keeshin, a fiery, opinionated businessman who would later become one of the prime movers for truck regulation, the firm languished between 1912 and 1925. When distribution patterns shifted away from the rail centers in the mid-1920s, Keeshin's company expanded rapidly. Within a few years, the firm brought overnight service to towns within two hundred miles of Chicago. The best the rails could offer was three-day delivery, and that was rare. By 1931 Keeshin Motor Express served an area from South Bend, Indiana, in the east, to Davenport, Iowa, in the west. Keeshin's organizing ability, good business sense, and understanding of trucking economics explain the success. He judiciously used 123 trucks, tractor-trailer rigs, and two-man driving teams to lower shippers' costs. Dispatchers could send trucks directly to shippers, loading the cargo in the reverse of how it was to be unloaded. This eliminated unnecessary handling of freight (thus reducing damage claims) and saved valuable terminal switching time. Moreover, Keeshin Express followed responsible business practices to ensure regular service and prompt payments for damage or loss. Once, for example, when a truck crashed and burned during an overnight haul, Keeshin ordered the fourteen shipments that had been lost duplicated at his expense and loaded onto another trailer; all were delivered no more than six hours behind schedule. Such commitment helped double company revenue between 1929 and 1930 to over half a million dollars.[15]

Consolidated trucking operations, then, emerged for a variety of reasons: to meet competition, to control the backhaul, to take over the growing lcl business, to meet shipper demands, and to exploit scale economies in trucking. Although the nature of trucking does not allow the massive scale economies of railroading, control of the backhaul and direct loading of shipments in reverse order of the unloading sequence constituted such economies for truckers. Several statistics reveal the extent of consolidation taking place. By 1932, 22,000 fleets of five or more trucks existed in the United States; between 1924 and 1931, the top fifteen fleets nearly tripled the number of vehicles used in consolidated operations; in 1924 the fifteenth largest truck fleet employed 790 vehicles, while in 1931 the twenty-ninth used 785. Not only did more fleets exist, but the largest ones were growing larger.[16]

Yet, the trend toward consolidation represented a small force in the trucking business. In 1932 nearly 65 percent of the trucks on the road belonged to one-man firms; 2.2 million truckers owned and operated only one vehicle. The remaining 1.2 million trucks were attached to terminals, but most of those were in two- to five-vehicle firms. Clearly, the business of motor trucking remained small-scale in the early 1930s.[17]

4

To this point, the story has focused on the economic and technological causes behind the rise of trucking. The same perspective can be used to describe and analyze the largest segment of the trucking business—the small-scale firms—but such an approach would ignore another important element in the story, namely the influence of transport law.

State motor carrier laws underscored the economic and technological factors that shaped transport competition in the 1920s and 1930s, and the transportation laws of those decades encouraged small-scale operations. By 1932 there existed three types of trucking services: common, private, and contract. Common carriers comprised 5.5 percent of all trucking firms. Like the railways, these firms held themselves out to the public at large, a position that historically had required certain duties. For example, common carriers had to serve all shippers who were willing and able to pay; they could not refuse shipments that were too small or were destined for out-of-the-way cities. They were further subdivided as regular-route common carriers (those who followed regular schedules over definite routes) and irregular-route common carriers (those who went where and when business dictated).[18] To ensure responsible service, state governments subjected common carriers to rate and weight restrictions and license fees. Railway Express, Keeshin Express, and Allied were all common carriers.

The vast majority of truckers, 85 percent, were private carriers. They used their vehicles only as adjuncts to their main business of producing or retailing. Private carriers included farmers, bakers, butchers, highway departments, oil companies, and many more. Farmers, who owned 26 percent of all trucks, represented the largest group of private carriers. Few state regulatory laws applied to private carriers, because their trucking was only a sideline to an otherwise private business not subject to state controls.

With the rise of motor trucking, a third designation appeared, the contract carriers. Composing 8.7 percent of all truck firms, contract carriers were engaged principally in the business of transportation, but they did not hold themselves out to the public at large. Instead, they selected shippers that suited the specialized nature of their operations. Those owning flatbed trailers served heavy-equipment manufacturers and pipe companies; those with refrigerated trailers served meat-packers and grocery chains. The contract carrier's legal status was unclear. Some truckers had so many contracts that they were indistinguishable from common carriers; others took title to the cargo, so as to appear to be private carriers; and until 1932 state governments had no legal grounds on which to control the contract carriers.[19]

In fact, as Chapter 4 will make clear, motor carrier law was in a condition of flux in the 1920s and 1930s. Trucking emerged so quickly that the economic changes outstripped the law's ability to control them. Some analysts have thus suggested that the situation represented a free-enterprise market in which natural economic factors guided the competition.[20] This was not really the case. The common carriers, by virtue of long-standing transport law, found themselves restricted in combating their chief competitors, the contract carriers. Had the common carriers not been required to serve everyone, regardless of the profit to be made, the outcome might have been very different. As it was, legal restraints combined with economic factors to place the common carriers—truck and rail—at a disadvantage.

5

Approximately 150,000 independent truckers appeared on the highways in the late 1920s and early 1930s to take advantage of the shifting economic and legal conditions in transportation.[21] Comprising only about 5.4 percent of all truck firms, these owner-operators intensified competition in the young business of trucking. They evaded the spirit and the letter of the state regulatory laws, whether they hauled only within one state or crossed state lines. They were chameleons, taking on the appearance of common, private, or contract carriers whenever circumstances dictated. They owned their rigs and held themselves out to the general public, which technically made them common carriers. Yet, the owner-operators shunned the responsibilities of common carriage. In some instances, they refused shipments; in others they bought the cargo, transported it, and resold it. Either way, whether contract or private, they mocked state law-enforcement efforts. Poor business practices added to the confusion. In too many cases, the owner-operators accepted cargo at rates that did not pay a profit. They did so because they were either unaware of basic business methods or desperate to take shipments in hopes that down the road there would be a paying load.

These were the free spirits, the "gypsies," "wildcatters," and "fly-by-night" operators. They first affected trucking in the 1920s when farm boys used the motor truck to escape to the excitement of the city. More materialized in the 1930s when laid-off factory and railroad workers took whatever jobs they could to survive. In part, their operations reflected the natural tendency of a young business toward competition; and in part, they took advantage of a market regulated only partially.

Gypsy truckers entered the business for a variety of reasons—the primary one, of course, to make money. Some did, most did not. The gypsy's truck, costing from two to five thousand dollars, was easy to purchase because overzealous dealers allowed low cash downpayments (from $125 to $250) and liberal payment plans of eighteen months. Thus, captive farm boys and the unemployed entered trucking, and too many of them knew nothing of basic business practices (not to mention depreciation, insurance, deadheading, and backhauls). The gypsy's overhead expenses were few, for his truck was at once his livelihood, his office, and his home. Too frequently, however, he only considered the cost of fuel, oil, and food to determine the rates charged; in some cases, not even those out-of-pocket expenses were met. In securing a shipment from a coal operator or farmer, moreover, the gypsy often neglected to grade the product. At the market, he met buyers who did not know what they were purchasing and thus understandably gave low prices that may not have paid all of his expenses. More than a few bankrupt drivers burned their rigs to collect insurance or to avoid repossession and the poor credit rating that entailed. The gypsy created uncertainty for all concerned—truckers, shippers, retailers, and truck dealers.[22]

Without the strengths of collective organization found in the large-scale truck terminals, independent trucking proved an arduous business. Gypsies had to pay cash for gasoline and repairs, for credit was unavailable to such a shifting population. As state regulations increased in number, severity, and enforcement, independents began to drive at night and sometimes miles out of their way to evade highway patrolmen, waiting, it seemed, to fine them out of existence. They faced not only the same hazards as the consolidated drivers—rough roads, steep grades, ice in winter, mud in spring—but also an uncertainty that did not plague drivers in the large-scale operations. The gypsy's backhaul problem was more acute. Consolidated terminals used scale economies to minimize the effects of backhauls. Almost every haul became a fronthaul to an allied terminal, and therefore a company driver could be assured of a load going home. By contrast, one independent spent six weeks on the East Coast driving short hauls before securing a shipment back to his home in the Midwest.[23] The uncertainty and the physical strain of independent trucking led to the large number of individual start-ups and failures in the trucking business.

Not all gypsies succumbed to the uncertainties and physical demands. Some prospered enough to expand into consolidated trucking firms; others, less ambitious, appeared content to stay with the one-truck operation. One of the latter was Harry D. Woods, a stocky, five-foot-nine, red-haired Midwesterner. Woods entered trucking in the late 1920s during high school summer breaks. After graduation, he turned full-time to the life of a gypsy trucker, driving for others until he could buy his own truck. He got used to the "southern route"—Chicago to Pittsburgh, Route 22 to Philadelphia, cross into New Jersey and over to New York City or traverse Connecticut and Massachusetts to Boston. After acquiring his own truck in 1932, Woods learned of the "northern route," which, though longer, encountered less dangerous mountain driving and fewer state police.[24]

Woods began a typical northern route trip at Doc Wirtz's gas station, located at Canal and Archer Avenue in Chicago. He contracted with a local broker (a freight agent) for an eight- to nine-ton eastbound shipment of dry goods, eggs, or meat at the rate of nine to ten dollars per ton. Leaving in the late afternoon and driving east on Route 6, he did not stop until he spotted a café in Walkerton, Indiana, eighty-five miles from Chicago. He drank a quick cup of coffee, checked on road and state trooper conditions, and offered tips on backhauls to truckers heading west. Then it was on to Jean and Slim's Truck Stop at the Indiana-Ohio border and perhaps a brief respite at Bob and Hazel's in Bryan, just inside Ohio. Just over 310 miles from Chicago, Woods stopped for fuel at Ted's in Sandusky, next to Lake Erie. If he had been driving well (with minimal braking and at a steady thirty-five miles per hour), he had coaxed from his ninety- to ninety-five-horsepower gasoline engine an average of 5 to 5-1/2 miles per gallon.

The truck stops Woods frequented proved important to his business. They were the underground information centers for the independents. Briefings on road and weather conditions and state trooper locations were a must to the wildcatter, who often drove overweight and without proper licenses. Inaccurate weight tickets or insufficient waybills landed Woods in jail on several occasions. A few truck stop owners, like Ted in Sandusky (purportedly a former bootlegger with ties to local authorities), assisted Woods and others in trouble with the law. Others worked with the police to catch illegal truckers. In addition to information, truck stops furnished fuel, oil, and maintenance facilities, hot food and coffee, showers, and bunks. Frequent contact between independents at the stops, moreover, led to the emergence of gypsy gangs in the early 1930s. As Woods himself recalls it, "The reason for getting into a gang . . . , not even knowing it [at the time], was because of protection for our business."[25] Gang members easily contacted one another by leaving notes on the truck stop bulletin boards.

After fueling in Sandusky, Woods drove on to Cleveland, where crossing the city consumed two hours in the days before interstate loops. After achieving the next goal, the Ohio-Pennsylvania border, the trip turned interesting, for the "state of Pennsylvania . . . was a holy terror as far as truck laws were concerned."[26] Gypsies helped each other by turning headlights off and on to signal when they had spotted state troopers lurking nearby. Once safely in New York, Woods pushed on to Hamburg or Orchard Park.

When he made it to Pop Bain's Truck Stop, he had traveled just over five hundred miles in two days with only catnaps and coffee to keep him alert. He had negotiated several steep hills that required skillful handling of an often overweight truck equipped with underpowered braking systems. (Several of Wood's friends failed to make it safely over those same hills.) Reeling from lack of sleep, his body was also sore and bruised, for he operated the double stick-shift mechanism with his sternum and right hand and steered with his left hand. The leather truck seat was hard and the trailer springs inadequate to cushion the jolts from rough roads. Feeling not unlike a football player after a hard-hitting game, Woods now "slept-out" for fourteen hours straight in a bunk room over Pop Bain's café.

Rejuvenated, Woods ate a good hot meal, talked with his friends, and then continued along the last half of his journey, made somewhat easier by the lax attitude of the New York state police at that time. After 250 miles, he arrived at Little Em's and Little Mike's Truck Stop in Little Falls. Only one day away from the Big Apple, Woods made delivery by the fifth morning of his thousand-mile trip. After unloading the cargo, he drove to a phone booth at Tenth and Fourteenth Streets where he handed a waiting man two dollars and received in return a slip of paper containing information on a load back to the Midwest. After paying for this information and for gasoline, which cost about seventeen cents per gallon in 1931, Woods had only twenty-eight to forty-five dollars left, depending on whether he hauled eight or nine tons and whether he was paid eight or nine dollars per ton. Out of this money he had to pay for oil, food, tires, and payments and repairs on his rig.

Several striking conclusions emerge from Wood's experiences. For one thing, although it was arduous, the trip provided fifth-morning delivery of goods from the Midwest, a service that railways could match only occasionally. Then too, even though Woods was not attached to a consolidated firm, he did engage in collective action. Like all truckers, Woods could not long have continued in operation without help from agents at both ends of the trip. Admittedly, his agents or brokers were not established ones like those who worked for Allied or the National Delivery Association, but they supplied similar services. Without the gypsy camaraderie on the road, moreover, breakdowns could have proven disastrous, rather than simply inconvenient. Wood's operations illustrate also, as he realized, that the truck created a momentum that at times outstripped its capacities. Gypsies frequently loaded trucks beyond the safe limits and often axles broke and brakes failed. Roads in the early 1930s lacked the engineering needed for such an extended trip as Woods undertook, as the deaths of truckers on the steeply graded mountain turns testify. Of course, some of the gypsies were irresponsible. In their efforts to compete with the railways, they drove longer than was safe, and thus created potential hazards for others on the road, not to mention the possibility that the shipment would not be delivered at all.[27]

Despite their small numbers (150,000 gypsy trucks, 3 million others), gypsies greatly affected the trucking market. One study estimated that "itinerant truck peddlers" hauled 60 percent of the nation's fruits and vegetables, a service that reduced prices substantially. Gypsies lowered Florida orange prices 50 percent in the Washington, D.C., area, and potato prices nine to thirteen cents per hundred pounds in Detroit. In the Southwest, independents invaded the railroad grain market, lowered prices, and forced dealers there out of business. Gypsy truckers in the coalfields of the central-eastern states disrupted the distribution of coal. They drove to the mines, loaded the trailers with ungraded coal, and delivered it direct to city consumers, thus bypassing the retail coal dealer and driving him out of business.[28]

On the surface, the actions of the independents seem to have benefited the society. The gypsies furnished direct service at lower prices, introduced milk and vegetables to people who had gone without before, and delivered cheaper coal during depressed economic times. Only the middlemen seem to have lost out. The departure of wholesalers and retailers, however, created marketing chaos in many areas. Sometimes the trade-off of low prices for chaotic supplies proved negligible; at other times it might be disastrous. For example, an urban dweller might find his coal bin empty, the weather turning colder, and no truck in sight. The independent truckers, then, brought some distinct advantages and disadvantages. [29]

6

In the early 1930s, the gypsy operations and the increasing numbers of consolidated truck terminals reflected a vibrant, though hardly stable business. In fact, as the construction, power, automobile, railroad, and related industries declined during the Depression, [30] trucking appeared to thrive on the circumstances. The economic structure of motor trucking, the contraction in other transportation industries, and government policies encouraged this expansion.

Trucking was especially well positioned to adjust to depression conditions. Minimal capital investment and low operating costs made entry easy; a large used-truck market and liberal payment plans promoted these advantages. Consolidation was possible without a significant increase in capital expenditures, for trucks could be added one at a time or whole terminal systems integrated with little extra costs. The flexibility that the highways and technology furnished enabled independent truckers to find business whenever and wherever it existed. The railways could not duplicate this flexibility, nor could they match the inherent personal contact between trucker and shipper. [31] The consumer culture, moreover, was founded on "hand-to-mouth buying," for which quick transport service allowed manufacturers to retain small inventories; if demand rose, output was increased and the goods delivered quickly. During the Depression, of course, small inventories reduced merchants' costs. The motor truck continued to furnish the flexibility and speed necessary for the sporadic movement of small shipments.

Specific industries contributed to trucking's vibrancy. Automobile manufacturers overproduced in the 1920s, and the resulting lower prices lured the unemployed into motor trucking. Ironically, laid-off railroad workers bought trucks and competed against their former employers. [32] The highway construction industry provided not only the arteries over which truckers hauled goods but also jobs that utilized trucks. These economic forces helped turn wholesalers and retailers away from the rails and to trucking.

Government policies also encouraged expansion. Quite simply, until 1935 the federal government regulated railways but not trucks. Regulatory procedures hampered railroad responses to the Depression. It is true, as one federal regulator pointed out, that "there is nothing to prevent the carriers reducing [their rates] in order to meet truck competition." The ICC could not prevent the railways from reducing rates below the published maximums, but to do so in many cases meant lowering rates below out-of-pocket costs. In any case, truckers could always respond by reducing their own rates still further, confident that the regulators could not control them. State laws inconvenienced many truckers, but for the most part, these laws were not enforced effectively. Certainly the government-sponsored highway construction bolstered the trucking business; only the timidity of the Hoover and Roosevelt administrations kept highway construction from further supporting the rise of trucking during the Depression.[33]

7

Not surprisingly, the factors that bolstered the fortunes of trucking also contributed to the transportation problem in the 1930s. As the Depression worsened, transportation became more and more a topic of discussion in business and government circles. Some believed the trouble to be too many facilities for too little freight. Others thought the imbalance in government policies toward the different transport industries had created the problem. Still others saw the situation as simply the evolution of a new technology, the truck, to replace a worn-out technology, the railroad. There is some truth in each explanation.

Most observers agreed that an oversupply of transportation facilities formed the basis of the problem. In this, the transport industries were no different from others during the Depression. The railroads since 1920 had invested six billion dollars in expansion and upgrading of terminals and rolling stock. The estimated capital investment of the rails' competitors during the same period equaled the cost of the entire railway system in 1920. Of course, each of the transport businesses did not compete directly against the other. Nonetheless, rapid and massive expansion combined with reduced tonnage to produce the oversupply situation. That the Interstate Commerce Commission and other government agencies encouraged the expansion lends more irony to the story.[34]

In fact, inconsistent government policies aggravated the basic over-supply predicament. Local, state, and federal agencies subsidized airline expansion, through mail contracts and airport construction, and motor trucking expansion, through public highway construction. The federal government paid capital and maintenance costs for inland waterways and even subsidized barge operations (some nonprofit). The railways, meanwhile, appear to have suffered from government pol-icies. They had to haul mail and military goods at rates lower than those charged for commercial traffic. The rails labored under stringent state and federal rate regulations while trucks, airplanes, and waterways operated under subsidies and relative freedom from government con-trol. Some states tried to protect the rails from truck competition, but for the most part, government policies encouraged other transport forms at the expense of the railways.[35]

Of course, the appearance of new transport technologies under-scored the oversupply situation and the inconsistent government pol-icies. As we have discovered, during its rise after World War I, trucking helped revolutionize freight transportation methods. It first facilitated railway terminal service, then competed directly with that service. Truckers, at first content with competing in the short-haul local category, later took advantage of improving technology in motive power and trailer design to launch into long-distance hauling. The absence of effective state controls and total lack of federal supervision allowed the truck to capture traffic from the railways, bogged down as they were in technological obsolescence and regulatory restraints. Although a trend toward rationalized operations in the form of trucking terminals was noticeable, more important was the trend toward disper-sion. One-truck firms made up nearly two-thirds of trucking. These operations not only affected long-established rail operations but also threatened the stability of the recently consolidated trucking terminals. The transportation problem, then, consisted of acute competition between railways and trucks and between consolidated trucking firms and independents—all occurring within a shrinking market and under inconsistent government policies.

Trucking represented the very qualities of the twentieth century that had so concerned Henry Adams at the turn of the century.[36] As we have seen, the trucking revolution spanned two very different epochs in American history and yet seemed to separate itself from both. It altered established patterns in the 1920s and thrived on the general economic decline in the 1930s.

The atomistic, competitive structure of trucking; the quickness with which it emerged; and the mixed economy in which it appeared prevented natural economic forces from forging a stable transportation situation. Instead, like the railroad experience in the last third of the nineteenth century, private sector businessmen and public sector officials sought to impose controls over the dynamic truck. Initial efforts to cartelize trucking occurred in the 1920s, well before the Depression magnified the transportation problem. These first attempts to rationalize trucking were diffuse, uncoordinated, and unsuccessful, but in hindsight, they proved to be rehearsals for public action in the 1930s.

PART TWO

**Public and
Private Responses,
1920–1932**

Cooperation is not a sentiment, it is an economic
necessity. Keen interest is one of the driving
forces of every Association.

> —AHFA flyer
> April 12, 1933

It is unfortunate indeed that so many interests in
America, all with the same objective in view,
should be travelling via so many diversified paths.

> —Tom Snyder,
> Secretary-Treasurer, TAEA
> August 22, 1932

3

State Regulation and the Truck Associational Movement:
An Illusory Quest for Cooperation and Uniformity

In 1924 Secretary of Commerce Herbert C. Hoover sponsored two national conferences on transportation problems in the U.S., the Transportation Conference and the National Conference on Street and Highway Safety. Hoover hoped to achieve uniformity in public policies through the cooperative efforts of business and government leaders. To that end, committees of businessmen and public officials drafted plans to alleviate urban congestion, reduce rising highway death rates, refurbish the railway systems, and coordinate all transport businesses into an efficient network.[1]

Hoover championed this alliance between the private and public sectors throughout his tenure at Commerce. As he told participants of the Transportation Conference called by the United States Chamber of Commerce, American businessmen were "passing from a period of extremely individualistic action into a period of associational activities." The Secretary believed that with limited governmental guidance private business groups could stabilize industry competition and thus establish a progressive economy with stable growth patterns. By his estimate, there were twenty-five thousand business organizations in America—chambers of commerce, professional associations, farmers' cooperatives, and trade groups. "With vision and devotion," Hoover was convinced, "these voluntary forces can accomplish more for America than any spread of the hand of government." He claimed, moreover, that this approach had already brought improved conditions in the lumber and bituminous coal industries, in which representatives from various firms had drawn up detailed rules for ethical conduct.[2]

Hoover was correct in at least one respect: American businessmen had been engaged in collective activities. In 1920 over two thousand trade groups had been formed by various industries to promote their interests. Through separate programs, the Commerce Department and the Federal Trade Commission encouraged hundreds more associations during the 1920s. Some trade groups were defensive and temporary, becoming active when competitive pressures appeared, only to disband when the threats subsided. Other, more permanent associations set up industrywide trade rules designed to produce steady growth in their industries. Whether defensive or planning-oriented, these groups all wanted to reduce competition and thus ensure profits for their members. Moreover, most operated within the hazy zone where private and public interests overlapped, either using government as a guide (as Hoover envisioned) or asking government to regulate (which Hoover did not want to do).[3]

Motor trucking did not escape this wave of associationalism; perhaps because of its youth, however, it did not attract attention from either Commerce or the FTC.[4] Instead, truckers engaged in collective actions similar in technique to but divorced from the mainsteam government programs. Trucking, to some extent, undermined commercial patterns, disrupting quality, quantity, and price controls that had been established for decades. Since it affected so much of the economy, motor trucking was bound to elicit collective attempts to control its development. The real issue was not whether the new technology should be controlled, but how and by whom.

That a quasi-public, quasi-private association of state regulators—the National Association of Railroad and Utility Commissioners (NARUC)—began the movement to bring uniformity to trucking laws underscores the control theme. The state commissioners, motivated in part by self-interest and in part by railway lobbyists, first promoted coordination of state and federal regulations. Yet they failed to convince either state or federal lawmakers that their plan was necessary. Consequently, a patchwork quilt of state laws appeared that obviously hindered the development of interstate motor trucking and less obviously curtailed intrastate business as well. In response, local truckers in the mid-1920s organized ad hoc associations and lobbied state legislatures for less restrictive laws. Simultaneously, a group of visionary truck association executives attempted to devise a national force that would coordinate responses to the state regulations. Meanwhile, truck manufacturers also viewed the state laws as threats to their business. Ideologically opposed to government intrusion in the economy, the truck manufacturers sponsored a national program to educate truckers in sound business practices and to encourage self-regulation that would make government controls unnecessary. A group of regulated interstate motor carriers joined the fray in the early 1930s, seeking federal controls that would standardize state laws and eliminate unscrupulous and inexperienced truckers.

Given this array of conflicting interests connected to motor trucking, it is not surprising that Secretary Hoover's hopes for cooperation and uniformity in transportation matters failed to materialize. It was not that the state commissioners and truckers and manufacturers lacked the "vision and devotion" Hoover had urged, but rather that the vision and devotion of some conflicted with those of others. The conflicts and failures nevertheless laid the groundwork for more concerted action in the 1930s.

I

The National Association of Railroad and Utility Commissioners, made up of state officials who regulated public utilities, prophetically recognized that trucking presented special problems of control that the railways had not.

NARUC had appeared in the late 1880s as a mechanism through which state and federal regulators could cooperate with one another. The idea of a private association of public officials was novel but perceptive. Chairman Thomas M. Cooley of the ICC, who had first proposed NARUC, recognized that the recently established federal commission did not have exclusive authority over the railroads; the states still exercised important controls. The experienced state regulators, moreover, had valuable information that the new federal commissioners could use. Thus, NARUC emerged in part as an organization through which state and federal officials could solve jurisdictional problems, exchange ideas, and suggest plans for more effective administration. NARUC was not just an intergovermental body, for at its annual conventions, its members listened to leaders of the business community who offered their ideas on particular regulatory issues: accounting, valuation, state-federal cooperation, and so on. In this comprehensive and cooperative manner, it was hoped, technical and theoretical matters of business regulation would be resolved to the satisfaction of all parties involved.[5]

The very jurisdictional conflicts that underlay NARUC's creation led ironically—if not inevitably—to strained relations between the state and federal commissioners. In the early 1890s, NARUC, the ICC, and the industry cooperated well under the leadership of Henry Carter Adams, statistician for the ICC, to devise a uniform system of accounting for the railroads. In this same spirit of cooperation, NARUC helped the ICC lobby congress for expanded authority to regulate railroad operations. The results—the Elkins Act of 1903 (which gave teeth to the antirebating clause of the original 1887 statute by allowing prosecution of shippers who received rebates) and the Hepburn Act of 1906 (which increased the number of commissioners from five to seven and gave the ICC authority to fix just and reasonable maximum rail rates)—inaugurated a two-decade period during which the states gradually lost power to the ICC. In the so-called *Shreveport* case of 1914, the Supreme Court ruled that the ICC could establish intrastate rates when those rates were found to unduly discriminate against interstate rates. For all practical purposes, then, the states no longer held authority over rate making. Federal management of the railroads during World War I further curtailed state control, and finally, the Transportation Act of 1920 gave the ICC still more authority over the rail industry. Despite the erosion of power, the states were not completely left out of the picture, for Congress in the 1920 act instructed the ICC to cooperate with the state commissions in investigating regulatory problems.[6] If the state officials had lost much of their authority, they had not lost the concept of cooperation.

Fortuitously, the young trucking business afforded the state commissioners an opportunity to regain lost power and status. In the early years of the postwar decade, even before trucking became important to the national economy, NARUC members discussed how best to control it. They concluded that since trucks operated essentially within local areas and used state highways, they were subject to state controls. Pennsylvania extended controls over trucks in 1914. In 1923 E.V. Kuykendall, director of the Washington (state) commission, submitted a model uniform statute that each state might use to standardize regulations. In his comprehensive plan—which included provisions for license fees, speed limits, route regulation, and control over common and contract motor carriers—Kuykendall foresaw problems that the Supreme Court and Congress would not resolve until the 1930s.[7]

In 1924–25 the model statute met a setback when the Supreme Court invalidated state laws that controlled interstate truck commerce (see Chapter 4). Although some NARUC members altered the model statute to meet the Court's objections, others worked on a new approach to regulating transportation. In 1925 NARUC's Committee on Motor Vehicle Transportation presented the first proposal for federal regulation of trucking. The philosophy behind the plan was the same as the one for the model state statute. Trucking represented a local business, and therefore the state was the proper agent for control. Recognizing that some truck commerce crossed state lines, the committee suggested Congress assign federal status to state commissioners who would man special joint boards; these state-federal officials would perform the usual regulatory functions as they applied to interstate trucking in the area covered by the joint board. Decisions of the joint boards could be appealed to the ICC, which would retain ultimate authority.[8]

The concept of power formally shared in this way represented a new idea in regulatory history that followed logically from the cooperative spirit in which NARUC had been conceived and from the inherent conflicts between the states and the federal government in regulating commerce. A few of NARUC's members were decidedly hostile to the proposal. One Minnesota regulator characterized it as "the most radical departure from the policies of this Association that has taken place, at least since I have been a member." This delegate and others, jealous of the federal power embodied in the *Shreveport* case, wanted no federal interference in the regulation of trucks.[9]

Yet, the fatal flaw embodied in the proposal was not its suggestion of shared authority. The trouble with the scheme was that it proposed controlling an industry that did not yet exist. Nearly a decade after NARUC's proposal was offered, only 7 percent of all trucks were engaged in interstate hauling; as late as 1932 the ICC maintained that federal regulation was simply unnecessary. When support for federal controls appeared after 1933, NARUC was no longer at the center of the movement; its old nemesis, the ICC, had assumed control.[10]

Without the cooperative spirit envisioned in NARUC's model statute and its joint board system, state lawmakers in the 1920s and early 1930s became susceptible to interest group pressures and to the complexities of regulating a business composed of tens of thousands of small-scale firms. Though different in detail from state to state, the truck laws fell into two distinct categories. Direct regulations controlled entry, service, and rates. They were direct because the state decided for the trucker whether and where he could engage in business, how he was to conduct that business, and what rates he could charge for his services. Truckers challenged these controls, however, and they remained ineffective until 1932, when the Supreme Court ruled that the laws did not violate constitutional boundaries. Indirect regulations limited the physical dimensions of the truck (height, length, width, and weight); these laws also imposed fees for licenses and taxes on gasoline. Such laws did not directly exclude a trucker from engaging in business, but they did restrict his ability to make a profit. In a few extreme cases, indirect controls could make trucking an unprofitable enterprise altogether.[11]

Whether direct or indirect, the state laws varied markedly from one state to the next. A glance at regulations in the Midwest and Northeast as they had evolved up to 1933 illustrates the lack of uniformity. If a trucker began a trip in Chicago, heading east, he could load a truck and trailer with a total of 39,000 pounds, 20,000 on the truck and 19,000 in the trailer. When he approached the Indiana border, he had to remove 16,000 pounds from the truck and 12,800 pounds from the trailer to meet the Hoosier State's limit of 10,200 pounds. Once in Ohio he could add a total of 7,000 pounds; Pennsylvania allowed an additional 14,000 pounds (to total 31,200). Obviously, interstate trucking from Chicago to Philadelphia in the early 1930s was difficult if truckers obeyed the diverse laws.[12]

In addition to the weight restrictions, states imposed different limits on the height, length, and width of commercial vehicles. Pennsylvania allowed heights to 174 inches, but Indiana only 144 inches. Maximum lengths of combination vehicles (tractor and trailer) varied widely, from forty feet in Connecticut, Illinois, and Indiana, to seventy in Pennsylvania and eighty-five in Rhode Island. Width restrictions were the most uniform: all the northeastern states limited widths to 96 inches, except Rhode Island and Connecticut, which placed the limit at 102 inches.[13]

State laws imposing license fees and gasoline taxes also created problems for the aspiring interstate truckers. Enforcement of these laws in one state often provoked retaliation in neighboring states. "Border wars" erupted in which highway patrolmen waited just inside the state line to fine out-of-state truckers who failed to have license and gasoline receipts. Such wars were usually short-lived because state truck association officials and public regulatory commissioners met to make temporary reciprocity agreements. These ad hoc agreements allowed truckers from one state to operate in the other. They fell far short of uniformity, however, for they often remained in effect for only several months. The uncertainty attending these changing conditions burdened consolidated and gypsy truckers alike. [14]

Several forces shaped the diversity of laws, and these same forces prevented NARUC from assuming leadership in any movement toward uniformity. In part, the state laws were adapted to local geographic necessities and road system limitations. States with winding roads and steep grades restricted vehicle sizes to forestall dangerous driving conditions. Similarly, states with radically shifting weather conditions instituted load limits to reduce wear and tear on roadways already damaged by intermittent frost and heat. The lawmakers, and later even the Supreme Court, remained unpersuaded by scientific evidence suggesting that more efficiently designed roads and vehicles could overcome the local conditions. [15] Skepticism of scientific evidence played a part in this intransigence, but more important were the effects of public opinion. Despite the benefits trucking presented to the economy, the public often focused upon the negative aspects of the new business. When confronted with a huge tractor-trailer rig crawling up a mountain pass at five miles per hour, the pleasure car driver was more concerned with the dangers of passing and the time lost than he was with the economic benefits that truck might bring him. Some truckers, moreover, did not know or chose not to follow safe operating procedures. Whether or not it was true, the public's perception was that most truckers were careless or dangerous. State legislators, acting on this perception, enacted restrictive legislation. [16]

Railroad interests also encouraged the legislatures to restrict trucking both directly and indirectly. Unable to compete profitably in the economic arena, the railways employed highway maintenance and safety issues to persuade lawmakers to control the new competition. For example, in 1931 the railroads in Texas successfully sponsored legislation that drove most contract carriers hauling cotton from the highways. Meanwhile, railroad pressure in Kentucky, Indiana, and Ohio brought restrictive laws to those contiguous states. In 1932 several midwestern systems hired a former truck association official, ostensibly to organize a coordinated rail-truck network. Instead, this person traveled to Iowa towns to persuade city councils to enact local weight laws; he then sold them new Black and Decker truck scales with which to enforce the laws. This same operator is said to have offered rewards to encourage state highway patrolmen to harass truckers. In a related example, Kentucky hired laid-off railway workers as highway sheriffs to enforce the state's truck statutes.[17] These railway tactics did not require a master conspiracy to be effective; the diversity in state laws was enough to slow the emergence of interstate trucking.

Whether based upon geographic necessities, public opinion, or railroad lobbying, state laws created problems for those engaged in or associated with the motor carrier business. Local, state, and interstate truckers suffered from increased operating costs, while manufacturers faced diverse production requirements and a growing used-truck market (caused in part by the bankruptcies of inexperienced drivers under pressure of the increased costs). Moreover, common carrier truckers appear to have been at a disadvantage because the laws controlled them but not the private and contract truckers.

This, then, was the complex background in which the associational movement in trucking emerged. Businessmen connected to trucking slowly realized that if they were to protect their interests they could not rely solely upon the technological advantages the truck provided. Competition now took place not only in the economic market but also in the political arena and the realm of public opinion. The truckers would have to organize and engage in political action.

2

North Carolina's law appeared especially onerous: it required truckers to pay three to four times as much for operating licenses as haulers paid in Georgia, New Jersey, or New York. In one extreme example, one businessman had to pay $960 per year to use one truck. A short time after the North Carolina legislature enacted the so-called Triple Tax Law in 1929, a group of twenty truckers and manufacturers met informally in Charlotte to discuss possible responses to the statute. The Charlotte group collected money and hired lawyers to challenge the law through the courts; they were successful until North Carolina's highest tribunal ruled against them and in favor of the state. Undaunted, the group met again in November 1930, with newly recruited businessmen in attendance, and formed the Truck Association of North Carolina. With no specific agenda guiding this meeting, the new association addressed a wide range of issues affecting trucking, including speed laws, license requirements, and weight restrictions. Members eventually agreed to meet with legislators before the next session to explain the truckers' position.[18]

Similar scenes were reenacted in a majority of the states during the late 1920s and early 1930s. In many states, several associations emerged, each one representing a particular kind of trucking that faced specific kinds of problems. Tank truck operators were subject to different restrictions than were cattle haulers; common carriers complained that they were regulated and others were not; cartage businesses objected to competition from out-of-state truckers.[19] These diverse, local associations, narrowly focused and defensive, followed the rhythms of state politics, becoming active when the legislative sessions opened, only to disappear when the lawmakers adjourned. In the early 1930s, as state controls increased in number and severity, more truckers became interested in organized response. By this time, however, too many associations competed with each other for the truckers' too few dollars. Rackets frequently appeared wherein unscrupulous organizers promised unsuspecting truckers immediate relief, took their money, and departed, never to be seen again. In such an atmosphere, many operators grew disillusioned and refused to join any more associations.

California presented a particularly complex situation, ripe for the emergence of numerous local truck associations. By March 1934, twenty to twenty-five such organizations existed. In general, the state was divided into two different trucking situations. The nine southern counties, from Los Angeles to the Mexican border, experienced rapid growth in the late 1920s and early 1930s, and numerous trucking companies came into existence. With that increase came sharp competition and conflict between those firms that were regulated by the California Railroad Commission and those that were not. Northern California trucking, however, was more established, with higher wages and closely connected trade associations that succeeded in barring entry to new firms. This situation led to disparate lobbying efforts during state legislative sessions. As Roy H. Compton summed it up, when truckers "try to influence the making of laws there is no unity of ideas."[20]

What was needed was legitimacy and national direction if truckers were to combat attacks on their livelihoods from regulators and railroads. The executive secretaries of three different groups—the most successful state associations, the national association of motor vehicle manufacturers, and an alliance of interstate operators—competed with one another to become the guiding hand that would shape the trucking business into a strong industry capable of withstanding political attacks. The strategies of each group, based on different perceptions of what was in the best interest of trucking, conflicted with those of the other two.

3

As early as 1920, an Indianapolis truck operator recognized the need for a national organization of truckers to promote uniformity in state laws. It took Tom Snyder until 1926–27, however, to persuade other leading truckers in Indiana, Ohio, and Kentucky to join him. At the Motor Transportation Conference in 1928, Snyder and officials from several other state truck associations established the Transportation Association Executives of America (TAEA). Among the members was H.C. Kelting, founder of the successful Central Truck Depot. Tom Snyder was named Secretary-Treasurer of the new organization, and he approached his job energetically as the self-proclaimed advocate of "industrial consciousness" in motor trucking. Synder mailed thousands of letters, extolling the virtues of organization, spent his own money when dues payment lagged; and took time from his own firm to organize trucking interests on a national scale. His enthusiasm played no small part in bringing about several regional conferences in which state association officials met to discuss common problems they faced in establishing effective trade groups.[21]

For example, at the Eastern Conference in New York City in July 1930, TAEA members discussed methods for overcoming the apathy of truckers and their suspicion of associations. The suggestions that came forth from these discussions reflected strategies common to other cooperative schemes in American history, particularly the Patrons of Husbandry and the Farmers' Alliance in the last third of the nineteenth century. Associations used important speakers, often war heroes, and outings such as picnics and Christmas parties to attract members; but special services like newspapers and cooperatives kept them attending and paying dues. Many associations published biweekly or monthly bulletins that reported on group activities, recent changes in the laws, road conditions, and current and future legislative issues. Financial support came from advertisements in the bulletins that were sold to businesses serving truckers, such as tire and truck dealers and oil companies. A few associations aided members in securing licenses and hiring lawyers to contest fines. Others organized employment bureaus, driver-training schools, and cooperative purchasing schemes, through

which members bought fuel, tires, and accessories at reduced prices.[22]
The discussions in the summer of 1930 revealed a growing sophistication in responses that truckers were making to attacks on their business.

Snyder did not confine his organizational energies to the conferences. Between meetings, he communicated with other groups concerned over the lack of uniformity in state truck laws, including the American Road Builders Association, the Society of Automotive Engineers, the Association of Highway Administrators, and the Bureau of Public Roads. In January 1932 Snyder put together a joint conference with the TAEA and the American Road Builders Association, during which rail-motor coordination, highway taxation, insurance, and regulatory issues were discussed. Eight months later, Snyder was working with the SAE on standardization of truck dimensions.[23] The exchange of information Snyder had generated convinced TAEA leaders that the ad hoc and defensive strategies of the past would have to give way to an ongoing political presence if their trade groups were to be effective in stabilizing the trucking business. That the TAEA failed to achieve its goal should not obscure the importance of the association, for it more clearly defined for truckers the issues that threatened their business and began the process that would eventually lead to concerted action among interstate truckers.

4

A growing used-truck market prompted the manufacturers to enter the truck associational movement and, for a while at least, to work with the TAEA. Manufacturers such as Mack, International, White, and GMC found themselves victims of unsound selling practices similar to those in the stock market and land booms of the 1920s. Dealers accepted low downpayments and offered liberal loan plans that attracted inexperienced truckers; once on the road, these drivers charged rates below the cost of service, bankrupted themselves, and returned the truck to the sales market. As the decade came to a close, the state truck laws began to exacerbate the manufacturers' problems. Efficient use of scale economies was curtailed, for different size trucks and trailers had to be designed to meet the varying standards. In some ways the restrictions encouraged technological progress in truck design, through the development of cab-over tractors and lighter materials, but they raised production costs and thus the price of new equipment. The truck laws and the unsound dealer practices, then, created for the manufacturers an unstable market for new trucks.[24]

The National Automobile Chamber of Commerce (NACC), the manufacturers' trade association, set up a Truck Committee in 1923. Over the next decade, under the leadership of Edward F. Loomis, the committee devised strategies to organize trucking into a sound service industry. Rather than the ad hoc and narrow-visioned local groups already in existence, Loomis preferred that each state contain only one organization that included all elements of the business: common, contract, private, and cartage operators, as well as manufacturers, oil companies, and tire dealerships. Through a wide representation of interests, Loomis believed, educational and lobbying efforts coordinated through one association would stabilize truck competition in each state.[25]

For reasons that are unclear, Loomis waited until the spring of 1929 to implement his organizational strategy. Given four thousand dollars for expenses from NACC, Loomis's organizers began their work in New Jersey. Their initial effort met with mixed success, but through this and later forays, they gradually learned how to organize truckers. State-by-state, field men first called on the manufacturers and explained to them that organized response was required to meet the problems trucking faced. With introductions from the manufacturers, the field representatives next contacted the dealerships. With dealer support, NACC organizers were able to locate and speak with the truckers. Since many states already contained several associations, the field men often tried to convince the different groups to merge into one state organization. And they contacted businessmen who used trucking services. If these meetings did not result in membership, at least they placed "information before important interests which [made] it possible to obtain their cooperation on legislation."[26]

NACC's associational program represented a cautious philosophy with respect to expenditures, combined with sophisticated techniques for organization. NACC paid the field men's salaries and the publishing costs of educational pamphlets, but it refused to spend money for further organization. The Truck Committee believed that initial support should come from local manufacturers and dealers, who, the committee suggested, could finance the costs through higher prices. Eventually, it was planned, the truckers would bear most of the costs of associationalism through increased revenues. The strategy of going through the manufacturers to get to the dealers did not always work, for some dealers were independent of the manufacturers, but this approach directly confronted the problem of distinguishing NACC organizers from the racketeers. Truckers were much more likely to listen to their immediate business contacts than they were to someone just off the train who, for all they knew, might be another con man.[27]

In addition to the organizational impetus, NACC furnished other services to the trade groups. For example, the Truck Committee hired lawyers LaRue Brown and Stuart Scott to offer legal advice and to formulate strategies for combating the state laws. In fact, NACC paid Brown's fees for arguing the pivotal Supreme Court cases in 1932. The Truck Committee also scheduled speakers for association gatherings, made available canned articles for state bulletins, and published educational pamphlets that included information on industry problems (taxation, safe-driving techniques, and regulation). By the end of 1932, for example, the NACC had 621 organizations—including chambers of commerce, trade and truck associations, manufacturers, and insurance companies—distributing pamphlets for a better truck-driving campaign.[28] Through these services, the NACC strengthened truckers' awareness of the problems they faced, both from outside and from within the business.

The efforts of the National Automobile Chamber of Commerce naturally attracted the attention of the Truck Association Executives of America. The two groups appeared to be moving in similar directions, and on occasion, they worked together. Yet, they disagreed over how to use the collective strength the state associations represented. The TAEA wanted to lobby state legislatures for positive truck controls—regulations that would not overly restrict trucking but would stabilize its development. The NACC, on the other hand, opposed all government controls. Its members believed that regulations would only raise the cost of doing business, and higher prices might force shippers back to the railroads, thus diminishing the need for the new trucks they manufactured. Loomis claimed that the NACC was not opposed to "experiments" in regulation but did oppose laws "designed to cripple truck operation for the benefit of the railroads." He also pointed out the problems of effectively enforcing protruck laws and noted that competition did not always decrease with the advent of regulation.[29]

It was a puzzling position. The NACC seems to have ignored the prevailing political climate in the early 1930s. There were already a number of laws in effect, and given the states' record of restrictive legislation, based on such varied issues as economics, road safety, and public opinion, it was unlikely that legislators would remove them from the books. At best, the laws might be altered to help trucking. As the TAEA argued, positive controls over trucking, while perhaps raising costs, would not necessarily result in prices higher than the railroads charged; the movement back to the rails that Loomis and the NACC feared was unlikely to occur. Yet, the NACC apparently did not understand—or chose not to accept—the argument that positive legislation could remove the inexperienced truckers who had contributed to the burgeoning used-truck market.[30] The NACC's position against government intrusion of any kind represents a case in which ideology proved stronger than political or economic realities.

The manufacturers' intransigence on the regulation issue would eventually separate the NACC from the major thrust of the truck associational movement. Yet, the organization, nonetheless, furnished an important contribution to associationalism. By 1932 thirty-three state trade groups were working directly with the Truck Committee. Indeed, the NACC's concept of one state association to represent all trucking interests formed the basic principle, and its associations, the basic structure for the national truck association that emerged during the New Deal.[31] Along with the TAEA, the NACC not only had schooled truckers in better business practices but had also shown them the importance of organization. Tom Snyder's dream of "industrial consciousness" seemed to be materializing.

5

Common carrier interstate truckers, for the most part, did not need associations to teach them how to be profitable businessmen; they were already successful. They did need associations to present a united political front against attacks on their livelihood. Subject to common law precedent, these truckers viewed themselves as an oppressed group. The same legal precedents that allowed state control over their operations also prevented the states from regulating their competitors, the private and contract carriers. Moreover, railroads could seek relief from state commissions and the ICC to meet competition, but the common carrier truckers could not, for neither the state agencies nor the federal commission possessed clear statutory authority to help them. A growing awareness of these problems prompted common carriers to organize, first, on the state level, then nationally.

The appearance of these regulated carriers' associations heightened tensions between the trucking groups. On the whole, common carriers did not object to regulation itself; good laws, properly enforced, could, they recognized, eliminate rate cutters and improve business conduct, thus bringing stability to their business. However, they did object to the lack of uniformity in the state laws, the absence of controls over all truckers, and the inefficient enforcement of laws already enacted. To redress these grievances, regulated truckers resorted to political pressure. In some cases, they worked with railroad lobbyists, a tactic that alienated other truckers, who viewed the railways as the chief villian behind the state laws. Notwithstanding the bad blood it caused, this strategy made sense, for it enabled truckers to dilute the rails' influence, and sometimes they successfully sponsored provisions beneficial to motor trucking. Besides, in most instances, the railroads and common carrier truckers faced the same problems. Both suffered from unregulated competitors who often cut rates below the costs of service, a practice the states prohibited for common carriers.[32] Consequently, in the early 1930s, state legislative sessions became miniature Roman senates in which lobbyists for the various transportation groups plotted against each other to enact legislation favorable to them and detrimental to their opponents.[33] In this contentious atmosphere, regulated interstate truckers found effective relief unattainable.

The rate-cutting practices, the state legislative situation, and the jurisdictional problems of controlling interstate commerce prompted the common carriers to organize a national association. In November 1932, led by Jack Keeshin, the successful midwestern trucker and an ambitious spokesman for the industry, the operators founded the American Highway Freight Association, limiting membership to common carrier truckers. The AHFA demanded federal legislation that would stabilize interstate trucking and strove, as J.P. Dempsey proclaimed, to provide for the "dissemination of educational and economic propoganda . . . together with a program having for its purpose the cleansing of the industry as a whole."[34] Thus, the AHFA was motivated toward goals similar to those of the TAEA and the NACC. The major difference separating the groups lay in the AHFA's emphasis on promoting federal regulation rather than uniform state laws (as the TAEA desired) or no laws at all (as the NACC preferred).

To implement its program, the AHFA first hired Charles E. Cotterill, an experienced utilities lawyer, most of whose clients had been large national transportation, mining, and chemical firms, to draft a fede al regulatory bill. Assuming that the logical agent for federal control would be the Interstate Commerce Commission, Cotterill, Keeshin, and their allies solicited ideas from ICC personnel as well as from interested Congressmen.[35] This represented a different approach from the TAEA and NACC efforts in that it circumvented such peripheral organizations as the SAE, the Bureau of Public Roads, and the state commissions and instead went directly to the source of power. Consequently, the focus of the associational movement shifted from a state-oriented defensive effort to a national one based on cooperation with the ICC and Congress.

The AHFA altered the focus in another way. Until late 1932, the major thrust behind associational activities was toward uniformity of indirect regulations. The common carriers, however, wanted stronger, direct controls that would eliminate the rate cutters. Since relief was not forthcoming from the states, the regulated operators sought help from the federal government. In requesting direct federal controls, the AHFA awakened other truckers to the possibility of federal intrusion into their business.

Not surprisingly, the AHFA efforts encountered numerous obstacles. From the outset, the choice to exclude all but common carriers confined the movement because it reduced potential financial support and lobbying strength. Then too, the history of the truck associational movement before 1932 also hindered the AHFA. Some carriers declined to join yet another association; others feared the new trade group was just another racket; and still others simply had no more money to give to the cause. Of course, many truckers disagreed with the AHFA's emphasis on federal regulation. AHFA officials, moreover, created confusion over just who was behind the trade group and exactly what its purpose was.[36] The AHFA's timing proved unfortunate in another respect, for the common carriers organized just as political power was changing hands in Washington. Early in 1933 the transport policy of the new Democratic adminstration was ill defined. Without momentum in Washington, the AHFA would encounter apathy in the field.

Despite these drawbacks, the emergence of the AHFA marked a watershed in the truck associational movement. The common carrier group forcefully argued that local problems would indeed have to be addressed on the national level, just as NARUC had foreseen nine years before. Further, the AHFA's very existence tended to polarize the numerous truckers' groups into two general camps—those who favored federal regulation and those who did not.[37] Several other conflicts remained, of course, but the issue of federal control clarified the directions the associational movement would take. By early 1933 the common carriers and a growing number of other truckers recognized that a national association represented the best device for responding to the various attacks from within and from without the trucking business. What was not clear was what form the association should take.

6

Herbert Hoover's vision of associationalism in transportation matters in 1924 had seemed especially relevant to the problems facing the trucking business, for the cooperative process he had outlined for transportation and other industries offered a dynamic solution for solving complex problems. Yet, as his defeat in 1932 at the hands of Franklin D. Roosevelt and the Democrats revealed, his vision of cooperative planning for the future had been overwhelmed by the ensuing Depression. The error in his vision lay in his assumption that enlightened self-interest would guide businessmen and government officials toward integrating their needs with those of the public. Instead, the trucking industry, state regulators, the TAEA, the NACC, and the AHFA competed one against another for support from the operators. Without a directing force, either an internal code of ethics or direct government controls, the truck associational movement unfolded as a story of disparate interest groups going separate ways with little comprehension of or responsibility for the larger picture.[38]

Despite the absence of a guiding hand, the movement in the 1920s showed positive accomplishments. Association lobbyists prevented the railroads from completely destroying the technological progress the truck embodied. These early defensive actions evolved into positive strategies that employed legislative activity and educational programs. Through the efforts of the NACC and the TAEA, truckers recognized that others endured similar problems. The educational pamphlets that the NACC distributed illuminated these common concerns and the TAEA-sponsored conventions furnished a forum through which solutions might be found. Both groups represented private sector attempts to rationalize business conduct, just as Hoover had envisioned. Even though the TAEA had shown signs of moving away from pure Hooverian associationalism (through sponsorship of legislation), it was the emergence of the AHFA in the fall of 1932 that permanently shifted the major focus toward federal regulation. Trucking leaders were recognizing that local problems with national implications could not be solved through enlightened self-interest and voluntarism.

While the private sector imperfectly engaged in associational activities, the public sector, too, confronted the problems the truck posed to the economy. By 1932, after addressing a series of truck cases, the U.S. Supreme Court had authorized state control of intrastate but not interstate trucking. Meanwhile, the ICC slowly discovered the problems that the truck presented, and by the time the Court had acted, the commission was delivering to Congress tentative proposals for national control.

4 Authority to Control: The Supreme Court and State Truck Regulation

Truckers in the 1920s found themselves in quick succession subjected to fierce competition in the economic market, in the political arena, and in the court system. Truckers' associations retaliated with educational programs, legislative lobbying, and legal appeals. This last strategy—challenging the constitutionality of the state truck laws—gave impetus to a series of Supreme Court cases between 1924 and 1932 that, taken together, outlined the limits of governmental control over the trucking business.

The truckers discovered that additional abilities were required to be competitive in the court system. Here, in the courts, the fate of truckers' interests hinged, not on technological advantages or managerial abilities or even on political skill, but rather on whether or not the majority of nine justices agreed with the truckers' interpretation of the legal issues.

The nature of the judicial story derived in part from the history of transport law and in part from the characteristics of trucking. As noted earlier, in transport law as it had evolved to the twentieth century, common carriers served any and all shippers willing to pay; private carriers transported goods only as an extension of another trade, such as farming or baking. The common law allowed government to control the former but not the latter. The new motor carrier business, however, included a third class, the contract carrier, who did not serve the public generally but rather held contracts with a select few shippers. Were contract carriers subject to government controls, or were they private carriers? How many contracts could such carriers hold—two, three, five—before the law could consider them common carriers? And what of the increasing number of trucks that crossed state lines? Could the state legislators control this interstate commerce?[1] The states maintained that in the absence of Congressional action, they themselves held the authority, through the police power, to regulate these movements. Lawyers for the trucking interests argued that the central issue concerned the commerce power; if the state laws restricted interstate commerce, then they were unconstitutional. The truck cases, then, clarified the three major classes of trucking, delineated state powers over each, and indicated that Congress should act to remove jurisdictional conflicts between the states and the federal government.

Viewed in a broader historical context, these trucking cases reflect a fundamental shift in the philosophy of the Court toward government intrusion in the economy. At first unwilling to sanction state controls, the Court gradually accepted the argument that in a period when technological changes and economic depression had outstripped the ability of the old political order to respond to change, new authority to experiment with public policy initiatives was necessary. During the 1920s and early 1930s, at least four members of the Supreme Court consistently disagreed with this view; even so, the high tribunal began to shift from a perspective that restricted government intrusion into private affairs to one that permitted the law to be used as a positive instrument for social change. The trucking cases may have influenced this shift more than legal historians have admitted.[2]

When the Court first addressed the state truck laws in 1925, it did so against a history of legal decisions extending back to medieval English law. It was a confusing legacy, for changes over time in the economy, in the political arena, and in the legal profession brought extensions and reversals on some of the central issues. The survey that follows shows that the truck cases were not decided in a vacuum, but rather against a rich and complex background of legal history. By no means a complete description and analysis of the legal history of business regulation, it is intended only as an outline of the essential principles involved in trucking cases and as an indication of the variability apparent in constitutional interpretation.

I

Throughout Anglo-American history, business has been subjected to varying degrees of government control. In medieval England, common law distinguished "public callings" from private ones through the concept of the "duty to serve" all who were willing to pay. By 1518 the "duty to serve" concept had expanded to make common carriers liable for damages occurring because of neglect, such as overloading a wagon or being robbed while driving through a dangerous area. Apparently, English common carriers varied their rates according to a shipper's ability to pay and his station in life, but in the U.S., the courts gradually expanded the "duty to serve" concept to mean that common carriers must charge equal rates to all customers.[3]

Confusion in government control of business appeared early in U.S. history because of the dual authority that the Constitution granted to the national government and the states. In general, the commerce clause of the Constitution, through which Congress regulated business transactions that crossed state lines, conflicted with the police power, a common law concept that gave states the authority to control business for the public good. The Supreme Court under Chief Justice John Marshall (1810–1835) usually emphasized the exclusivity of the commerce clause, but Chief Justice Roger B. Taney's Court (1836–1864) most often favored the police power.[4]

After Reconstruction, new cases addressing new problems, such as the due process clause of the Fourteenth Amendment, the doctrine of "affected with a public interest," and the notion of freedom of contract, further obscured the issues of business regulation. The most famous of these cases, *Munn* v. *Illinois* (1877) appeared to open the door to extensive government control of commerce. The case involved the 1870 statute regulating the maximum prices for storage of grain in Chicago. The warehousemen claimed, first, that the state could not set prices and, second, that the state could not regulate business engaged in interstate commerce.

Citing English and American precedents, Chief Justice Morrison R. Waite clearly showed that the police power had been used in times past "to regulate ferries, common carriers, hackmen, bakers, millers, . . . etc., and in so doing to fix a minimum charge to be made for services rendered." In other words, the police power, when used to advance the public good, had superseded the rights of private property. The Fourteenth Amendment, moreover, did not abrogate this power, according to Waite; it only declared that the state could not deprive a man of property without due process of law. In a somewhat circular fashion, Waite found due process in *Munn* to rest on the doctrine of "affected with a public interest." When private property was devoted to a public use, (if it were affected with a public interest), it ceased to be only private property and thus became subject to public control. To the warehousemen's complaints that they could not earn a profit at the regulated levels, Waite declared that that problem should be addressed to the legislature, not to the courts.[5]

As for the issue of whether the Illinois statute violated the commerce clause, Waite argued that it did not because Congress had not acted on the issues; in the absence of federal law, the state could legislate to protect the public welfare. Even though *Munn* concerned state powers, it held wider implications for later national regulation of business. The decision reflected a philosophy of judicial restraint, wherein judges allow the lawmakers wide latitude in devising public policies, that apparently opened a broad area for government control of commerce. Felix Frankfurter, for example, viewed *Munn* as the progenitor of the Interstate Commerce Act of 1887.[6]

Yet the precedents in *Munn* did not take hold immediately, for judicial concern for the rights of property intervened. Justice Stephen J. Field, who wrote the dissent in *Munn*, declared the majority's decision to be "subversive of the rights of private property."[7] Nine years after *Munn*, Chief Justice Waite accepted some of Field's arguments when he asserted that the police power to regulate business was not unlimited and that regulation without regard for profit "amounts to a taking of property for public use without just compensation, or without due process of law." In the 1890s Field won over a majority of the Court and extended protection of private property when he insisted that the courts should review the findings of the state regulatory commissions. This position, in effect, protected private rights from public infringement, but it also emasculated the ability of the states to correct abuses in the economy. Field's concept of judicial review was formalized in *Smyth* v. *Ames* (1898), when the Court decided it had the authority to review all rate-making decisions of the regulatory agencies.[8] The legislature might enact a regulatory law, and it might furnish the commission with authority to administer the law, but the Court could still intervene to protest special interests.

Thus, by the time Henry Ford began producing the Model T in 1909, the legal extent of government regulation of business was unclear. *Munn* had seemed to open the door to reform of business conduct, but the vagueness of its doctrine allowed the courts to restrict the number of businesses "affected with a public interest." The ascendancy of Field's views on judicial review combined with the narrow interpretation of *Munn* to block attempts to regulate the industrial society. And a tortured definition of commerce in *United States* v. *E.*

C. Knight Co. (1895) further restricted government control of business. In that case, the Court ruled that production was only incidental to commerce and so was not subject to federal control.[9]

During the first quarter of the twentieth century, the Court considered numerous issues in government control of business, among them laws pertaining to antitrust, child labor, and wage-and-hour regulations. The Court upheld some new laws and invalidated others. Justice Oliver Wendell Holmes began to develop the "stream of commerce" concept that would eventually overturn the *Knight* precedent and open up congressional authority to control business.[10] With the appointment of the Republican former President William H. Taft as Chief Justice in 1918, however, the rights of property appeared to be secure against state encroachment. In 1923, for example, Taft informed state lawmakers that they could not simply declare that a business was affected with a public interest and proceed to regulate it. The courts would retain the authority to determine businesses affected with a public interest. Taft further protected business from government intrusion when he declared, "Freedom is the general rule, restraint the exception."[11]

Meanwhile, by 1927 the Taft Court established guidelines for determining when a business was affected with a public interest. A business was considered public if the state had granted it a license or if the business had been recognized from early parliamentary and colonial laws as subject to government control or if it was devoted to the public and thereby itself granted the public an interest in it.[12] The state could regulate businesses that fit any of these tests. Four justices dissented in the decision, and by 1934, after Taft's departure, the Court had discarded the guidelines, electing instead to return to the precedents in *Munn.* If the state could show that a business posed a danger to the public and if the authority behind the laws did not conflict with the Constitution, then the state could regulate that business. Significantly, the Court also ruled that the consequences of such legislation were not a judicial matter. All that concerned the Court was whether or not the state held the authority to regulate and whether or not the state followed due process. If the police powers were abused, remedy was to be sought in the political process, not through the courts.[13]

The trucking cases appeared during this period of confusion and transition in the Court's thinking on the regulation of all business. The initial truck decisions protected the rights of property from state intrusion; the later cases reflected the Court's shift toward supporting government regulation of business.

2

State regulation of motor carriers first came before the Supreme Court in 1925. In *Michigan Public Utilities Commission et al.* v. *Duke*, the Court analyzed the two major legal problems facing the states—regulation of contract carriers and of interstate trucking. At issue was a Michigan statute of 1923 that required both intra- and interstate truckers to obtain permits before they could conduct business over the state's highways. To secure a permit, and thus be able to use the state road system, the operator had to prove his service met the test of "public convenience and necessity." In other words, the carrier had to show that his proposed operation was both advantageous and desirable to the economy and public welfare. It was an ambiguous phrase, but it generally alluded to the adequacy, or inadequacy, of the present service. The law instructed the state commission to refuse a permit if other truckers already provided adequate service. Allegedly for purposes of administration, the law defined all trucking operations as common carriers. Duke Cartage Company's business consisted of three contracts to haul car bodies from Detroit, Michigan, to Toledo, Ohio. The company filed suit, claiming that because Duke was a contract operator and also engaged in interstate commerce, it was not subject to state control.[14]

Writing for the majority, Justice Pierce Butler concluded that the Michigan statute violated the commerce and due process clauses of the Constitution. Since the state had not granted a franchise to motor carriers and the purpose of the law had "no relation to public safety or order," the law's provisions unduly interfered with interstate commerce. In this case, Butler argued, the state's police power was limited to reasonable license fees as compensation for the use of the highways. Furthermore, in imposing common carrier status on a private contract carrier, the state had violated the due process clause by depriving the company of its property without just compensation. (In this case, the contract carrier was viewed as a private carrier.)[15]

The *Duke* decision established two important precedents. First, contract carriers were held to have distinctive characteristics from those of common carriers. Second, the states could not unreasonably impede interstate commerce by denying truckers access to the highways. The Court indicated, however, that it would view future legislation more favorably if the purpose were related to "public safety and order."

Two other cases in 1925 considered state regulation of interstate commerce. *Buck* v. *Kuykendall* concerned the State of Washington's denial of a certificate of public convenience and necessity to an interstate bus line operator who wanted to establish service from Seattle to Portland, Oregon. Oregon had granted Buck a certificate to operate in that state, but the Washington commission refused the matching certificate on grounds that four other firms adequately served the area. Justice Louis D. Brandeis, who wrote the opinion for the majority, noted that the *Duke* case had focused specifically on the use of the highways; in contrast, the *Buck* case involved the prohibition of competition. In light of Oregon's action in granting a permit, Brandeis declared that Washington's refusal to do so constituted an obstruction of interstate commerce.[16] However, since the case involved only interstate competition, Brandeis did not consider the issue of regulating intrastate competition.

The companion case, *George W. Bush & Sons* v. *Maloy,* presented a different set of facts. The state of Maryland had denied a permit to Bush to engage in interstate commerce over roads whose construction was financed solely with Maryland state monies. Nevertheless, the Court found against the state because the instructions the legislature had given to the regulatory commission were too broad, and their administration tended to obstruct interstate commerce. The majority opinion implied that the legislators must write specific instructions in future statutes.[17]

Justice James C. McReynolds dissented in both of these decisions, and his views furnish a vivid illustration of the complex regulatory problems the motor truck presented. "The problem arising out of the sudden increase of motor vehicles presents extraordinary difficulties," he wrote. "As yet nobody knows what should be done. Manifestly, the exigency cannot be met through uniform rules laid down by Congress." For McReynolds, the problem seemed a local one that was not answerable to precise federal regulation. He pleaded that the states should be allowed to control trucking "unless and until something is done which really tends to obstruct the free flow of commerce."[18]

The *Duke*, *Buck*, and *Bush* decisions also drew harsh criticism from the state commissioners. To the members of the NARUC, the Court's actions appeared to reverse earlier rulings that the states could, in the absence of national legislation, regulate commerce, including inter-state trade, to protect public safety and order. In *Hendrick* v. *Maryland* (1914), the Court had upheld state regulation in the absence of national legislation.[19] NARUC responded to the judicial setbacks in several ways. The association lobbied Congress for the enactment of federal legislation and submitted a bill of its own for consideration. It changed its proposed uniform statute to eliminate the' Court's objections, particularly the one concerning regulation of contract carriers. NARUC also encouraged discussion among its members as to what the decisions meant. To this end, the governor of Maryland asserted that the *Bush* case only prohibited the state from blocking interstate trucking; the state commission, he believed, could still require interstate carriers to comply with licensing and weight and height requirements (indirect regulations). In addition, the decision did not appear to affect regulation of intrastate truckers. The Washington state commission continued to require certificates of all truckers, but it no longer granted or denied them on the basis of public convenience and necessity.[20]

In 1926 the Court decided another contract carrier case, *Frost et al.* v. *Railroad Commission of California*. A six-to-three majority invalidated a state law requiring contract truckers to obtain certificates of convenience and necessity. Writing for the majority, Justice George Sutherland concluded that the statute's "primary purpose evidently is to protect the business of those who are common carriers in fact by controlling competitive conditions." Regulation of the highways to protect the citizens of the state was not involved. Sutherland invoked the *Duke* precedent and again held that contract drivers could not be forced to assume common carrier status. He implied, however, that the state's power to prohibit the use of its highways might, in certain cases, allow the states to regulate a contract driver as a common carrier. Sutherland addressed the dissent of Justices Holmes, Brandeis, and McReynolds, which argued that a state had the power to regulate the use of its highways. The controlling point for Sutherland, however, though he agreed in principle with the dissenters, remained the lack of specific reference to the police power. He further suggested that the Court would not invalidate legislation that prohibited truckers from maintaining the appearance of contract carriers when, in fact, they were common carriers. Apparently, some truckers claimed contract carrier status even though they actually served just about any shipper that came along.[21]

The *Frost* case implied that the state could control the burgeoning trucking business through the police power if only the legislatures properly invoked that authority. The Court recognized the possibility that the states might use the authority to regulate competition in order to promote one economic group over another. In fact, Sutherland indicated in *Frost* that this potential abuse of the police power would be upheld, arguing that the Court was concerned only with the authority to regulate, not the consequences of that regulation. The Court, through dicta and implication, led the lawmakers toward a constitutionally correct form of state truck regulation.

3

Five years later, the Court in *Smith* v. *Cahoon*, informed the states that they would have to specifically define contract and common carrier truckers and regulate them separately.[22] This decision, together with the *Frost* opinion of 1926, apparently guided the states in writing new statutes that the Court would accept. Three strategies designed to control contract truckers appeared in these new laws. First, they declared contract truckers to be engaged in a business affected with a public interest; second, they separately defined common and contract truckers; and third, they forced contract carriers to file minimum rate schedules that were not lower than those of common carriers of rail or truck. In further distinguishing contract carriers from common carriers, the laws required the former to secure permits, rather than certificates.[23]

In 1931, for example, the state of Texas included all these strategies in its Motor Vehicle Act. Following the *Frost* lead, the lawmakers based the entire statute on the police power to protect and conserve the highways. This declaration, which ensured the constitutionality of the law, was really a smoke screen hiding the true intentions of the Texas legislators. Competitive business conditions, not highway conservation, had motivated the lawmakers. Between 1927 and 1931, two trends related to trucking converged in Texas: a state highway expansion program and an increase in the trucking of uncompressed cotton to the Port of Galveston. Truck hauls originated as far away as Oklahoma farms, sometimes 425 miles from the coast. As more and more trucks entered the cotton-hauling market, other business interests—railroads and the interior cotton compresses in particular—lost revenue. These groups prevailed on the legislators to enact a truck law that effectively regulated contract cotton trucks off the roads of Texas.[24]

Provisions in the law clearly reflected the political influence the railways and compress owners had exerted to control the trucking of cotton. For example, the statute limited trucks using Texas highways to hauling containers no more than thirty cubic feet in size nor greater than five hundred pounds in weight. Uncompressed bales of cotton usually were larger than thirty cubic feet and weighed more than five hundred pounds, but they were the only items of freight that approximated the dimensions listed in the act. Also, the act prohibited loads over seven thousand pounds, except when hauled from origin directly to the nearest common carrier loading dock. Contract carriers claimed that the seven-thousand-pound limit restricted profits; the exception meant, of course, that a trucker could haul a paying load of cotton to the nearest railroad station, but not to Galveston.[25]

LaRue Brown, attorney for the NACC, filed two briefs, and R. C. Fulbright, counselor for the Industrial Traffic League, filed another in support of an appeal from the district court that challenged the Texas statute. The case, *Sproles* v. *Binford*, was argued before the Court in April 1932. Chief Justice Charles Evans Hughes wrote the opinion (a unanimous one), which rejected the trucking lawyers' arguments and upheld the Texas statute. In his opinion, Hughes first reviewed the findings of fact on which the earlier decisions for the state had rested. The number of trucks in Texas had increased 300 percent during the previous six years; the average annual maintenance cost for highways in Texas during the past three years had been twelve million dollars; excessive truck loads were damaging the Texas highways; only 5,500 trucks of a total of 206,000 had a rated capacity over seven thousand pounds.[26]

The fact that only a small number of trucks then had the capacity to exceed the Texas limit made the law seem innocuous. In fact, however, the limit could have prevented future expansion of trucking in Texas. LaRue Brown complained that the trucking industry was losing the regulation cases because the opposition was utilizing such distorted facts. Hughes's acceptance of the district court's findings of fact reflected the problem Brown faced. As he noted before the case was rendered, "Important results [will] turn on assumptions by the trial court as to the effect of certain vehicles upon the highway, as to the location of 'common carrier receiving points' and as to other matters of fact which seem, to those familiar with the situation, utterly unsupported by the evidence."[27] This is precisely what happened in the *Sproles* case.

After accepting the findings of fact, Hughes turned to the questions of law brought to the Court's attention. He ruled that the seven-thousand-pound limit did not violate the due process clause because limiting size and weight of vehicles fell within the broad authority of the police power. In a classic statement of judicial restraint, Hughes dismissed testimony from engineers that the highways could sustain a load greater than seven thousand pounds if it were distributed correctly over the axles and wheels. "To make scientific precision a criterion of constitutional power," he wrote, "would be to subject the State to an intolerable supervision hostile to the basic principles of our government and wholly beyond the protection which the general clause of the Fourteenth Amendment was intended to secure." In addition, the Chief Justice declared, "questions as to reasonableness" of a law's provisions were for the legislatures alone to decide, and actions within this range of legislative discretion could "not be set aside because compliance was burdensome."[28]

The Texas statute applied to interstate as well as to intrastate truckers. Utilizing an argument similar to McReynolds' dissent in *Buck* and *Bush*, Hughes upheld the right of the states to enact regulatory laws in the absence of national legislation. He relied heavily on the policy statement of the Texas law and declared that when safety considerations and conservation of the highways were involved, the states could control commerce that might cross state lines. Similarly, Hughes dismissed the appeal that the Texas law violated the freedom of contract rule. "Freedom of contract" was a concept, not found specifically enunciated in the Constitution, that was used to protect private business from public control. Citing numerous cases, he claimed that the state could not be burdened with maintaining existing private contracts in conflict with legislative policy directed toward preserving the general welfare.[29]

The Texas law did allow for exemption permits for loads greater than seven thousand pounds that were hauled from origin to the "nearest practicable common carrier receiving or loading point" by way of the "shortest practicable route." The truck lawyers claimed this exemption was arbitrary and could therefore lead to discriminatory administration of the law. Hughes disagreed. The word "practicable" saved the clause from being capricious; had the lawmakers used the word "possible" instead, then the provision would have been vague. Apparently, "practicable" was more specific and directive than "possible." The former did not bind the Texas Railroad Commission in mapping exemption routes; it allowed flexible decisions determined by specific, local conditions.[30]

Trucking lawyers also attacked the law for its clear attempt to regulate competition, claiming that it favored one business over another, railroads over trucks. Hughes might have declared regulation of competition was simply a by-product, or consequence, of a valid assertion of the police power and, as such, was an issue for the legislature, not the courts. The Chief Justice, however, went further and asserted that within the police power lay the authority to foster the use of all transportation facilities for the common good. "The State has a vital interest in the appropriate utilization of the railroads which serve its people, as well as in the proper maintenance of its highways as safe and convenient facilities. . . . The use of highways for truck transportation has its manifest convenience, but we perceive no constitutional ground for denying to the State the right to foster a fair distribution of traffic to the end that all necessary facilities should be maintained and that the public should not be inconvenienced by inordinate uses of its highways for purposes of gain." Without mentioning the term, "affected with a public interest," the Court expanded its meaning.[31]

It was now clear not only that the states could regulate the trucks but that they could do so to protect the railways. The dictum suggested that the power to promote business interests, in this case the railways, was equal to the power to protect the highways. Indeed, railroad spokesmen hailed the decision as a vindication of their pleas for equal regulation of competing forms of transportation.[32]

Sproles was important, for it sanctioned state power to interfere in the economy generally and to regulate contract truckers specifically. The unanimity of the decision, moreover, underscored the Court's findings. Such support for government regulation should have been repugnant to at least four of the justices in 1932: Sutherland, McReynolds, Butler, and Willis Van Devanter, collectively known in the mid-1930s as the "Four Horsemen" of conservatism, dedicated to protecting property rights from government intrusion.

Given the shroud of secrecy that surrounds the decision-making process of the Court, explanations of its acquiescence to government intrusion in *Sproles* can be only tentative. Of course, McReynold's concurrence in the case seems consistent with his dissent in *Buck* and *Bush*. Perhaps he convinced the other justices that state regulation was preferable to federal controls and that a unanimous opinion would forestall movement toward national legislation. Sutherland and Butler, in particular, might have been receptive to his arguments because both had been counselors for railways before beginning their terms on the Court.[33] Chief Justice Hughes may have been the key figure. He directed Court conferences in an ordered and knowledgeable fashion that impressed even those colleagues who disagreed with him. Hughes, moreover, held no economic philosophy hindering his ability to adjudicate strictly upon legal principles; he preferred to allow the lawmakers wide latitude in most cases, following Holmes's belief in judicial restraint. Yet, he did not always defer to the legislators, for he had joined the majority in invalidating the Florida law in *Smith* v. *Cahoon*. His flexibility in these matters may have solidified the unanimous decision.[34]

These tentative suggestions make a larger point: the fortunes of truckers in the early 1930s hinged not only upon the technological, managerial, and political talents of themselves and their competitors but also upon the personal beliefs and abilities of nine justices.

Even though the reasons behind *Sproles* remain hazy, the effect of the decision was clear. Through the Court's unanimous reliance upon legal principle and its insistence on judicial restraint, the decision left open the possibility that lawmakers could enact laws that equated special interests with the interests of the general welfare. Of course, definition of the "general welfare," or "public interest," was the issue. The Court preferred to leave the defining to the legislature, and in Texas at least, the lawmakers declared that protection of the railways promoted the common good. To the legislators, the technological improvement that the truck presented was less important than preserving the rail system.[35]

Toward the end of 1932, the Court upheld another Texas law that regulated contract carriers. Hughes assigned the opinion, *Stephenson* v. *Binford*, to Justice Sutherland. The Chief Justice habitually gave cases to those of his colleagues who normally would have disagreed with the decision; in doing so, he lent more authority to the Court's position. Such was the case in *Stephenson*, for the opinion expressed was hardly the characteristic laissez-faire argument one would expect from Sutherland.[36]

The *Stephenson* case, reflecting the new strategies that the states had followed to control trucking, alleged that increased truck traffic and its unregulated operations had heightened dangers on Texas roads and had increased highway expenditures. The legislators declared that the statute was designed "in the interest of the public." To that end, the Texas lawmakers, acting only eleven days after the *Cahoon* decision was rendered, separately defined common and contract carriers and instructed the Texas Railroad Commission to establish rules and regulations for contract operators. These rules were to include rate schedules that were not lower than those for common carriers, railroads and trucks.[37]

Sutherland confined the Court's opinion to whether or not the law was "a constitutional exercise of the legislative power to regulate the use of the highways." Lawyers for trucking interests had attacked the statute's definitions of contract and common motor carriers as being more form than substance because, in reality, both types were regulated similarly. The Court rejected this argument, for "it does not follow that regulations appropriately imposed on the business of a common carrier may not also be appropriate to the business of a contract driver." Sutherland next discussed the precedents from other truck cases that might affect the *Stephenson* case. Since the law did not require a contract carrier to become a common carrier, *Duke* was not applicable. The case did not involve interstate commerce, so *Buck* and *Bush* were irrelevant. The requirement that contract truckers secure a "permit" distinguished the instant case from the *Frost* decision, which had struck down the attempt to require "certificates" for contract drivers. Apparently, the Texas legislators had found the correct formula to satisfy the Court. They separately defined contract and common motor carriers and required permits for the former and certificates for the latter.[38]

Other aspects of the legislators' actions impressed Sutherland. The Texas Governor's message to the legislature, which outlined the truck problem in his state, and the legislator's contention that regulation would foster a safe, dependable transportation system in Texas greatly influenced Sutherland's opinion. Indeed, the facts listed by the district court indicated that a truck problem did exist. Texas railways had lost freight to the more convenient and efficient motor trucks; this transfer of freight had resulted in crowded highways, which placed a strain on the road system; heavy traffic conditions destroyed road surfaces and made them unsafe for all motorists. Sutherland concluded that, given these circumstances, the provisions in the statute were means "to the legitimate end of conserving the highway."[39]

In a stunning extension of regulatory power, moreover, Sutherland ruled not only that the state could regulate business conditions in order to protect the highways but also that the state could use price control to achieve these ends. (The minimum rates required of contract truckers were the same as those for common carriers.) Here was a justice who normally espoused the principles of laissez-faire upholding price regulation by the government.

Sutherland apparently reversed himself on another issue in *Stephenson*, the freedom of contract rule, which had been used in years past to protect private property from state intrusion. In this case, however, the Court believed the state's duty to provide for the safety and welfare of its citizens superseded the right of contract. Normally, Sutherland conceded, freedom of contract would rule, but the protection of the inhabitants of a state overrode this generality. Sutherland's biographer suggests that this line of reasoning was consistent with the judge's usual position because he was upholding protection of property, though it was public, not private, property. Nevertheless, protection of state property in this instance fostered the domination of one property interest, the railroads, over another, the truckers. Sutherland recognized this, but dismissed it as beyond the consideration of the Court. "If the Legislature had other or additional purposes which, considered apart, it had no constitutional power to make effective, that would not have the result of making the act invalid."[40] Sutherland and the Court, then, seemed to leave the door open to further experiments in regulating business.

Yet Sutherland avoided using the affected with a public interest doctrine in *Stephenson*, even though the Texas attorneys had mentioned it in their briefs. The omission is significant. The police power was usually associated with state laws; by emphasizing it rather than the more encompassing doctrine of affected with a public interest, Sutherland may have been attempting to forestall federal intervention into truck regulation. He had apparently given in on the price regulation provision; to do so on the public interest doctrine would have been truly liberal.[41]

Support for this analysis of the Texas cases is found in the conflict surrounding the five-to-four decision in *Nebbia* v. *New York* (1934). The Four Horsemen dissented from the decision, which upheld a law authorizing the New York Milk Control Board to regulate the milk industry through price controls. McReynolds, in dissent with Butler, Sutherland, and Van Devanter, reminded the majority that *Duke* and *Frost* had declared that lawmakers could not convert a private business into a public utility simply by legislative fiat. The dissenters believed that the New York lawmakers had not based their actions on legitimate police powers. The majority, on the other hand, did not distinguish between the police power and the public interest doctrine. They required only that the provisions of the act be designed to meet the stated purpose. Judicial restraint in this case followed that in the *Sproles* and *Stephenson* truck cases. In fact, the majority cited *Stephenson* as one of many cases that supported the Court's decision.[42]

Ironically, then, the conservatives' acquiescence in *Sproles* and *Stephenson* contributed to their defeat in *Nebbia*. The emphasis on judicial restraint in the truck cases, although based on the police power, emerged in *Nebbia* as the controlling perspective. "Affected with a public interest" was rendered moot. If the lawmakers believed circumstances existed that warranted government regulation, then the Court would not interfere, as long as the Constitution was not abrogated.[43] Intrastate trucking could now be regulated by the states. Still, Congress would have to act to control interstate trucking.

4

The decisions in the trucking cases of *Sproles* and *Stephenson* reflected a shift in the philosophy of the Court, a trend Chief Justice Hughes led in response to the need, as he perceived it, for promoting new power relationships in the American political system. No mention of the Depression appears in the Texas opinions. Yet, although the trucking situation in that state was not directly related to the Great Depression, the economic dislocations it caused paralleled Depression-caused problems. The private sector, Hughes believed, had failed to master the changes wrought by new technological and economic forces in the 1920s and 1930s. Bold experiments in public policy were called for and he believed the Court should actively facilitate the shift in power from the private to the public sector. The judicial system could contribute, he believed, if it sanctioned a return to democratic principles that elevated the common good over the protection of private property. Judicial restraint was the prime instrument for encouraging this shift of power from private business interests to the legislatures. The courts, of course, would reserve the authority to restrain democracy run amok, but in general, it would allow wide discretion for public policy experimentation.[44]

What Hughes failed to act upon, although he recognized it, was the problem of special interests. In some instances, the workings of democratic government allowed narrow interests to dictate policy not necessarily beneficial to the general welfare. It seems plausible, for example, that the seven-thousand-pound limit in Texas could have curtailed experiments with heavier trucks, experiments that might have benefited the common good more than protection of the railways did. In fact, as is so often the case in regulation, unintended consequences appeared. The law did not help the railways after all; instead, private motor carriers now supplanted the regulated contract operators.[45] The central issue, of course, was the common good, and the Court decided to give the democratic systems in the states a wide berth, under the police power, to define the common good.

Yet, there was a limit to how far the state police powers could be used to determine the national common good. A similar story had unfolded during the last quarter of the nineteenth century. The Granger cases established the public interest doctrine on the state level; indeed, in *Munn* regulation of prices became a legitimate force under the police power. In 1886 the Court decided that the boundary had been reached in the police power's authority to control interstate commerce. The case involved state regulation of long-haul and short-haul rates, which the Court found intolerable if the property rights of the railroads were to be adequately protected.[46] The following year, using the state regulatory powers as a model, Congress enacted the Interstate Commerce Act.

The truck cases followed a similar pattern. *Sproles* gave the states broad authority, under the police power, to regulate trucking. *Stephenson*, although limited to intrastate operations (like *Munn*), nevertheless held implications for national legislation because it furnished a precedent for regulating the contract truckers. By 1932 the Court had identified three classes of motor trucking. Common and contract carriers could be controlled directly through price regulation, but private carriers were subject only to indirect controls. Additionally, common and contract carriers were divided into regular route carriers (between fixed terminals) and irregular carriers (routes that varied in time and place).[47] These distinctions would form the basis for national legislation when Congress decided to assert the commerce power.

Thus, through an adversarial process in the 1920s and 1930s, private business interests, state legislators, and the courts began to define the nature of the public interest as it related to trucking. Conspicuously absent as a partner to the debate in the 1920s was the Interstate Commerce Commission. For numerous reasons, the ICC discovered motor trucking later than did the other interest groups. Nonetheless, as the motor truck had contributed to the Supreme Court's period of transition, so too would the truck motivate a transitional period in the history of the ICC.

5 Pragmatic Public Policy: The Interstate Commerce Commission and the Public Interest, 1887–1932

Throughout the 1920s and into the 1930s, public and private groups attempted to harness the motor truck revolution. As we have seen, economic responses (consolidations and rate cutting) gave way to political activity; all efforts fell short in bringing order to the competitive business. No one group—the state commissioners, the manufacturers, the railways, the common carrier truckers—gained sufficient power to forge a consensus policy toward trucking. The Supreme Court lent some semblance of order in 1932 when it outlined the authority of the states to regulate truck operations. The Court indicated, however, that Congress would have to act if interstate trucking was to be controlled. None of the interested groups had the influence to persuade Congress that a national policy toward trucking was necessary.

One institution that might have been expected to assume such a role, but did not until after 1932, was the Interstate Commerce Commission. Even though the ICC during the 1920s enjoyed a highly visible and respected position in the political economy, it failed to anticipate and deal with the trucking revolution. The many and complex reasons why can be seen in the history of the commission, its origin and its methods of operation. The story exposes the inherent conflicts associated with a mixed system of public control of private business, the changing nature of the "public interest" in the twentieth century, and the bureaucratic context in which federal regulation eventually was extended to motor trucking.

I

Prolific construction of railroads after the Civil War created not only a national transport network but also numerous public policy problems. As the railroads expanded (to 200,000 miles by 1890), many businessmen took advantage of the unfettered scramble for tonnage. Many could not. Though state legislators attempted to regulate competition in the Gilded Age, by the mid-1880s, lack of uniformity in the laws threatened not only the rights of the railways but also the free flow of interstate commerce. Numerous interest groups (farmers, manufacturers, wholesalers, retailers, railroads—in short, anyone who had lost out to the competition) pressured Congress to assume responsibility for controlling railway abuses. The federal lawmakers passed on that responsibility to a new kind of federal institution (which the states had developed), the independent regulatory commission. The Interstate Commerce Commission, established by the Act to Regulate Commerce of 1887, constituted the first tentative institutional attempt on the federal level to control the consequences of the industrial revolution.[1]

The central purpose of the ICC was to eliminate the discriminatory rate practices of many railways, particularly rebating and long-haul/short-haul rates. In rebating, the railways gave preferred shippers lower rates than others for the same tonnage, and in setting rates over the same line, the railways charged more for a short haul than for a long haul. These tactics seemed to many to violate the American principles of equal opportunity and fairness. (Of course, both were also grounded in the pressures of competition and the economics of railroading.) The five-member ICC found, however, that its authority to eliminate these practices could not stand up to the complexity of railroading, the uncooperative spirit of railway management, and adverse court rulings. The commission therefore made little headway in eliminating the discriminatory practices for over a decade.[2]

Not until 1903 did Congress respond to ICC pleas for adequate authority. The Elkins Act of that year established procedures that, it was hoped, would rationalize the rate structure and protect the railways from destructive competition and thus provide a stable market for the shipping public. In practice, the law fell short of its goals, for most shippers could not afford the time or money to file a complaint. Even for those who could file against the railroads, relief was minimal because the ICC could award only the amount of money at issue, not compensatory damages. Nevertheless, rebating did subside somewhat. Publicity from commission hearings and reports forced the railways to eliminate the more blatant discrepancies in rate levels.[3]

The notion that publicity was enough to bring about moral actions from businessmen (the guiding philosophy of late nineteenth-century regulation) underwent revision after 1900, and the ICC became the central institution marking that change. Regulatory activity during the Progressive Era rested on the assumption that experts in a commission setting could make business more responsible for the broader interests of the public than could capitalists whose goals were too narrow (profit for and survival of the firm). Thus, at the request of the commission, Congress in the Hepburn Act of 1906 furnished additional authority to control railway abuses. Now, the ICC, expanded to seven members, could adjust maximum rate levels. The object, once again, was to protect shippers from unreasonable charges.[4]

The railways, however, pushed as always by competitive pressures, evaded the controls and continued to charge some shippers less than others. A simple tactic was to raise and lower rates frequently so that shippers and regulators would be confused. Even though the Hepburn Act had required a thirty-day waiting period before a new rate could go into effect, it was not enough to stop the railway practices. Therefore, in the Mann-Elkins Act of 1910, Congress added more controls over rates. The ICC could now suspend new rates immediately and force the railroads to prove the rates were just and reasonable. The railways found still another tactic to avoid ICC scrutiny. In order to offset the ICC-mandated lower interstate rate levels, the rails set related intrastate rates higher. (Usually, state commissioners went along with railway increases.) The ICC, despite objections from the railways and the state commissioners, began to set the intrastate levels. The Supreme Court sustained this broad use of federal authority in the *Shreveport* case of 1914. After 1910, for all practical purposes, the railways could not increase rates or engage in expansion programs without the consent of the commission.[5]

During the first twenty years of its existence, then, the ICC obtained from Congress more authority to supervise railway activities. Even though the railways sometimes joined the ICC in requesting more controls, the major regulatory thrust of this period was protection of the shipper, for that was considered to be in the public interest.

Yet, the period 1910–17 brought into question the nature of the public's interest in transport regulation. During that time, the commission denied a series of rail requests for rate increases. Railroad managers failed to convince the regulators that a growing economy demanded a better rail system and that such a system had to be funded through rate increases. Instead, the commission sided with shippers' groups, which argued that the rails were trying to abuse their position in the economy and that the railroads could fund expansion through greater profits derived from more efficient management of rail operations. While the railways must share the blame (through their past abuses and poorly prepared arguments), the ICC nevertheless failed to recognize that the economy of the 1910s was changing and that that demanded new perspectives.[6]

The result was chaos. The U.S. entered the Great War in the spring of 1917 with a transportation network inadequate to the task of mobilization. The increase in war material production spilled onto the railway systems; soon boxcars languished in East Coast terminals—some full, others empty—while more and more goods piled up in manufacturing centers. In December 1917, therefore, President Woodrow Wilson placed the railways under a new Federal Railroad Administration, and for twenty-six months the federal government managed rail service. The experiment succeeded. Freight moved again and efficiently. Success occurred in part because the Railroad Administration granted the rate increases that the ICC had rejected before the war and in part because more efficient operations were implemented.[7]

The war experience pointed to new directions for regulation of transportation in peacetime. A few public policy theorists now believed that direct government ownership and control of the railways would better serve the public interest than the mixed system of ICC regulation, but the American fear of centralized power overcame the sentiment for efficiency in 1920 when Congress returned the railways to ICC supervision. However, the lawmakers had learned something from the war experience, for they shifted from a narrow perspective of the public interest that protected shippers to a broader perspective that attempted to protect and promote the transportation network as a whole.[8]

2

During the first thirty years of its existence, the ICC developed a bureaucratic style with elements of both the ad hoc and the pragmatic that, together with congressional politics, defined the public's interest in transportation. The commission often faced economic, political, and legal obstacles in its attempts to administer the regulations that Congress had put forth. As each obstacle appeared, the ICC members and staff considered the problem from many angles, discussed the issues among themselves and with other interested parties, and eventually drew up a consensus strategy. This pragmatic preparation (along with shipper and railway lobbying) persuaded Congress in 1903, 1906, and 1910 to grant additional authority to the commission. In this manner, the public interest came to be defined through a bureaucracy of negative controls over the railroads.[9]

The early history of the ICC thus reflected the growing belief in the early twentieth century that man could use institutions to alter the economic environment to benefit the common good. The pragmatic process involved in ICC-congressional relations fell short of William James's detailed concept, but it nevertheless reflected the basic tenets of developing theories of action based upon experience. Although political, economic, and legal factors prevented the clear process James would have propounded, it is important to note that deliberations behind each amendment were based upon a grand scheme of social controls.[10] Yet, the ICC's denial of requests from the railroad for rate increases between 1910 and 1917 and the wartime transport crisis suggest that the commission had failed to serve the common good. Other evidence suggests that the belief in institutions was not entirely misplaced.

The real worth of commission regulation was found not in the controversial rate hearings but rather in the day-to-day activities of the members and their staff. Answering shippers' complaints, discussing uniformity of operations with rail executives, cooperating with state regulators on jurisdictional disputes, and conducting investigatory hearings—all of these proceedings lent a sense of order to the railroad industry that had not appeared during the frenzied competition of the 1880s. For example, ICC-sponsored negotiations resulted in uniform accounting procedures and simplified tariff schedules, two improvements that helped reduce railway abuses.[11] So, as it had done with the lawmakers, the ICC had earned the respect (if grudging in some cases) of the railroads. The commission had also impressed the courts through its careful attention to procedure and due process, and consequently, after 1900 the courts usually sustained ICC decisions. By the 1920s, the ICC was accepted as an institution of reform. The rate controversies apparently had not tarnished its image; in fact, most observers gave the commission high marks.[12] The good will would continue, but the previous rate controversies would have an effect, for the ICC would now be asked to shift its perspective toward regulating private business.

3

Congress mandated the shift in regulatory activity in the Transportation Act of 1920. Convinced that the lesson of the war experience was that restrictive controls alone did not constitute wise public management, the lawmakers now ordered the ICC to develop strategies that would preserve and enhance the transport systems. The public interest had been redefined: not only the particular needs of shippers but also the financial health of the railways would be safeguarded.[13] The act of 1920 assumed that a financially sound and efficiently coordinated transport network would prevent a repeat of the 1917 crisis.

To this end, the lawmakers gave the ICC authority to set minimum rates. This would head-off disastrous rate wars that had often plagued the railways and threatened the continued existence of some. Another provision underscored this shift toward sustaining corporate stability. Any road earning more than a fair return on investment (later set at 5.75 percent) would have to share the excess with other, less fortunate roads; the ICC would lend the excess to the weaker firms. This "recapture" provision promoted a sound transport network through the protection of weaker companies, but not at the expense of the stronger firms. Congress granted still broader authority in the Transportation Act of 1920. It ordered the commission to devise a consolidation plan that arranged the railways into several efficient systems, to encourage combinations and traffic agreements, and to monitor the financial plans of the railways to ensure stable growth. More specifically, the commission could now order railroads to pool their equipment, could determine the routing of shipments, and could command the use of common terminals.[14] These powers served the twin goals of strengthening the rails and protecting shippers by using the available resources more efficiently.

The Transportation Act of 1920, then, reflected new departures in regulation. It included, however, the old restrictive view as well, for the act instructed the regulators to enhance competition whenever possible. The commissioners thus faced a contradiction (to coordinate and enhance competition) that would prove difficult to resolve. The commission had been organized into divisions in 1917, when its membership was increased to nine. Now, although the act of 1920 had increased membership to eleven, the ICC confronted a Herculean task in administering the ambitious transport policies the act embodied.[15]

The sprawling ICC bureaucracy of two-thousand persons in 1930 was quite unlike the small office of the late 1880s. Over the intervening four decades, steady increases in appropriations and in the number of published reports reflected the ICC's mounting responsibilities. From $113,000 in 1888, the budget ballooned to $8.1 million in 1930; the *ICC Reports* expanded from 11 volumes during the first nineteen years to 113 during the decade of the 1920s.[16] A general list of the regulatory responsibilities in the 1920s reveals the wide range of activities that took place at the ICC offices in the Transportation Building in Washington, D.C. The Bureau of Informal Cases adjusted rates, interpreted tariffs, and mediated claims—all through a process of correspondence with shippers and carriers. The Bureau of Formal Cases followed more rigid procedures, in which complaints were officially filed, answered, and determined through hearings. The Bureau of Finance reviewed applications for certifications of operation and extensions of operating authority and plans for acquisitions, abandonments, and consolidations. It also dealt with claims from the wartime federal control period, administered the recaptured earnings provisions, and monitored the buying and selling of railway securities. In addition to all these activities, the ICC exercised limited authority over water carriers, electric railways, express companies, and pipelines.[17]

Five divisions formed the basis of the ICC. Although the scheme changed from time to time, in that some functions were switched from one division to another, for the most part, Division 1 handled valuation cases; Division 2, rate suspension; Division 3, long-haul/short-haul complaints; Division 4, financial questions; and Division 5, rail operations. In 1930 outgoing member Thomas F. Woodlock described the yearly workload of a commissioner. Of the 277 working days, 127 were devoted to docket, or formal, cases related to a specific division. The remaining 150 days, members typically spent in conferences with other commissioners, hearing arguments from carriers and shippers, and deciding issues sent from the divisions. On the average, each member heard seven hundred cases per year, roughly one-third of the total. (All cases were heard by more than one member at a time). By the end of the 1920s, one volume of the *ICC Reports* constituted roughly one month of docketed work. These reports, however, represented only the formal aspects of the ICC workload, for the informal activities were not reported in detail.[18]

Over the years, few commissioners worked only the required seven hours per day that most government workers enjoyed; many members labored during evening hours and on Sunday. Besides division work and full-commission meetings, the regulators engaged in many other tasks. Congress demanded their time, of course. In a one-year period, for example, the commission submitted sixty-five reports to the lawmakers. These opinions represented long hours of collecting data, discussing issues among members and staff, and rewriting drafts. ICC personnel often attended congressional hearings to present the regulators' position on impending legislation. Jurisdictional problems required close cooperation with state regulators. So, each year one of the eleven members became official liaison with NARUC. Finally, each autumn, the members contributed to the Annual Report. The chair of each division summarized his division's work, and the others read and commented upon it before it was submitted for publication.[19]

The commmission could not have done so much paperwork without support from a capable staff. The two-thousand-member work force shouldered the technical, routine (and tedious) tasks of regulation. They read the initial complaints, (averaging fifty million words per year) and reduced them to the basic arguments for quick review by each commissioner. ICC examiners conducted fact-finding investigations and drafted reports from testimony taken at public hearings. Overtime for staff was not uncommon. With such an exhausting workload, many qualified, diligent government workers moved to the private sector, where better-paying and less-demanding duties beckoned.[20]

The heavy workload for the staff and commissioners underscored a significant flaw in the bureaucratic structure. The commissioners lacked time in their busy schedule to *think* about the overall strategy. The division scheme certainly helped integrate ongoing strategies, but it did nothing to encourage development of new ones. The commission lacked a forward-looking vision.

The ICC was captive of its environment. Put simply, the political economy of the United States prevented both the planned rationalization of the railroad systems and the anticipation of new economic problems and their effects. The structure of railroading and the common law tradition, for example, fused together to anchor commission work to the cumbersome case-by-case method of regulation. Railroading was a complex enterprise with hundreds of rate classifications, thousands of shipping contracts, and an apparently infinite number of dissimilar transport situations, and passenger service complicated freight regulation. While the regulators established general rules to address specific problems (such as long- and short-haul discrimination), they still had to investigate each complaint on the basis of the particular facts involved. The Anglo-American legal tradition, which guaranteed every citizen's day in court and which protected him through procedural safeguards, consumed many hours of the regulators' time in the hearing rooms at the Transportation Building. Bogged down in detail, the regulators could not escape the case-by-case approach.

Also contributing to the lack of forward vision was the democratic process. Congress, pushed and tugged by numerous interest groups, failed to indicate precisely the balance to be struck between public and private management in creating a transport network. Apparently, Congress wanted it both ways: a private thrust that encouraged entrepreneurship (competitive), and a public thrust that ensured fairness, coordination, and planned growth (cooperative). Congress left to the regulators the task of untangling the conflicting instructions and developing an effective administrative bureaucracy in the process.[21]

Brief analysis of three special regulatory projects of the 1920s—the valuation project, the consolidation plan, and the agricultural rate adjustment investigation—reveals the difficulties the regulators faced in carrying out the wishes of Congress.

From its inception, the ICC had encountered difficulties in dealing with freight rates. In 1898 the Supreme Court put forth a rather vague rate-making rule designed to produce a fair return based on a fair value of railway properties. Yet, what was a "fair return," and what was "fair value"? Should the value of railroad properties be based on original costs, replacement costs, or some combination of the two? In 1913 Congress ordered the ICC to look into this problem and establish standards for rate making. To do this, the commission had to know the value of the railway properties. Consequently, a field force began the tedious task of inventorying all railroad properties, from the nineteenth-century land grants to stock sales to the number of iron spikes used to secure the rails. The valuation project extended into the 1920s, in part because of the immensity of the task and in part because the railways could and did protest the conclusions of the regulators. Those protests, of course, had to be heard and decided, and that took time. In the so-called *O'Fallon* case, moreover, the commissioners challenged the Supreme Court's rules on rate making, arguing that the ICC held more expertise to set rates than did the justices. The ICC lost this confrontation, but the proceedings also consumed the regulators' time and they did not result in the hoped-for standard rate-making rules.[22]

Meanwhile, after 1920, the commission had to deal as well with the consolidation plan that Congress had ordered drawn up. Notwithstanding the success of consolidation during the war and the penchant for efficiency then current in public policy circles, the consolidation plan would prove impossible to devise and implement. First, the commission had to take into account the maintenance of competition whenever possible; this, of course, often worked against the goal of consolidation. Second, the railways simply did not cooperate with the regulators. Each railroad, of course, wanted to lose as little and gain as much as it could in any consolidation plan. The regulators grew weary of the struggle and in 1929 released a plan, not so much with the hope that it would work as with the hope that it would simply satisfy the congressional instructions. The plan was modified in 1932, but the Depression prevented implementation.[23]

In 1925 Congress added another project to the burdens of the ICC. The Hoch-Smith Resolution ordered investigation into and adjustment of the entire railway state structure, with special attention to be given to agricultural rates. It amounted to political buck-passing. Congress had stated for public consumption (especially for the farmers) its desire for a comprehensive and fair rate structure, even though the goal was probably impossible to achieve and despite the ongoing valuation project. Nonetheless, the ICC created a new Division 6 to deal with the entire rate structure.[24]

The time involved and the manpower utilized in pursuing the valuation project, the consolidation plan, and the Hoch-Smith Resolution, in addition to other duties, prevented the ICC from anticipating and dealing with the motor truck revolution. More generally, these activities of the commission reflected a bias in transport regulation that constricted the view of the ICC in dealing with changes in the economy.

In the 1920s transport policies were based in large measure on the assumption that the railroads were in trouble and that the government should bring relief. The Transportation Act of 1920 clearly reflected this perspective. To take another example, in 1922 Secretary of Commerce Herbert Hoover appeared before the commission and presented his views on the problems in transportation. While Hoover focused most of his remarks on the need for better rate-making rules, the secretary also emphasized the need for more railway facilities. In fact, he suggested that government loans might be necessary to help the railroads expand to meet the changing needs of the economy. Even though Hoover noted that change was occurring, his bias toward railroading blinded him to the larger picture. Hoover, like most other public officials, narrowly conceived the transportation problem to be a railroad problem. The ICC concurred and in the 1920s encouraged the railways to spend $5.72 billion on expansion programs. The war experience still haunted the regulators.[25]

Meanwhile, the transportation situation was changing rapidly. Not only were the new motor trucks altering the market, but so too were airplanes, pipelines, and the Panama Canal trade. The impact on railways is clearly seen through a few statistics. In 1926 carload tonnage stood at 1,296,651,000 tons; by 1932, that figure had dropped to 630,989,000 tons. (The drop was not consistent, for the rails experienced a strong year in 1929 of 1,303,048,000 tons.) Less-than-carload traffic showed a consistent drop from 39,491,000 tons in 1926 to only 15,234,000 tons in 1932. Revenue for all railway tonnage was $4.906 billion in 1926, but by 1932 that had dropped to $2.485 billion.[26]

The ICC, mired as it was in the technical, case-by-case method of regulation and provincially focused on the railways, failed to recognize these trends soon enough. Thus, even as railway tonnage and revenue dropped, the commission continued to encourage upgrading and expansion of facilities. The regulatory structure was apparently incapable of responding to rapid change.

4

Only slowly did the ICC discover the competing forms of transport. The commission's awareness evolved from indifference immediately after the war to an exploratory investigation between 1926 and 1928 to a more in-depth analysis between 1930 and 1932. By early 1932 the regulators agreed that a problem existed, but they could not seem to decide on how to respond.

In the mid-1920s, a few of the commissioners and staff recognized that trucking presented a challenge to railway regulation. Several events awakened them: the Supreme Court truck cases of 1925, an increase in applications by railroads for the abandonment of lines that were losing revenue to motor carriers, and more and more informal complaints from shippers and railways that trucks engaged in unfair competition. Although it lacked specific authority, the commission launched a general investigation of the extent of motor trucking in 1926. ICC staff travelled to a dozen cities, heard four hundred witnesses, collected five thousand pages of testimony, and issued a report.[27]

The report (released in April, 1928) noted that transport conditions were in a state of rapid transition. While conceding that the new and unregulated forms (mainly trucks) had removed tonnage from the rails, the commission also indicated that these losses had been offset through increased freight in other areas: the rails had indeed lost short-haul goods to the more flexible trucks, but they had gained tonnage through the shipment of truck bodies, tires, and motor vehicle parts. The situation did not warrant federal supervision in 1928, but the ICC acknowledged that conditions could change.[28]

The future arrived quickly, for less than four years later, the transportation situation had changed. Now, not only were railways complaining about truckers' competition but so too were other truckers. The ICC, therefore, embarked on a second investigation. In 1932, Leo J. Flynn, an ICC examiner, prepared the report, entitled "Coordination of Motor Transportation." He noted that depressed economic conditions had reduced freight tonnage and thereby exposed an oversupply of transport facilities. To deal with this immediate problem and future ones, Flynn envisioned a broad program of government supervision of all forms of transport—rail, motor, and water. Government regulation, Flynn believed, could bring about a coordinated network in which each mode of transport performed the tasks for which it was best suited (rails for long hauls, trucks for short hauls and deliveries, for example); each form would supplement but not compete with the others. At least one major participant in the truck associational movement praised Flynn's fair-mindedness, and a British public policy figure claimed his report was "really the only statement yet available as regards the position in any country which assembles sufficient data on which a policy may or can be based." The report bore the unmistakable imprint of progressive beliefs in institutions, experts, and efficiency; yet it was more the product of Flynn's experience and biases than of the ICC's, for the commissioners were not ready in 1932 to propose such an ambitious program.[29]

Despite the commission's rejection of Flynn's broad views, the agency was at least beginning to move away from its narrowly focused perspective. As it had done before, the ICC now approached Congress with a request for additional authority (specifically, investigatory powers) to deal with the motor carrier business. In response, Congress held hearings on the issues.

Republican Senator James Couzens of Michigan, chairman of the Senate Committee on Interstate Commerce, led the congressional hearings. Couzens, a former executive at Ford Motor Company, was well acquainted with transportation issues, but like most other observers in 1932, he was unsure how much the depressed economic conditions had contributed to the present problems. Thus, the bill he sponsored called only for the collection of more data. Nevertheless, the hearings he chaired early in the year furnished a forum for a free-for-all discussion among groups interested in transport policies.[30] At Couzens's request, ICC examiner Leo Flynn appeared as the first witness. Despite the bold conclusions in his report, Flynn now tempered his testimony to fit the ICC policy. He suggested that any regulation contemplated "should be moderate and with a view to changing conditions in the future."[31]

In subsequent testimony, shipper representatives opposed regulation of trucks because they feared that it would raise shipping costs. The state regulators also opposed federal controls, taking the position that no agency in Washington could regulate what was essentially a local problem. Officials from the Bureau of Public Roads testified and put forward their belief that elaborate administrative machinery was needless, since trucks hauled only .3 percent of all freight in the United States. Testimony from the National Automobile Chamber of Commerce included more statistics designed to show regulation was unnecessary. Since over 85 percent of all truck traffic consisted of privately owned vehicles and since the common law prohibited state control of these operators, regulation of the remaining 14 to 15 percent appeared to be of dubious value.[32]

Railway corporations, however, disagreed with this entire line of reasoning. Citing very different books of statistics, rail executives attempted to persuade the senators that federal control over trucking was in the public interest. They resurrected time-tested arguments about promoting existing rail systems as a means of ensuring economic progress and strengthening national defense. In a new twist, the railroads laid before the committee copies of recent regulatory statutes passed in England and in several European countries. The British

Parliament had sustained a regulatory scheme that coordinated truck and rail operations and, according to the rail executives, benefited both. The Congress should follow Parliament's example.[33]

As it turned out, the 72nd Congress did not act on Couzens's bill (in fact, it was not reported out of committee). Controversies between the lawmakers and President Herbert Hoover rendered the entire session impotent on essential matters such as relief to the unemployed, much less on the still unfocused problem of truck regulation. The absence of shipper complaints and trucking lobbyists, along with the lack of ICC commitment to a broad program, also explains why Congress ignored the truck bill in 1932.[34] The transportation problem, along with all economic matters, would have to await the incoming Democratic administration.

5

By the early 1930s, railway securities holders were anxious about their investments. Too many transport facilities existed for the available freight, and general chaos, not planned coordination, appeared to be the rule in transport matters. The mixed systems of private ownership and government supervision had failed to construct a sound transport system.[35]

The alterations that the industrial and technological revolutions brought to society in the late nineteenth and early twentieth centuries strained the constitutional framework established in 1787. In response, reformers developed the independent regulatory commission, a concept based on the notion that institutions staffed with trained experts could effect positive change in the political economy. The reformers and other interests (shippers and railways) persuaded Congress to give trained regulators quasi-executive, quasi-legislative, and quasi-judicial powers; with these powers, the regulators were supposed to end abuses and to guide diverse economic interests into a national whole.[36] On the basis of their professional training and supposedly apolitical beliefs, the experts were expected to make decisions that would enhance "the public interest." Given the context of the political economy, no other strategy appeared likely. American ideology opposed government ownership of utilities, and as the outcry against monopoly abuses indicated, unfettered competition was also unacceptable. Thus, the independent regulatory commission was to be the engine of the middle course.

By the 1920s, the Interstate Commerce Commission was the leading example of such "independent" agencies. Yet, it seems that "the public interest" changed faster than the ICC could react. In the early years (1887–1917), the public interest (as inferred from congressional and ICC policies) seems to have glorified competition and shipper protection over pernicious bigness; restrictive controls became the method of regulation. After the transportation debacle of 1917–18, however, the public interest included the idea that financially sound railways were necessary to ensure a healthy economy. The ICC remained out of step in both periods, for it restricted railroad expansion when it was necessary and encouraged it when no expansion was needed.

Interest group politics, uncooperative railway executives, and a cumbersome pragmatic method of regulation together explain why the ICC was unable to produce a coordinated transport network in the 1920s. Congress, driven by diverse lobbying efforts, gave the ICC conflicting instructions. Contrary to expectations, moreover, the regulators found their positions to be anything but apolitical. The same interests that moved Congress also appeared in the ICC hearing rooms, each one presenting a different version of reality and a different view of the public interest. Recalcitrant railway executives also hindered effective administration of the regulatory laws. Instead of working with the regulators to plan the future of their industry nationally, railway leaders more often than not succumbed to their ideological fears of government intrusion into private business. They took advantage of common law legacies and due process requirements to frustrate the work of the experts. Bogged down in procedural, case-by-case detail, the regulators could not break free to look about them; consequently, they did not see that fundamental changes in transportation were occurring very quickly. Even when some in the ICC recognized the changes, they could not effect rapid movement in the bureaucracy.

The commission form of regulation, therefore, emerged as an imperfect response to the desire for order in a rapidly changing economy. It was an attempt to address the basic conflict between the desire for private management and the need for public supervision of private decisions. If private management could not make decisions based upon the consequences for the wider public interest, then the ICC experts should do so. Yet, the powers of the regulators were always circumscribed by conflicting instructions from Congress or by procedural detail.[37] Decisions based upon careful investigation of the problem, moreover, were subject to private management input. Inevitable disagreement between regulators and businessmen led to hearings, reports, and protracted appeals. Meanwhile, the conditions upon which the initial decisions had been based invariably changed, thus starting the cycle all over again. In effect, then, the political economy that gave birth to the regulatory commission prevented the realization of a coordinated transport system and an early public response to the trucking revolution.

Franklin Roosevelt's landslide victory over Herbert Hoover in November of 1932 signaled the American electorate's extreme dissatisfaction with the manner in which the political economy had performed in recent years. The transportation issue was only one of many facing public policy makers, but it was a problem that interested Roosevelt less than those in the banking and securities industries. Thus, it would be left to the interest groups, Congress, and the ICC to work out a solution to the transportation problem. The significant differences between the earlier period of railway controversies and the one approaching on trucking would be the quickness with which the strategies were debated and implemented and the extent to which federal agencies furnished a guiding hand in the process.

PART THREE

**Toward Federal
Truck Regulation,
1933–1940**

Disinterested students know that the theory [of
private enterprise] is to a very considerable extent
fallacious, and the results are not what they
should be.

—Joseph B. Eastman
January 30, 1933

6

Strategy for Control:
The Mixed Results
of Industry
Self-regulation

I

Unlike most businesses in the Great Depression, motor trucking seemed impervious to the economic crisis. The truck's low operating costs lured the unemployed to try the business and the truck's flexible services attracted shippers anxious to reduce expenses. To be sure, acute competition between established firms and the new truckers tended to temper the expansion, but this was to be expected in a new business. In contrast, the railroads languished. Railway executives found themselves victims of reduced tonnages, acute competition, and government regulation. By 1933 most businessmen and government officials recognized a transportation problem that consisted, for the most part, of a shrinking market and acute competition within each industry and between the industries. They agreed that the problem would have to be addressed politically if the country was to recover from the Depression. What they did not agree upon was how to respond to this situation.

Several remedies competed for public acceptance. A small minority believed a laissez-faire, or free-market, policy was the answer; unfettered competition would determine winners and losers and would best serve the public interest. Others noted that since the market included political intrusion already in the form of government subsidies and regulation, a laissez-faire policy toward the newer forms of transport would be unfair to the older forms. They desired, instead, that the government establish and enforce a competitive system. Still others believed the industries themselves could eliminate the problems if given the chance. Like the laissez-faire advocates, they ideologically opposed government intrusion into private affairs; unlike the laissez-faire champions, they wanted the firms within an industry to cooperate with one another to construct a strong, progressive industry. Given the antitrust tradition, of course, government would have to sanction such cooperation. Widespread public demands for government action in 1933 muffled the free-market advocates, relegating them to obscurity within the other groups. Thus, the debate over the transportation problem centered generally on two alternatives: industry self-regulation or government regulation. In each, the goal was the same—to control economic forces to bring the industries out of the Depression and to foster programs that would prevent such disasters in the future. The difference between the two approaches lay in the extent to which government would be involved.[1]

The newly installed Democratic administration of Franklin D. Roosevelt tried both alternatives in 1933. The National Industrial Recovery Act (NIRA), through the National Recovery Administration (NRA), attempted to erect a system of private controls over trucking. Simultaneously, the Federal Emergency Railroad Transportation Act, through the office of the Federal Coordinator of Transportation (FCT), attempted to devise a comprehensive system of public control over the railways and their competitors. Although seemingly working at cross-purposes, the two programs were not mutually exclusive. Information and experience gained during the abortive NRA experience helped those working in the FCT to draw up a comprehensive system of regulation. In fact, the NRA truck experience lent positive influence to the movement toward federal regulation.

The NIRA emerged from the feverish legislative activity in early 1933 that historians have labeled the First Hundred Days. Congressional haste stemmed in part from the election mandate of the previous November, from the personality of the new president, and from groundwork laid in the 1920s. Herbert C. Hoover's devastating defeat in 1932 clearly signaled a popular desire for government action to end the crisis facing American capitalism. Roosevelt understood this and prodded the lawmakers to enact a plethora of relief, recovery, and reform programs. The central reform issues of the previous decade—public power production, securities regulation, and railroad revitalization—now also became important recovery issues. The heightened crisis mentality in the spring of 1933, and FDR's manner of serving all political needs, regardless of conflict, resulted in a hodgepodge of haphazard, confusing, and contradictory laws that seemed to address every conceivable interest group except the truly powerless. The NIRA reflected this haphazardness more acutely than perhaps any other piece of legislation.[2]

The NIRA, although a product of the perceived need in 1933 to reform business conduct and thus save capitalism, nevertheless had antecedents back to the Federal Trade Commission Act of 1914. Businessmen, reformers, and public officials had grappled with the inherent tensions in capitalism during the Progressive Era, trying to foster situations in which industries could control competition and its negative effects without appearing to create monopolies. The impossibility of the task was reflected in the quirky path cartelization followed from 1914 until the New Deal. Conflict between the Commerce and Justice Departments and the Federal Trade Commission forestalled progress in the 1920s.[3] The advent of the National Recovery Administration brought some hope that the government might be able to guide businessmen in cleaning their own houses through industrywide codes of fair competition. The NRA, composed of public and private officials, would direct the code-writing process to make sure each code promoted cooperation, eliminated unfair trade practices, increased purchasing power, expanded production, reduced employment, and conserved the nation's resources. In short, the NRA was designed to save American business from itself and to do so without fostering monopolies. Not surprisingly, the entire scheme had fallen into disarray by the fall of 1934, well before the Supreme Court struck it down in May 1935.[4] Some benefits came out of the NRA experiment. For example, the automobile manufacturing industry was stabilized, and labor was given a voice in the political arena. Nevertheless, the NRA did not bring about the desired recovery.[5]

2

The NRA experiment benefited trucking more than most industries, but that was because trucking had more to gain. Trucking did not have a national trade association in 1933. Local and state associational activities in the 1920s had failed to draw together into a national organ, for the infancy of the business and the divisive issue of federal regulation had prevented concerted action. Thus, the first step in the NRA experiment was to form a national trade association that represented all trucking interests. This would prove difficult, however, for in

1933 there existed two major trucking groups, and each held different views toward the experiment in self-regulation.

One group, consisting of the NACC and the TAEA, saw the NRA as an opportunity for trucking to clean house. Leaders of these two organizations believed they could manipulate the NRA program to set rates, oust wildcat truckers, and stabilize the highly competitive business. If they were successful, they would prevent federal regulation, a calamity they feared would raise costs and eliminate natural advantages truckers enjoyed.

The second group, formally organized as the American Highway Freight Association in November 1932, viewed the NRA as a chance to prove that federal regulation was necessary. The AHFA believed that self-regulation was sure to fail. Subjected to conflicting state regulations, these common carriers knew firsthand the problems of enforcing regulatory laws, and they believed industry controls would fare no better. Instead, they desired uniformity under the watchful eye of the Interstate Commerce Commission.[6]

The task ahead, then, was a formidable one. Business and government officials first had to agree on the structure of a national trade association. Then a code had to be proposed, discussed, drafted, and approved. Once accepted by industry, labor, and government officials, the code had to be put into operation and enforced. Complex relationships within trucking and between it and other businesses, shifting government policies, and competing forces from the Federal Coordinator's office defined and limited the cartelization experiment.

Enactment of the NIRA prompted Jack Keeshin, AHFA president, to move quickly to secure recognition of the AHFA as spokesman for all of trucking. Keeshin's motivation grew out of his experience as a common carrier. He believed the unregulated status of "not-for-hire" (private) truckers created an unstable and unfair situation for the "for-hire" (common) carriers. The situation was exacerbated by the contract truckers, who were "for hire" in the sense that they struck contracts with a number of shippers but not "for hire" in the way a common carrier was. AHFA members not only lost freight to unregulated truckers but also suffered the public's and the shippers' wrath over unsafe and unscrupulous operations. In gaining control of the code, Keeshin hoped at best to dictate trade and rate agreements beneficial to common carriers; at least, he could influence administration officials to consider federal regulation.[7]

Keeshin's plans ran counter to NRA policy. Industry codes were to be drawn and approved by a wide range of interests, including business, labor, and consumers. Nonetheless, Keeshin made overtures to the TAEA in an attempt to check his opponents in the NACC. In the largest gathering ever of trucking delegates—over 250 attended—the AHFA and the TAEA met in Chicago on July 11 and 12. A joint committee proposed alterations in the AHFA constitution that liberalized membership requirements, and AHFA leaders apparently accepted the changes. The modifications, however, did not satisfy the NRA, for on July 24, Deputy Administrator Malcom Muir announced that any association requesting official status must represent all types of trucking.[8]

Muir's letter encouraged disgruntled members of TAEA and others affiliated with NACC to form the Truck Owners National Emergency Code Committee in early August. The committee met in Washington on August 10. The following day, a new association appeared, the Federated Truck Associations of America (FTAA).

Officials in the NRA thus faced a bitter and complex situation during August and September. The rival organizations submitted separate codes containing different definitions and policies for NRA review.[9] The FTAA opposed domination of the code by any one group; for its part, the AHFA protested the inclusion of manufacturers in the FTAA. By the middle of September, government officials had had enough. They informed the truckers that the internecine warfare could not continue and ordered them to organize one association that represented all trucking interests. NRA personnel would write a code if the operators failed to do so.[10]

At this point, one man fused the contending factions into the NRA-mandated association. In contrast to many trucking leaders who began their careers during the World War and early 1920s, Ted V. Rodgers came to the business late. Born in 1889, Rodgers worked in Pennsylvania coal mines as a teenager. With little formal education, he advanced to clerk for the general manager of the Lehigh Coal and Navigation Company in Lansford. Rodgers left the coalfields after a short stint as a mine contractor, to manage truck dealerships for Maccar Truck Company in Baltimore, Scranton, and Wilkes-Barre. In 1927, he and a partner established the Eschenbach and Rodgers trucking firm; their principal customer was the Great Atlantic and Pacific Tea Company. By 1932 Rodgers was well known and respected in the area and was elected president of the Pennsylvania Motor Truck Association.

From his position as head of one of the more active state associations, Rodgers maneuvered his way into the national scene. During the
summer of 1933, he bided his time and, at the right moment, rose to
succeed Jack Keeshin as president of the AHFA. His election reflected
genuinely widespread respect, for Rodgers was a contract trucker, not a
common carrier, and his dealerships tied him to the manufacturers.
Unlike the abrasive Keeshin, Rodgers possessed the native ability to
foster cooperation among strong-willed individuals. Often working
night and day, with little attention to his wife and five children,
Rodgers persuaded the contending factions to unite. By the end of
September, the truckers had agreed to form the American Trucking
Associations, Incorporated.[11] The NRA had forced the truckers' hand
and Rodgers had risen to the challenge.

Naturally, Rodgers became the first president of the ATA. He
himself preferred industry self-regulation and looked forward to the
NRA experiment. Rodgers deftly staffed the new association with
equal numbers from the now defunct AHFA and FTAA, but with the
appointment of Edward F. Loomis as secretary, it became clear that
proregulation forces had lost influence. Loomis was not a trucker, but
rather a professional organizer who had established the NACC's Truck
Committee in the 1920s; he had engineered the development of over
thirty state associations, which now formed the nucleus of the ATA.
His appointment sparked protests, but his organizational abilities
eventually quieted fears that he was a spy for the manufacturers. That
he officially resigned his position with NACC also helped. Meanwhile, though proregulation forces lost influence in the code-writing
process, they did not give up the fight for regulation. Keeshin established the National Highway Freight Association as a proregulation
lobby.[12]

By the fall of 1933, the ATA was recognized as the spokesman for all
trucking interests, but the association was not born intact. Initially,
confusion over the name of the organization caused some con-
sternation, for as one of the founders noted, "when one speaks of a
trucker, we immediately think of one growing produce or farm products and not a transporter of property." Nearly a year elapsed, moreover, before Rodgers could resolve organizational, policy, and
personality conflicts. The delays of the summer had alienated some
truckers, but others awoke to the understanding that collective action
would protect and extend their interests. This realization sustained
Rodgers in the months to come.[13]

3

At first, negotiations on the proposed truck code progressed rapidly. By mid-November, ATA and NRA officials had agreed on the form and most of the substance of a draft. Then, the chief NRA negotiator was promoted, and his successor proceeded to rewrite the draft, ignoring the accords already reached. After strenuous objections from the ATA, the NRA replaced the substitute with Charles L. Dearing, a respected student of transport policy. Under Dearing's direction, the draft returned to its earlier form. It was then sent to the several NRA advisory boards, as the NIRA directed. Objections to the labor and rate sections arose, and the draft was returned to the negotiators. At this critical point, Division Administrator Muir resigned and Sol Rosenblatt assumed his duties. Overworked with other codes, Rosenblatt could not attend to the labor and rate controversies before the winter holidays.[14]

Early in 1934, another delay materialized. Democratic Congressman Sam Rayburn of Texas introduced a federal truck regulation bill. General Hugh S. Johnson, the gregarious Administrator of the NRA, halted action on the truck code to await the fate of the Rayburn bill. Stunned, ATA leaders, lobbying against the bill while working on the details of the code, protested that the legislation stood small chance of passage that session and that NRA inaction would delay organization of the industry. In mid-January, Rosenblatt apparently intervened, spoke with Johnson, and announced talks would resume.[15]

For several days thereafter, ATA and labor leaders debated the issues of hours and wages. Labor representatives demanded a forty-hour work week and time and a half for overtime after eight hours, with a ten-hour maximum. They hoped that such requirements would spread the available work around and would increase consumer purchasing power. Trucking managers countered that meeting the labor demands would be detrimental to all in the industry. Higher costs would lead to higher rates, which in turn would force shippers to seek other carriers. Compounding the impasse was the seasonal nature of much of trucking. Drivers often worked long hours for a few weeks (to deliver a perishable crop, for example), only to be faced with reduced hours when demand dropped. Differences in wages North and South snagged the negotiations as well. In an ironic twist, business leaders from Charlotte, North Carolina, petitioned the NRA to keep wages in the South low enough so that black truckers would not be left out. As one of them put it, "If the wage scale for labor is made unreasonable it will means [*sic*] practically the elimination of colored labor in this section of the country. With conditions being the same the great majority of employers of labor will hire white men to the total exclusion almost of negro men." Adding to the difficulty were the apparently poor relations between Rodgers and Thomas O'Brien of the Teamsters. Eventually, to force action in the stalled labor talks, ATA officials went to Congress and persuaded Robert F. Wagner, Democrat of New York and principal supporter of the labor provisions in the NIRA, to use his influence. William Green, president of the American Federation of Labor, was also consulted. In the end, compromise prevailed. The code would specify hours and wages, but the ATA agreed to investigate further and report to the NRA for possible revisions.[16]

The issue of rate control was just as tangled and ended in a similarly unsatisfactory way. The ATA viewed rate agreements as the only method through which the industry could be stabilized; without them, unscrupulous truckers would continue to undermine established firms. Consumer advocates in the NRA, however, opposed rate agreements. They predicted shipping costs would rise and pointed out that the NIRA forbade such government-sanctioned monopoly practices if they harmed small businesses. In fact, the NRA officials refused to incorporate rate agreements into the code. Instead, they agreed that a cost formula could be used to establish rates. Although less than the ATA desired, the cost formula represented the best its leaders could get, given the NRA neurosis over monopoly power.[17]

Other disputes (particularly attempts to exempt certain kinds of trucking), continued confusion over policy objectives, and a typographical error in the labor section protracted the negotiations into February.[18] Finally, on February 10, 1934, President Roosevelt signed the Code of Fair Competition for the Trucking Industry. In a letter to the President, General Johnson furnished insight into what the code was designed to accomplish. He admitted that the structure of trucking prevented more stringent labor provisions, and he believed that administration of the code would furnish statistics never before available. Apparently, Johnson recognized the code would not be a panacea for the business, but rather a stepping stone to future stability.[19]

Nevertheless, the ten articles comprised in the truck code reflected an ambitious attempt to cartelize the young industry. The industry was defined as "the transportation of property and all services ordinarily incidental thereto in connection with any trade, industry, or business to

the extent that such transportation is over publicly used roadways by"
vehicles for hire and not for hire. Exemptions included household
goods carriers, farmers, and farm cooperatives. To administer the
code, the negotiators had designed an elaborate structure of national,
state, and local agencies. The cartelization plan created an Industrial
Relations Board to deal with violations of the labor sections. Hours
and wages were set for clerical personnel (forty hours and fourteen to
fifteen dollars per week, according to the size of the city) and for
drivers and helpers (37.5 cents to 55 cents per hour in the North and 25
cents to 30 cents in the South for unskilled workers). Overtime was to
be computed on the basis of one and one-third regular pay. Drivers and
helpers could work an additional twelve hours in any two-week period
over the 108-hour two-week maximum, if seasonal demands required
it. Dictated by the flexible nature of the business, the labor provisions
were the most liberal of any in the NRA codes.[20]

Other articles listed registration procedures, guidelines for rate-
making and trade agreements, and trade-practice rules. The latter
prohibited improper use of bills of lading (the freight bill), rebating,
false billing, false advertising, harassment of competitors, bribery, and
operation of vehicles beyond the prescribed hours.[21] The truck code,
then, represented a unique document. Under the auspices of the federal
government, private business leaders were to establish and enforce
rules of competition for an industry still in its infancy. Clearly, the
crisis mentality attending the early years of the Depression and the
structure of the new trucking technology shaped the cartelization plan.

4

The first eight months administering the truck code evolved into an
exasperating period for Ted Rodgers and the ATA, perhaps more trying
than the contentious months leading to the code's acceptance. Not only
did exemption, labor, and rate questions continue to plague the truckers, but also code machinery had to be established, industry members
registered, and compliance and enforcement procedures carried out.
The structure of trucking, the NRA bureaucracy, lack of enforcement
powers, and a weak rate-making program prevented a true test of
industry members' ability to regulate themselves. Nevertheless, the
first eight months brought some important gains for those desiring a
stable trucking industry.

The NRA's placement in Washington and the localized nature of trucking imposed a mixed administrative structure on the cartelization experiment. The National Code Authority (NCA), headquartered in the nation's capitol, oversaw fifty State Code Authorities (SCAs)—one each in the forty-eight states, Washington, D.C., and New York City. Not surprisingly, the industry elected Ted Rodgers Chairman of the NCA. From his position, Rodgers played the super organizer and compromiser. He exhorted the SCAs to sign up truckers, establish democratic procedures, and raise money for code expenses, even as he acted the conciliator, negotiating with NRA officials on points of procedure and interpretation. The pressures on Rodgers were enormous. Each SCA had numerous administrative problems that required his attention; simultaneously, NRA agents watched every move that he and the SCAs made. No decisions could be reached quickly, for the NRA required reports on every issue the NCA addressed, reports that passed through the hierarchy, susceptible to rejection on every desk they crossed. Rodgers had a secretary and an assistant to aid him, and the NCA also employed a general counsel and a treasurer. Its structure provided for a Labor Division, a Litigation Division, a Government Contracts Division, and sections to deal with statistics, publicity, and accounting. Later, the officials added an Educational Division to better inform truckers on the proper procedures to follow with the cost formula and other NRA rules.[22]

As Rodgers was both Chairman of the NCA and President of the ATA, so too were many of the state chairmen presidents of the state associations. Such a wedding of business and government interests suggests, on the surface, that the ATA leaders controlled the self-regulation experiment. That was not the case. ATA officials conscientiously tried to avoid conflict of interest, and Washington leaders instructed the SCAs to charge the state association for expenses rather than the NRA-supported SCA whenever any doubt about propriety arose.[23] Moreover, numerous organizational and administrative snafus suffocated any conspiratorial motivations the truckers might have had.

For example, the structure of the SCAs prohibited any one interest from dominating the others. The code required the state authorities to include representatives from the various classes of trucking—one regular-route common carrier; one contract hauler; one local cartage member; and one not represented by the other three. Inherent conflict between these classes erupted often. One, emanating from the evolution of transportation, existed between local cartage groups and over-the-road operators. The former had performed local transfer duties for the railways long before the interstate truckers appeared in the nation's cities. The cartage men resented the invasion into what they considered their business by historical right. Common carriers, moreover, protested the flexibility contract haulers exercised in choosing customers.[24] Friction between these natural competitors prohibited conspiratorial activities.

Rodgers realized that the SCAs had to be strong, or the experiment would fail. He faced, however, geographical, economical, and political factors in each state that delayed formation of state associations, which in turn slowed construction of the SCAs. For example, California presented a difficult situation. When the code was signed, twenty-five or so associations existed in the Bear Flag state, all of which had to be fairly represented in the SCA. Further, trucking operations appeared divided between older firms in the north and new enterprises in the south. Already organized, the northern truckers enjoyed solid management-labor relations, high wages, and established rate structures. Southern California truckers, however, suffered intense competition and factional divisions. New York presented a special case also. Cartage operations within and long-distance hauling to the Big Apple had little in common with the trucking found in rural, upstate New York. In the South, Accomac and Northampton counties in Virginia held closer economic relations to Maryland than to Virginia; the question here was whether or not to add these counties to the Maryland SCA or retain them under the Virginia authority. Intense factional and rail-truck politics delayed progress in Louisiana, while organization of trucking in New Mexico occurred in a vacuum. These local situations consumed much of Rodgers's time, but by the winter of 1934–35, all fifty SCAs were operating.[25]

After an SCA was organized, the next step was to register vehicles so drivers could display the NRA Blue Eagle emblem as a sign of compliance with the code. Registration did not go smoothly, for the long and contentious wait for the code, the delays in establishing the SCAs, the remaining unresolved conflicts, and geographical factors frustrated code officials and truckers alike. Some operators took advantage of the confusion. When their services appeared to fit two codes simultaneously, they refused to register at all. Rodgers and the NCA engaged in time-consuming arbitration with NRA officials and agents of Retail Trade, the Retail Solid Fuel Industry, the Household Goods Storage and Moving Trade, and the Construction Industry, to name a few, to clarify jurisdictions. The ATA took the conflicts seriously; unmonitored truckers could undercut rate and wage levels, thus defeating the goal of eliminating cutthroat competition. The drive-it-yourself business posed a particularly troublesome problem in this regard, for it was possible that truckers could undermine the code by renting trucks under the guise of occasional operators.[26]

Black truckers in the South presented a poignant problem. Many simply refused to register their vehicles, mostly one-mule wagons and Model T Fords. Sometimes the southern style of intimidation forced registration; other times, the logic of the black's position in the region stymied the program. The following exchange occurred between an SCA official and a black trucker from Georgia:

Do you want to register?

Go away boss. You know us niggers can't register and vote.

You are not registering to vote. You are registering your vehicle with the Government under the Code of Fair Practice [*sic*] for the Trucking Industry.

Cap'n ah ain't got no truck.

Well, the Code applies also to horse-drawn vehicles.

Yowsah, but I drives a mule.

You see the Code applies to horse-drawn and mule-drawn vehicles, even if it is called the Code of Fair Practice for the Trucking Industry.

Boss, anybody kin tell you I'se always practiced fair. Do this heah thing cost any money?

Yes, the authorities have fixed a $3.00 assessment as the proper charge for the cost of registering the vehicles under the Code.

(Heading toward the door) Boss, I am sho' sorry, but I ain't seen $3.00 since Buck was a calf. Tell Uncle Sam I sho' hates it, but if I had $3.00 I wouldn't even speak to him.

Many other truckers, black and white, did not have the three dollars or the confidence in the authorities to register.[27]

Slowing down registration was the NRA's insistence that each SCA establish committees to hear protests against the fees. Clearly a democratic procedure that protected operators from excessive manipulation by those in positions of power, it confused the process of registration. Yet, despite complications arising from NRA policies and the unwillingness of truckers to register, the registration process produced some impressive statistics. Through persistence, the SCAs eventually registered 300,000 trucks; perhaps as many as 75,000 were not registered. Nearly 80 percent of the registered vehicles represented one-truck firms, an indication both of the composition of the industry and of the diligence of SCAs. Not all of those registering paid the three-dollar assessment, for the NRA exempted those on relief.[28]

Registration, compliance, and enforcement were the basic elements of industrial cartelization. When a trucker registered and paid the fee, he also filed a schedule of minimum rates. He then received a metal plate with the Blue Eagle emblem and a number stamped on it. Display of the plate indicated only that the operator had registered and filed a tariff schedule. How could it be determined if the trucker was in compliance with the fair-trade practices? In fact, truckers found it rather easy to hide behind the Blue Eagle and cut rates and work longer hours at lower pay than the code allowed. When a trucker filed a complaint against a cheater, he put his faith in the enforcement committee of the SCA.

At this point, the concept of self-regulation broke down. As with most attempts at cartelization before it, the NRA program omitted an effective method of enforcement. No real authority existed at the local or national levels. A complaint followed carefully constructed procedural steps from the SCA to the NCA. Once the complaint had been filed with the NRA, it was shuffled from the Control Section to the Analysis Branch to the Division Assistant for Compliance to the Assistant Counsel to the Deputy Administrator to the Division Administrator, who returned it to the Assistant Counsel, who presented it to the National Compliance Board, which could remove the Blue Eagle. The complaint could still go to the Litigation Division for further enforcement procedures. In the final analysis, the offending trucker could, and often did, ignore the findings of his fellow industry members. From February 17, 1934, until May 25, 1935, the SCAs dealt with 4,445 labor complaints. Of those, the authorities adjusted 3,640, finding the defendants either not guilty or victims of bookkeeping discrepancies. Over 250 were referred beyond the local agencies, and 533 were still pending when the code ceased operation in May 1935. The NCA initiated forty-three court proceedings in an attempt to discourage cheating, but the unwieldy judicial process proved ineffective and demoralizing. As of August 6, 1934, litigation had resulted in eight convictions, three permanent injunctions, twelve restraining orders, and thirty-six adjustments. There were attempts to blackball recalcitrant truckers, but the NRA blocked them.[29] In short, even if all the truckers had registered, widespread commitment to enforcement of the rules did not exist.

Ironically, but in typical New Deal fashion, actions of other agencies interfered with enforcement of the truck code. Relief and recovery officials hired truckers who were not complying with the rules. Only ad hoc enforcement resulted from the NCA's Government Contracts Division's efforts to hold agencies accountable to the code. Another constant source of conflict was the Office of the Federal Coordinator of Transportation. After the ATA had successfully stalled consideration of the Rayburn bill in the spring of 1934, its leaders had to combat the publicity and interest surrounding the release of the Coordinator's Second Report and his bill for federal truck regulation. An in-house memo noted, "These two actions create a destructive conflict between two Government Departments and place the Trucking Industry in an untenable and impossible position." These events undermined registration and enforcment and distracted the ATA's attention from the self-regulation experiment.[30]

Perhaps nowhere was the conflict between ATA desires and NRA policies so clear as in the area of rate controls. Though hardly a unanimous sentiment in the industry (a few truckers feared inflexible rate agreements might benefit railways), support for rate control was widespread, and complaints about lack of enforcement were numerous.[31] In a classic memorandum on the subject, NRA official Sol Rosenblatt outlined the problems involved. Administratively, he argued, enforcement of rate controls was impossible. First, a price cutter received immediate results that were often beyond reparation unless a time-consuming hearing ensued. Even then, the complainant was not assured his efforts would be worthwhile. Second, the relative nature of cost of service complicated administration of rate controls. Variations in volume created variations in cost that were difficult to determine. Third, Rosenblatt believed that enforcement of price agreements in an industry comprising so many firms was next to impossible. Fourth, lack of enforcement of rate agreements adversely affected enforcement of other provisions in the cartelization scheme.[32] Consequently, the ATA faced a dilemma. Efforts toward strict enforcement of rate agreements would be viewed as monopolistic and therefore illegal. Yet, failure to enforce rate levels would undermine other sections of the code. Aware of the problems, the NCA counseled the SCAs to take care in holding rate hearings and in formulating rate committees. Officials suggested that the SCAs cover their actions with euphemisms such as "Compliance Committees" and "Tariff Filing Committees" to ward off charges of monopolistic practices.[33]

The NCA's cost formula, not approved until October 16, 1934, did not resolve the dilemma. Several months in the making, it proved too complicated for the majority of one-truck operators to comprehend, and the NCA was unable to launch an effective educational campaign to teach truckers how to add costs and determine rates. The cost formula introduced many for the first time to the basic principles of accounting, but that was small consolation to ATA leaders who had hoped for a more effective method to stabilize rates.[34]

Continuously, it seemed, during 1934, complaints flooded the SCAs and the NCA about the lack of enforcement of rates and other provisions in the code. Rodgers and his staff responded as best they could. They used publicity to embarrass operators into compliance, instituted court proceedings in cases they thought could be won, and continued efforts to change NRA attitudes toward rate agreements. Still, the rank-and-file truckers remained disenchanted with self-regulation. In September 1934, one New York trucker summarized the thoughts of many when he wrote, "The Code, as at present constituted, in this area is dead."[35] Perhaps it was. Yet, the complaint had been mailed to a central organization, and that had been impossible only twelve months before.

5

If the NRA experiment was indeed dead in the fall of 1934, the spirit of associationalism was not. Frustration born of the code could not mask evidence that truckers were thinking and acting collectively. Begun in the early 1920s, the associational movement matured during the NRA experience. Conflict continued, to be sure, but from it materialized what one early advocate of associationalism, Tom Snyder, had labeled an "industrial consciousness."[36] Discussion revealed that all truckers faced similar difficulties obtaining insurance, initiating safety programs, negotiating labor contracts, and meeting rate reductions of chiselers and railways. Enhancing the appearance of industrial consciousness was the dialogue developing between industry leaders and government officials. Contact among the ATA and NRA and FCT indicated that self-regulation was not working but that other strategies for industry control were available.

The truckers recognized these positive accomplishments during the First Annual ATA Convention, held in Chicago, October 22–24, 1934. Relative harmony in the Windy City now appeared to replace the earlier strife and to boost ATA morale. Over 350 delegates took part, including such early activists as Edward Loomis, Henry C. Kelting, Joe C. Carrington, and Jack Keeshin. C. W. Duke and Edward Sproles, litigants in the pivotal Supreme Court cases, attended, as did observers from the NRA, the Department of Labor, the National Industrial League, and the Brookings Institution. Most importantly, the Federal Coordinator dropped in to deliver an address.[37]

"The attendance at this meeting today is proof that trucking is an industry and that it is organized," asserted Ted Rodgers proudly in his opening remarks. Rodgers reviewed events of the preceding year and noted the problems encountered in administering the code. He then emphasized the progress achieved in ATA activities distinct from those of the NRA. The Legislative Committee had lobbied successfully against the Rayburn and Federal Coordinator bills, opposed the Connery thirty-hour bill, and supported Roosevelt's crime bills pertaining to interstate commerce. ATA members had met with ICC officials to oppose railway rate reductions, to discuss the implications of railroad store-door deliveries, and to devise regulations for the transport of dangerous explosives. The Publicity Department had published an *ATA News Bulletin* that informed members about code and industry issues. Perhaps the most telling indication that the ATA represented a maturing organization was Rodgers's list of activities carried on with other associations. ATA officials attended the National Conference on Street and Highway Safety (to lobby against restrictive weight laws), worked with the Chamber of Commerce of the United States (to design a rate structure), and joined the National Highway Users Conference (to fight restrictions imposed on industry members).[38]

Although not recognized at the time, the most important accomplishment of the ATA's first year was the cordial relationship it forged with the Federal Coordinator of Transportation, which allowed productive exchange of statistics and ideas. Thus, when Federal Coordinator Joseph B. Eastman approached the rostrum after Rodgers's speech, the delegates welcomed him warmly. Characteristically, Eastman's remarks struck at the heart of the matter when he candidly told the truckers that the code was not working and federal regulation would be necessary. That the warm reception did not cool indicated the coordinator's ideas were not far removed from those of most of the members in attendance.[39]

The ATA Policy Committee confirmed the apparent transition in thought when it released a new resolution during the convention. No longer did the truckers view the code as the only strategy for industry control. In fact, the resolution declared, the ATA would "cooperate with the Federal Coordinator of Transportation and the Administration in the development of a sound national transportation network." By no means a full capitulation to federal regulation, the statement included the desire to maintain as many aspects of self-regulation as possible in any future programs. Indeed, a separate resolution called for a more viable rate-making provision in the code.[40] Industry leaders wanted to control the industry themselves, but they recognized that they needed federal authority to be successful.

Despite the movement to embrace federal regulation in the fall and winter of 1934, the ATA did not give up on the code. Remaining dedicated to self-regulation, Rodgers continued to exhort the SCAs to register recalcitrant truckers and to upgrade administrative procedures, a difficult task, considering that some SCA members were not complying with the code. On the national front, Rodgers ordered NCA lawyers to step up prosecutions of operators who violated code provisions. Meanwhile, other officials pressed the NRA to accept modifications that would allow groups of truckers to initiate rate agreements.[41]

Contrary to the Chairman's glowing report and enthusiasm, the experience in industry self-regulation was deeply troubled in January 1935. Incomplete registrations hampered enforcement and kept SCA coffers constantly low on operating funds. When the NCA ordered another registration campaign to open the second year of the code, truckers lost interest. Not the least of the NCA's problems was securing NRA approval for the changes in registration procedures for the second code year. Aggravating the situation, the Roosevelt Administration gave conflicting signals to the industry. For example, rumors circulated throughout Washington that the Coordinator's bill would be enacted in the coming session; others suggested the entire NRA would be scrapped.[42]

Thus, the ATA faced a crossroads in early 1935. While industry self-regulation was preferred, the code experience had suggested it was unworkable without federal support. The Coordinator was drafting an authoritative regulatory bill, but it excluded code machinery. The truckers responded with a dual political strategy. On the one hand, the Policy Committee shifted course on the Eastman program. It went beyond mere cooperation to embrace the Coordinator's plans outright, but with two qualifications. The ATA insisted that it be included in the administrative machinery of federal regulation and that the Interstate Commerce Commission (the agency that would oversee controls) be reorganized to ensure that those supervising trucking were not "railroad minded." On the other hand, the ATA continued to administer the code and to appeal to the NRA for changes. The NCA stepped up enforcement by filing forty additional cases, and Rodgers continued attempts to strengthen the SCAs by inviting SCA secretaries to travel to Washington to see the national operations at firsthand.[43] The businessmen truckers played both ends against the middle to increase the chances that they would be in a position of power when the strategy for regulation was finally decided. The second part of the truckers' strategy became moot on May 27 when the Supreme Court invalidated the NIRA. Only then, however, did the ATA place its full weight behind the Coordinator's program.[44]

6

The NRA experience produced mixed results for the trucking industry. It reflected the classic case of the failure of self-cartelization. As with the doomed pooling ventures of the railroads in the late nineteenth century, the code lacked the power of enforcement, even though the government was participating in the attempt to cartelize trucking. Stabilization was not achieved, for unfair trade practices, especially rate cutting, continued. Liberal labor provisions prevented the intended increase in employment. Wages rose a little in the South, but they were low there to begin with. The truck code, then, failed to achieve some of the key goals of the NIRA. That the industry continued to grow was more the result of inherent economic and technological advantages than of the government-sponsored experiment in self-regulation.[45]

The progress in associationalism offset the failure of the code. Annointed by the NRA, the ATA became, in the short span of fifteen months, an effective national association. Not only could the ATA organize diverse interests into associational activities (insurance, labor, and safety programs), but it could also influence national public policy. The code experience, moreover, had compiled statistics on trucking never before available, and the ATA could now use those statistics and its political power to influence the movement toward federal regulation of trucking.[46]

7 Pragmatic Public Policy: Joe Eastman and the Motor Carrier Act of 1935

Concurrent with the National Recovery Administration's abortive attempt to cartelize trucking, another New Deal agency strove to find a comprehensive approach to the transportation problem. The Federal Coordinator's office, under the direction of ICC member Joseph B. Eastman, rejected industry self-regulation in favor of public supervision over all transport forms. Apparently at odds and in competition for congressional support, the two agencies nevertheless complemented one another. Indeed, the dialectical relationship begat the Motor Carrier Act of 1935.

In the Emergency Railroad Transportation Act (signed just minutes apart from the National Industrial Recovery Act), Congress created a Federal Coordinator of Transportation (FCT). The Coordinator was to organize the railroads into an efficient national system, investigate competing forms of transport, and design a program for the extension and coordination of regulation. Not since World War I had the national government assumed such broad authority over the nation's transport industries. Unlike the war experience, however, the New Deal program fell far short of the intended goals. The railways were not reorganized and regulation was not coordinated. The only substantive result—aside from the data collected—was the Motor Carrier Act.[1]

As Federal Coordinator, Joe Eastman exercised no overt political power, relying instead on the progressive spirit of the disinterested expert. This approach failed to reorganize the rails but proved to be just what was needed to reconcile the contending interests involved in trucking. Following the pragmatic process the ICC had developed since 1887, Eastman shaped congressional understanding of the public's interest in trucking.[2]

I

That President Roosevelt tapped Joseph Bartlett Eastman to assume the role of Federal Coordinator came as no surprise in the spring of 1933. A member of the Interstate Commerce Commission since 1919, Eastman had compiled an impressive record of public service based on hard work, incisive analysis, balanced judgments, and political independence. Eastman antagonized nearly every interest group at one time or another during his career, but he remained highly respected, even liked, by most in the transportation industries.[3]

Although born in Katonah, New York, in 1882, Eastman's early life reflected a New England heritage. He grew up, as his biographer described it, within a family background "of plain living and high thinking, simplicity, conscientiousness, and devotion to duty—in short, the essence of Puritanism at its best." An independent nature surfaced early. Although he absorbed from his Presbyterian minister father the virtues of public spiritedness, unselfishness, and a sense of humor, Eastman abandoned formal religion. When he was fourteen, his family moved from the idyllic wooded hills of Westchester County to the grimy, poverty-ridden coal town of Pottsville, Pennsylvania. Despite the privations of his new community, Eastman did not awaken to issues of social justice until after college.

At Amherst College at the turn of the century, Eastman was an above average, but not outstanding student. He honed his writing skills as reporter and editor for the college newspaper and refined his abilities in public speaking and chess. He was one of the first of his class to part his hair on one side, rebelling against the Gilded Age fashion of parting it down the middle. Eastman's five-foot, nine-inch frame presented an "easy-going affability" at graduation in 1904. Hazel eyes, a "faint suspicion of a double chin," and a less than modest girth enhanced his calm manner. Indifferent to female companionship, Eastman remained a bachelor all his life.[4]

Having made no plans for postgraduate employment, Eastman readily accepted a fellowship to the South End House that was offered by another Amherst alumnus, Robert A. Woods. The settlement house in Boston gave young people firsthand experience of the rigors of urban life in hopes they could devise programs for social improvement. Following the footsteps of earlier reformers such as Jane Addams, Eastman in 1905 turned to political activism when he joined the Public Franchise League, a Gilded Age citizens' reform committee. He promptly became a protégé of Louis D. Brandeis, the so-called people's lawyer. Eastman enlisted in the battle to return decision-making power for the Boston Elevated to the citizens, and in 1912–13, he helped prepare the Brandeis brief against the New Haven Railroad. The student of reform naturally developed a style similar to his mentor's but he discarded some of Brandeis's questionable practices. While he developed a capacity to research the issues at hand thoroughly and to write copious briefs filled with novel ideas, he resisted the Brandeisian use of slanted publicity to influence court decisions.[5] Eastman was uncomfortable with deception and relied instead on intense preparation and a cordial, though professional debating style.

By 1916 Eastman's reputation landed him an appointment to the recently strengthened Massachusetts Public Service Commission. Established in 1869 as the Railroad Commission, a "sunshine" agency through which commissioners used publicity to change unethical and unsafe railway practices, its effectiveness had waned over the years until, by 1913, the agency had evolved into a rubber stamp for the railroads. In the new PSC, the commissioners had more authority and power to direct change. Members could subpoena railway records, employ outside experts for special investigations, and issue orders against unreasonable rates.[6] The student now found himself in the forefront of regulatory reform.

Eastman's appointment marked the beginning of a continuous process of reflection on and practical application in public regulation of private business. He believed the actions of the PSC would determine whether public supervision of private management could work or whether government ownership would be necessary. That he leaned toward the latter view was radical but not without a basis in the intellectual community. In characteristically independent fashion, however, Eastman reversed the assumptions implicit in government-business relations in the Progressive Era. Most leading progressives believed the government had the right to control private utilities because their operations affected the general welfare; Eastman, in contrast, saw the utilities as performing tasks the state could (should) have performed.[7] The distinction illuminates Eastman's independent nature and a curious irony. One of the most respected public regulators in American history would have preferred a socialist political economy.

Socialist underpinnings aside, Eastman held a fluid and aggressive view toward his job as regulator. To him, the PSC was to ensure that the utilities furnished reasonable service at reasonable rates. Rates were to be high enough to attract financial backing to sustain and expand services, but not so high as to be unreasonable. Eastman saw no simple formulas that would aid in balancing these requirements of the public and private sectors. The reasonableness of services and rates represented to Eastman a theoretical issue that demanded investigation, discussion, and debate.[8]

As a state commissioner, Eastman encouraged the exchange of ideas on such issues. He joined the National Association of Railroad and Utility Commissioners and implemented several programs to encourage discussion. He supported the establishment of a NARUC general solicitor in the nation's capital to monitor national issues affecting state regulators, and he served on several NARUC committees, particularly the railroad Valuation Committee. Despite the general ill-feeling existing between the federal and state commissioners (the latter were jealous of power lost to the former), Eastman advocated cooperation between NARUC, the Railroad Administration, and the ICC during the war. In fact, he served on the first joint hearing ever held between the commission and NARUC.[9]

Early in 1919, on the advice of Louis Brandeis, President Woodrow Wilson appointed Eastman to the Interstate Commerce Commission. The Senate confirmation met minimal resistance, even though the independent had recently advocated outright government ownership of public utilities. As it had before and would continue to do, Eastman's reputation as a fair-minded, hardworking public servant overcame uneasiness about his radical leanings.[10]

Eastman's quarter of a century on the commission only enhanced his earlier reputation as an independent. The ICC consumed most of his life, often sixteen to eighteen hours per day. He continued to support cooperation with the states after his appointment. He wrote more than the usual share of opinions and orders, and more often than the others, he dissented from the majority. His most frequent complaint was the lack of time to think about what it was the ICC was supposed to be doing. The busy and tedious schedule prompted Eastman on several occasions to propose reorganization plans for the commission that would streamline procedures, delegate more authority to staff, and thus release members to concentrate on broad policy concerns. Believing in the progressive ideal of independent commissions, Eastman jealously protected the ICC from outside intrusions. He took on the Supreme Court in 1927–29 in the *O'Fallon* rate-making case, attempting to influence the decision through material he sent privately to Brandeis. He opposed the President in 1932 when Hoover interfered in the railway consolidation controversy and in the late 1930s when FDR attempted to bring the independent agency under his control.[11]

Eastman's independent nature was backed by progressive training and acceptance of the pragmatic method. These things shaped his bureaucratic style and thus his approach to regulation. When a regulatory issue arose, he collected all the available information, studied it, made initial judgments in a preliminary report, and circulated it for comment among fellow commissioners, other interested persons, and business associations. After analyzing the responses, he drafted another report. When satisfied with the general policy and substance, he went public, testifying before congressional committees and presenting his ideas to business groups. Thus, he forged consensus through a fluid interchange with other interested parties, relying on pragmatism and associationalism to come up with workable policies. This style of investigation, consultation, and compromise reflected the professional public servant dedicated to finding the common good.[12]

Such commitment to the regulatory process appears to belie Eastman's desire for government ownership. Indeed, his work in the 1920s induced a metamorphosis in his thought about public policy and regulation; and the rise of the trucking industry in no small measure affected the shift.

By 1919 Eastman's views on government ownership had crystallized. He believed the theory of private enterprise did not work in practice, and he viewed regulation as "wasteful duplication" of managerial effort. Historical facts convinced him that private initiative and the pursuit of profit had brought about undesirable results. "It can be argued with much reason," he wrote, "that its [competition's] disadvantages have been as great as its advantages. Moreover, the assumption that private railroad owners have a peculiar self-interest in efficient management and economical operations has slender foundation." Intense railway competition in the 1870s and 1880s had produced unnecessary construction and destructive rate wars. The young regulator noted that the Boston Elevated had performed more efficiently after a board of trustees assumed control in 1918. The trustees system bypassed the duplication of effort found in public regulation, where commissioners reviewed and often altered private management decisions. Eastman was particularly impressed with the success of the Railroad Administration, which had untangled the chaotic railway systems and established an efficient transport network during the Great War. "Disinterested students," he wrote to Felix Frankfurter, "know that the theory [of private enterprise] is to a very considerable extent fallacious, and the results are not what they should be."[13]

The rise of new transport competition in the 1920s shook Eastman's faith in government ownership. For a brief time, he thought the railways might evolve into transport firms in the broadest sense, each firm engaging in all kinds of transportation—rail, water, road, and air. He then realized, of course, that the American political economy would not accept such a concentration of economic power in so few hands. Thus, he reasoned, if the state were to gain control of the railroads (as he preferred), then some method of supervision of competing forms would have to be developed. Otherwise, the competitors would take unfair advantage of the rails.[14] During the hearings on the Emergency Railroad Act early in 1933, Eastman indicated to Congress the extent of his thinking on the transport problem: "The transportation of this country is in a period of grave unsettlement pending important changes. New transportation agencies have appeared on the scene in great force. The proper place for each of these agencies must be found, and in some way they must be coordinated and welded into a well-knit whole, into a transportation system operating more nearly as a unit, without cross purposes and all manner of lost motion."[15]

In the progressive tradition, Eastman had recognized changes in the economy and offered a response to rationalize the resulting chaos. Although a classic statement of scientific management ideals, the prescription the regulator offered lacked an institutional approach; yet to be determined was the mechanism that would coordinate the various transportation forms. As Federal Coordinator in 1933, he was charged with finding that mechanism.

2

The Coordinator was not working in a vacuum. He brought sixteen years of experience and the historical perspective of forty-five years of national railway control. In addition, proposals for federal truck regulation had been circulating since the mid-1920s when the state commissions first discovered trucking. Several bus and truck bills had been introduced, the most recent by Senator Couzens in the 72nd Congress. Several studies, moreover, furnished material that complemented the experience of state and federal regulators—the "Flynn

Report" from the ICC in 1932, the report of the National Transportation Committee, and the Brookings Institution publication, *The Transportation Problem,* released in 1933. Eastman had followed the progress of these events before his appointment as Federal Coordinator.[16] His task, then, was to reexamine the issues, gather new information, and devise a regulatory structure that would rationalize the complex transportation situation.

Trade journals had been debating the issues for some years, and their editorial perspectives furnished Eastman with information on where each interest group stood. In the leading railroad journal, *Railway Age,* R. H. Aishton, Chairman of the Executive Committee of the Association of Railway Executives, candidly observed that the rail problems in 1932 stemmed from three interrelated causes: a severe and lengthy business depression, defects in the regulatory system, and competition with unregulated forms of transport. *Railway Age* editors also admitted that "the decline in railway freight business during the depression has been partly due to increased competition of trucks and waterways, but mainly to the fact that production and commerce have declined much more than ever before."[17]

Despite the effects of depression, *Railway Age* consistently pointed to the regulatory system as one of the main sources of the rails' plight. The ICC, according to the editors, had failed to follow the intent of Congress, as stated in the Transportation Act of 1920. Through restrictions on rate increases, the hoped-for 5.75 percent return on investment had not materialized. Consequently, the railroads had no surplus funds with which to weather depressed business conditions.[18] The unregulated status of motor carriers also harmed the rails because it underscored the technological advantages the truck enjoyed. Truckers made more pickups and deliveries per day and demoralized established markets—all because they were not regulated. Such conditions, the rails argued, brought low prices and low profits for all—farmers, merchants, railways, and truckers alike. A balanced approach to regulation of transportation was needed, the editors believed.[19]

Connected to the unequal regulation theme was the subsidy issue. Railway executives consistently maintained that they had to acquire, maintain, and pay taxes on roadbeds, but truckers rolled virtually free on the nation's highways. Actually, by the early 1930s, motor vehicles were apparently paying their fair share. Even so, the subsidy issue opened a Pandora's box of conflicting statistics and analyses; debate often deteriorated into emotional diatribes based upon skewed and self-serving studies. As the Federal Coordinator would discover, one central problem framed the subsidy issue: how could the value of service to the general welfare be calculated? Certainly both trucks and railroads contributed to the common good; how much of the costs should be recovered through general taxation and how much charged directly to the firms?[20]

Although their perspective would shift by mid-decade, trucking leaders in the early 1930s countered every allegation the rails made. Protruck journals noted that the truck represented the latest in American economic and technological progress and reminded the rail executives that when their business was new and innovative, the government had not tied their hands. A few truck enthusiasts called for less regulation for all transport modes; they believed free competition should be the regulator, with the law of survival of the fittest determining who would succeed and who would fail. Others maintained that regulation of trucking was impractical, for experience with state laws indicated motor carriers too easily evaded the controls. Since little public support existed, some truckers believed regulation was unjustified. Still others forcefully contradicted the charge that their operators disrupted commerce. Trucks took less-than-carload freight that had proven unprofitable to the rails anyway, furnished additional tonnage for the railways (in the form of high value shipments of automobiles, trucks, tires, parts, and accessories), and gave farmers improved service, for they could now more quickly react to fluctuations in market prices. Finally, trucking furnished more jobs for more people than did the railways—a telling argument in years of high unemployment.[21]

These industry arguments in part defined the task facing the Federal Coordinator. Of course, Eastman had rejected the laissez-faire approach out-of-hand. In devising a comprehensive regulatory scheme, he would have to consider the issues of technological progress, unequal regulation, and depression conditions. Beyond these broad considerations, the details of regulatory legislation—the piecing together of the sections and paragraphs of a statute—would require a firm understanding of the structure of trucking. That the industry was still developing complicated the Coordinator's mission.

3

Historian Paul K. Conkin has suggested that the real charm, the real substance of the New Deal, was found in the agencies and subagencies of the burgeoning Washington bureaucracy. In this vein, the Coordinators's office surfaced as the clearinghouse for information pertaining to the transportation problem. Through the force of his bureaucratic style and reputation, Joe Eastman made the FCT a highly respected agency, thus relegating other agencies and officials concerned with transportation (the NRA and Secretary of Commerce Daniel Roper) to relatively minor parts. [22]

From the moment of his appointment in June 1933, Eastman took a comprehensive approach to studying competing forms of transport. He first assembled a small group of experts, in some instances ignoring Civil Service requirements to hire the people he wanted. Staff members compiled information from which the Coordinator's four reports and other specialized studies were written. The FCT examined the flow of merchandise traffic, labor problems, subsidies for transportation, and a host of related issues, including the controversial cost-of-service rate-making approach. Despite this impressive list, Eastman did not complete all the work he had contemplated. Congress had imposed a two-year limit on his office (though the lawmakers extended it to three). [23]

Following a favorite technique of Eastman's, the FCT mailed out questionnaires to a variety of interest groups—truck and railway organizations, the National Highway Users Conference, the National Industrial Traffic League, oil companies, and farm groups. For more specific information on truck operations, the FCT relied on the NRA-sponsored American Trucking Associations. Despite trucking opposition to regulation in 1933 and 1934, ATA officials passed on the Coordinator's queries and encouraged industry members to support the FCT's efforts. In conferring with these private associations, a practice Eastman had long advocated in regulatory administration, the Coordinator's office collected data on operating costs, competitive conditions, through-rate agreements, and industry opinions. [24]

Eastman also conveniently and efficiently drew upon the experience and manpower of several government agencies. The Bureau of Public Roads furnished traffic surveys and much of the data and methodology for analyzing the subsidy question. The Bureau of Labor conducted a study of working conditions and the Bureau of Standards offered expertise on uniformity in sizes and weights of motor vehicles. NARUC proffered historical, theoretical, and technical information on state regulation and the NRA, especially after February 1934, provided up-to-date statistics on the extent of trucking.[25] NARUC and the NRA looked like strange bedfellows to the FCT. State regulators were jealous of federal power, and the NRA's strategy of self-regulation contradicted the notion of extending regulation. On occasion, conflicts erupted between the agencies but apparently did not arrest the flow of information to the Coordinator.[26]

After less than a year of study, Eastman released the Second Report and submitted several bills to Congress; all dealt with the extension of regulation. (The First Report had dealt with railroad revitalization.) In characteristically pragmatic fashion, Eastman admitted the program, though "sound in principle," was subject to revision in particulars. In fact, not all the special studies had been completed. Released in March 1934, the Second Report described the changes in transportation that had occurred recently and concluded the present problems could be reduced to the simple proposition that an oversupply of transport facilities existed for the available freight. The remedy, in principle, was to coordinate the various kinds of transport so that each performed the tasks for which it was best suited. Such an approach required extension and coordination of regulation to truck and water carriers. Eastman believed "the guiding hand of government control"—through ICC regulation—would bring order out of chaos.[27]

Eastman's decision to extend regulation, rather than reduce it, and to put the controls under the authority of the ICC came as no surprise. His philosophy of public control, his experience with commission regulation, and his understanding of railroad history all shaped his decision. The Coordinator recognized a historical parallel in operation. Just as the railways had suffered intense and wasteful competition before the ICC was established in 1887, so too was transportation suffering under chaotic competition in the 1930s. He understood that the Depression—perhaps only temporarily—was exacerbating the situation, but Eastman did not believe this important enough to alter his basic views.[28]

Although the Coordinator's report and proposed bills generated excitement in the spring of 1934, numerous political causes prevented serious consideration of them. As noted earlier, at the time, the ATA opposed federal regulation and effectively stalled action on Eastman's truck bill and another one that Sam Rayburn had submitted. Aiding the

ATA in blocking the measures were a busy session and a widespread desire to adjourn early to prepare for the off-year elections. President Roosevelt's lack of interest also impeded progress, for congressional leaders would not push for action without the go-ahead from the White House.

Another problem, as Eastman recognized, was the bill's complexity. It was a comprehensive plan to regulate a private industry that was still in its infancy.[29] Such a program might have passed Congress during the frenzied beginnings of the New Deal, but not during the more sober weeks of 1934. As respected as Eastman was, he still required help in explaining the particulars to members of Congress. The one group that could have helped him, the ATA, opposed him.

After returning from a vacation in mid-August (a respite Roosevelt had ordered for all agency chiefs), Eastman intensified efforts to revise his program. He requested still more information from private associations and government agencies and ordered a survey of industry journals to ascertain just where interest groups stood on the issues. The Coordinator delved more deeply into the experience state regulators had amassed in controlling contract and private truckers. The FCT staff also collected more data on motor carrier taxation, highway subsidies, hours and wages of trucking labor, average lengths of truck hauls, fuel consumption by size of vehicle, average truck speeds, factors involved in accidents, and the increase in the number of trucking brokers.[30]

A convergence of events occurred in the early fall that at once aided Eastman's revision process and improved chances for acceptance of his program in 1935. In effect, he found the help he needed to persuade the lawmakers that trucking should be regulated. The ATA, faced with the shortcomings of the NRA, with growing support for federal regulation, and with the widespread respect for Eastman's abilities, decided to work more closely with the Coordinator. Curiously, Eastman had remained aloof from the ATA at first; the one trucker he knew and liked was Jack L. Keeshin, a misfit midwestern common carrier who did not represent the majority of truckers, though he did favor federal controls.[31] Now, meetings between the FCT and the ATA were held, differences discussed. The relation between the two groups matured through stages: first, mutual respect, then wary cooperation, and finally, outright agreement when the NRA suffered defeat at the hands of the Supreme Court in May 1935.

Even though he remained pessimistic in early 1935, Eastman had strengthened his position from that of a year before. His program had been enhanced through more investigations and further consultations with the interest groups as well as through the emerging ATA support. He had begun, moreover, to solidify his political base, going public in speeches before transportation and business associations. As before, the ICC endorsed most of the Coordinator's program and this support was crucial, for not only would the ICC be the coordinating mechanism, but its members could also influence Congress. The off-year elections also strengthened Eastman's position. The American people had signaled the Roosevelt Administration that further reform was desired. While the President's agenda concentrated on social reforms, it included institutional reforms as well. Eastman now focused his energies on Congress.[32]

<h2 style="text-align:center">4</h2>

The Coordinator submitted to the 74th Congress bills for motor and water regulation, an ICC reorganization plan, and several railway-related measures. In late February, the Senate Committee on Interstate Commerce convened to hear from those interested in the Eastman program; the testimony was supposed to help the Senators decide whether or not the bills served the public interest.

Coordinator Eastman appeared before the committee as the foremost authority on transport issues. He informed the Senators that he and the ICC had concluded that there existed in America "an oversupply of transportation facilities and a tremendous increase in competition, all of which has been greatly accentuated by the depression." Oversupplies, Eastman maintained, made profits uncertain, perhaps unattainable, and thus threatened the future of private enterprise. The truck bill, S 1629, attempted to alleviate uncertainty and therefore, it was designed "from the standpoint of the public interest." Eastman explained further that the economic provisions would eliminate "wasteful and destructive competition." To compel "equal treatment of shippers," the bill included direct controls that would prevent excessive and discriminatory rate schedules; other provisions would ensure "adequate financial responsibility" among the carriers, monitor broker operations, and provide ICC authority to supervise mergers and consolidations.[33]

In keeping with his broad perspective toward transportation, Eastman included indirect controls in S 1629. The ICC could establish safety rules, uniform accounting procedures, and maximum hours of operation. To the suggestion that industry code authorities could implement such regulations, Eastman replied, "There are so many interests outside of the industry that have the right to be heard and that are interested in one way or another essentially with the operations of these carriers, that you must have some public tribunal which has final authority and to which controversies can be presented." An industry code authority could not deal with these numerous interests in an effective manner, but Eastman believed the ICC could.[34]

Eastman admitted the bill would tend to encourage the rise of large-scale trucking firms and to increase rates, that it favored common over contract carriers. Protection of large-scale businesses appeared to violate the American ideals of independence and private initiative; higher rates appeared to go against the public interest. Eastman thought not. Reflecting one school of progressive thought, the Coordinator maintained that large units represented efficient use of resources. Senator James Couzens challenged Eastman on this point and argued that "the mere size of an institution is no assurance of efficiency or competent management." The exchange was a classic, for it exposed the gulf between those who believed efficiency should determine the public interest and those who believed competition between small-scale firms better served the common good. As for higher rates, Eastman firmly believed them to be in the public's interest because levels as they now stood were below the cost of service and that harmed truckers and shippers alike.[35] The Supreme Court had already suggested that protection of existing firms was a legitimate use of the police power, and the appearance of large-scale firms was already evident in the industry. So Eastman's program was not as radical as it may have seemed at first glance.

Eastman informed the Senators that support for S 1629 appeared to be widespread. From 401 questionnaires tallied (those indicating railway bias were eliminated), 367 favored federal controls, and only 34 opposed them. The sample included individuals, transport companies, and trade associations. Of the thirty-one replies from truckers, twenty-one local cartage firms favored regulation while three intercity operators and three of seven associations opposed it. In general, the state commissioners, most common carriers, a few private and contract operators, and the railroads favored the truck regulation bill.[36] Most of the support, then, came from the transport industries and government agencies, not from the general public.

The Coordinator emphasized that S 1629 alone would not alleviate the transport situation; the reorganization and water carrier bills had to be enacted as well. In defending the ICC reorganization plan, Eastman lucidly explained the principles underlying his entire program.

Plainly it is to the success of the proposed legislation that each form of transportation shall be regulated with a full understanding of its peculiar conditions and special problems. In each case the pattern of regulation, and also its administration, must be somewhat different and fitted to the peculiar conditions; yet regulation of them all must be harmonious and consistent with the development of a well coordinated national system of transportation in which each of these transportation agencies will play its proper part. The organization of the Commission for this new task must, therefore, provide for both specialization and unity of action.[37]

Not all on the commission agreed with Eastman. Frank McManamy informed the committee that the ICC supported S 1629, but not the reorganization bill. Privately, Eastman claimed to have support from some of the commissioners, but he concluded that the ICC believed a united front against reorganization was better than presenting a diversified viewpoint. At this point, the committee chairman, Senator Burton K. Wheeler, a Montana progressive, announced he would abandon S 1629 if the ICC were not reorganized.[38] The squabble, however, was not unusual for Eastman and his fellow commissioners; nor would it prevent movement on the truck bill, Wheeler's vow notwithstanding.

Eastman's and McManamy's testimony before the Senators was orderly, exhaustive, and based upon a broad conception of the public interest. In contrast, the parade of witnesses following the regulators blurred the issues and sometimes confused the lawmakers. Shipping representatives, railway executives, state commissioners, and farming lobbyists each attempted to persuade the committee that his special interests defined the public's interest. A few examples illustrate how confusing and complex the trucking problems appeared in the winter of 1934.

A midwestern grain dealer testified that unregulated truckers bought grain directly from the farmer, refused to grade the crop, bypassed the grain elevators, and thereby depressed prices and created chaos in what had once been a reliable and predictable market. The witness favored S 1629 if it would eliminate the wildcat truckers. Apple growers from the eastern states, however, opposed S 1629. Truckers had provided fast, flexible service for the perishable crop and the growers feared losing the advantages if the ICC regulated motor carriers. Livestock producers opposed the bill for similar reasons. Trucks had improved service, lowered rates, and offered a quick means with which the cattle growers could respond to changing prices. Further, the ranchers believed the American people should have the right to choose the most efficient transport service without ICC interference. Common carrier truckers from Wisconsin favored federal control because it would subdue brokers who had monopolized delivery markets. The Minnesota Regulated Carriers' Association (intra- and interstate contract and common carriers) desired stable rates, uniformity in state laws, safer highways, and help against unregulated competitors; it wanted Congress to enact S 1629.[39]

Spontaneously, at one point in the testimony, Senator Homer T. Bone, a Republican from Washington, lashed out at the self-serving witnesses. In so doing, he illuminated the nature of congressional hearing procedures and the complex nature of government-business relations.

When a man comes before a Senate Committee and states that any set of regulations should not injure one company for the benefit of another, he is merely suggesting something that is utterly impossible, if you believe in the ordinary rules of mathematics in business or law. If you base a rate on investment, and then some devices like the bus or truck come along, you are not going to sacrifice progress for obsolescence, are you? . . .

You are not going to spurn and throw away the achievements of science? . . .

Men come here and make a suggestion, and then make another, and the two are directly inconsistent. Somebody has to be hurt in this game of business. . . .

It is just progress in the world of science. It is a question of which is going to be hurt the most, and how society is going to be protected. . . .

The public gets skinned all the time.[40]

As Bone's outburst implied, the crux of the matter was defining the public interest. Should technological progress be restrained to protect one or more groups, or would the public interest be served better if progress were left unrestrained and those unable to compete allowed to wither away? Eastman, of course, rejected the latter idea, but he was not totally committed to the former. He preferred that each technology be allowed to perform the tasks for which it was best suited, and he believed the commission could do a better job of deciding what those tasks were than could the invisible hand of competition or the collusive decisions of industry code authorities.

Some witnesses did not appeal to self-interests directly but instead used timeworn rhetorical exhortations to impress the lawmakers. They attempted to arouse sympathy for the ideals of progress, protection of the "little man," and animosity toward bureaucratic growth and interference. Though not in all cases related specifically to trucking, these arguments nevertheless contributed to the confusion surrounding the public interest. We have already noted how trucking journals belabored the progress theme and how Senator Bone conceived the issue; witnesses repeated the arguments. Ironically enough, as Eastman noted, progress could also be served by regulation. "The result [of laws limiting size and weight of trucks] had been to stimulate the designing by the truck manufacturers of a very efficient and economical truck of a smaller type."[41]

Allied to the rhetoric of progress was testimony focusing on the "little man." In fact, the lawmakers raised the subject. Senator Couzens challenged the Coordinator's reorganization plan because it appeared to favor large-scale firms that could hire lawyers to decipher commission rulings. Chairman Wheeler interjected that the objects of commission regulation over the years, as he understood the concept, were first, protection of the public interest and, second, protection of "the smaller business man against the larger business man." One shipper representative noted that in state regulation cases, the small-time truck operator always faced a coterie of lawyers for the railroads when applying for authority to establish a truck line; how could he stand up to such an impressive showing? Yet, a Wisconsin trucker believed that commission control would help the little man, for it would discipline the brokers who monopolized the one-truck firms.[42] The "little man" was an issue, but just where he fit in was unclear.

Other witnesses challenged S 1629 because it represented an extension of bureaucracy and government power. Introduced into the record was an editorial from the *Chicago Tribune* on an earlier motor carrier bill, which, the paper said, "represents bureaucracy in its historic stand against invention, ingenuity, and progress. Traditionally and almost inevitably such governmental control seeks to reduce the thing it controls to the lowest level of progress. There is no such incentive in bureaucracy and distinctly its effort is to procure routine and maintain it. The defenses are up against the injection of new ideas and new methods. In private enterprise exactly the opposite must happen or the enterprise suffers under competition." Of course, Coordinator Eastman had maintained that a regulatory bureaucracy would preserve the free-enterprise system, not suffocate it as the editorial charged.[43] He agreed that regulation sometimes stifled innovation but viewed this as less of a problem than the undersirable effects of competition.

Some observers charged that S 1629 represented a conspiracy among the railroads, the state commissions, and the ICC to gain control over trucking. Certainly each had vested interests in truck regulation, but there was no conspiracy. The charge is specious because it assumes a concert of interests that did not exist. The three groups had always been adversaries. Railways had complained about ICC restrictions of rate increases for years, and the failure of the Coordinator to revitalize the railroads has been traced to the inability of the two interests to cooperate one with another. The state commissions, moreover, remained jealous of ICC authority. True, the state regulators wanted to regain power through extending controls over the essentially local trucking industry, but Eastman's program lodged final authority in the ICC, not the state agencies. In fact, as Senators Bone and Wheeler recognized, the witnesses before them often contradicted themselves. Those who objected most vocally to government interference in the economy were often found asking Congress to protect their interests through another statute. How could there exist a conspiracy in such an atmosphere of cross-purposes? Indeed, how could the lawmakers reconcile the contradictions?[44]

Coordinator Eastman lent a sense of focus, if not rationality, to the lawmakers' decision-making process. His bureaucratic style of investigation, consultation, and compromise defused differences. In fact, he continued to insert changes in S 1629 as the hearings progressed. Although he was unwilling to alter the overall policy approach—ICC regulation was assumed—Eastman willingly accepted minor modifications in the provisions.

Apparently, the ATA influenced some of the changes, perhaps as many as fifty of them. One of the negotiators, Harold Shertz, remembered, "During all of these conferences, which were almost daily, there was never a dispute in principle between the industry and Joe Eastman. But he insisted upon it being reduced to what he called, legislative language."[45] These efforts paid off, for the Senate committee, apparently convinced that the public interest was being served, reported out S 1629 favorably on April 12.

Chairman Wheeler guided discussion on the Senate floor. He assured his colleagues that the bill did not favor the railways over trucks because the policy provisions instructed the commission to consider the "peculiar features" of each business in administering the regulations. On the second day of full Senate debate, a group of agricultural and shipper interests attempted to block the bill, but Wheeler effectively countered the charges that public demand was lacking, that regulation would foster greater transport costs, that progress would be impaired, and that the ICC would become too powerful. S 1629 easily passed the upper house on April 16.[46]

5

Joe Eastman was surprised at the turn of events in April; he had expected a tougher battle in the Senate. Instead, as he soon learned, the delays would occur in the House. Members of the House subcommittee studying S 1629 viewed the bill as too complicated and drastic a measure; sentiment surfaced for a simpler plan of control. Thus, the subcommittee wrote a new bill that removed many ICC powers, emphasized regulation of large-scale common carriers, and simplified procedures. Meanwhile, several groups opposed the measure outright. Farming interests continued to maintain—despite assurances to the contrary from the Coordinator—that the bill would raise transport costs to railway levels and restrain farmers from casual backhaul activities. Others, including shippers and truck and trailer manufacturers offered objections.[47]

Truckers and the state commissioners were the major stumbling blocks. The ATA, as Ted Rodgers saw it, had evolved to such strength that it now had a hand in the "writing of its own ticket." Rodgers would not accept just any plan of regulation; he wanted definite protections for the industry. Thus, when the ICC reorganization bill appeared doomed in May, the ATA asked House members to amend the truck bill in two ways. The truckers wanted code provisions inserted and a separate ICC truck division established. Their efforts proved successful to a point. Code provisions were left out and, indeed, code provisions in conflict with the bill were expressly invalidated. But lawmakers added a clause directing the ICC to work with industry organizations. Several clauses, particularly the policy provisions, instructed the commission to consider the characteristics of trucking, not those of railroading, in developing administrative policies. Simultaneously, since the NRA was still alive (if just barely), ATA leaders lobbied to extend code regulations under the NIRA. Either way, the ATA had positioned itself to be able to contribute to, if not control, whatever mechanism Congress chose to impose—commission regulation or industry self-regulation.[48]

The state commissioners did not engage in such duplicity. They knew exactly what they wanted, and as the originators of truck regulation ten years before, perhaps they felt justified in blocking the bill. The issue was power. NARUC opposed two features of the truck bill: final authority of the ICC and inclusion of the *Shreveport* doctrine, which allowed the ICC to set intrastate rates. NARUC's lobbying efforts succeeded, for the final House version ensured that the rights of the states would be preserved and stated flatly that the commission would have no authority over intrastate truck operations. Coordinator Eastman accepted these changes readily, for in the pragmatic tradition, he maintained the legislation could be amended in the future if experience indicated changes were necessary.[49]

Deliberations continued through June and into July. On July 15, the full House Committee on Interstate and Foreign Commerce rejected the subcommittee's simplified bill and sent S 1629 to a reconstituted subcommittee. ATA officials, by now more committed to federal regulation (*Schecter* had been decided in late May), launched quite a professional lobbying blitz, considering the youthfulness of the industry and the relative inexperience of its leaders, who went against seasoned railroad and state commission lobbyists. The lobbying force the ATA had begun to build earlier in the year met with ICC members, the Coordinator, and House and Senate members. They also enlisted help from truck enthusiasts who pressured hometown representatives in Congress to support the Eastman program.[50]

By the end of July, the House had added several amendments to relax controls over farmers, in addition to the NARUC-sponsored changes. The amended bill passed the House on August 1 by the vote of 193 to 18. Senator Wheeler presented it to the full Senate on August 5. Curiously, when asked if the House version contained any major changes, Wheeler replied that only minor agricultural amendments had been added; he omitted mention of the *Shreveport* issue entirely. With slight discussion, then, the Senate passed the amended version on

August 5. On August 9, President Roosevelt signed the Motor Carrier Act of 1935.[51]

Two other interest groups ought, perhaps, to have been more deeply involved in the deliberations that led to the passage of the Motor Carrier Act. The White House might have been expected to take a more active interest in the legislation, but Roosevelt did not really understand the MCA. *The Traffic World* reported: "The President said it had taken him a long time to read the measure. On account of its provisions he . . . asked Mr. Eastman to summarize it and . . . the latter had done it in two pages. . . . The bill, the President added, was terribly long and frightfully confusing.[52] In a "long-awaited" transportation speech on June 7, FDR noted that "the public had been inadequately served" because the nation's transport policies were unconnected, but he spent only two sentences recommending passage of Eastman's bill. FDR had evaded transportation issues throughout his first administration and never labeled the truck bill "must" legislation, a sign that could have ensured earlier passage; instead, he informed Congress the bill was "desirable." Speaker Rayburn sent the President a memo in which he asked if FDR wanted him to influence the passage of the truck bill. The answer was, "Yes, MHM" (Marvin McIntyre, the President's secretary). Beyond this sparse answer, no other direct evidence of FDR's influence on the MCA was found. Apparently, the only connection between the White House and the MCA was the President's signature.[53]

Perhaps personal philosophies and temperaments interfered with a strong executive showing in the story. Eastman and Roosevelt began as potential allies, but they never developed a close working or personal relationship. The former refused to be enamored of the latter, remaining fiercely independent of presidential meddling in commission affairs. This staunch independence may have angered the President, and in fact, FDR's easygoing, flattering, and gracious style irritated Eastman. When the Coordinator suggested the President release a strong statement in support of S 1629, Roosevelt did not respond. As with other legislation, the President appeared content to leave the details to Congress and government agencies.[54]

Another group that might have shown intense interest was organized labor, especially since the MCA gave the ICC authority to establish "qualifications and maximum hours of service of employees" for common and contract carriers and, if the commission thought it necessary, for private carriers as well. One Teamster official testified before the House subcommittee hearings, but no direct influence surfaced during the negotiations on S 1629. Unlike the railway brotherhoods, truck unions had not developed a viable national presence by the mid-1930s. As was the case in the automobile manufacturing industry, trucking labor groups were preoccupied with interunion competition and with local power struggles that precluded a unified national front. Unlike the NRA, the Coordinator's office did not have a mandated labor review process. Moreover, since Eastman recognized the need for further investigation, he put in the MCA wide discretionary authority for the ICC to formulate labor rules. The Teamsters would have the opportunity to affect subsequent decisions.[55]

Federal Coordinator Eastman, with self-congratulation that was somewhat out of character, considered himself the father of the Motor Carrier Act. Certainly he orchestrated the process in many respects, but he was operating within a complex political economy that prevented any one person or group from determining the outcome. Indeed, he admitted the MCA would not have passed without help from the ATA. If there must be a father, then NARUC would be a better choice, for it was the state commissioners who first suggested the idea in the mid-1920s. Perhaps Eastman could be viewed as the midwife of the MCA, for it was through his bureaucratic style of investigation, consultation, and compromise that the various interests reconciled differences in the final statute.[56]

6

Whether father or midwife, Coordinator Eastman failed to achieve his major goals in the late summer of 1935. Without the statutes for controlling water and air carriers, and the ICC reorganization bill, Eastman's dream of a coordinated regulatory scheme remained just that—a dream. Congress, perhaps put off by the centralized power inherent in the Coordinator's program, rejected his broad conception of the public interest. Instead, the lawmakers construed the public interest to require only the extension of ICC control over interstate trucking.

An overview of the MCA's provisions indicates the extent to which coordination was missing. The direct economic controls (entry, rates, and financial stability) applied to only 20 percent of all interstate trucking and to only 2 percent of all trucking in the country. Except for the policy provision, the MCA included neither provisions for coordinating truck and railway operations nor directions for coordinating interstate trucking with intrastate trucking. The policy statement, moreover, explicitly instructed the commission to "preserve the inherent advantages of" the industry in administering the statute.[57]

No, the Motor Carrier Act did not represent the coordinated system of controls Eastman had envisioned. Yet it did include the very cartel features the ATA had attempted to install through the NRA Truck Code; the truckers had convinced the lawmakers that their interest in stability matched the public's interest in transportation. Common carriers were fully regulated as to rates, continuous service, safety, accounting procedures, mergers, and consolidations. Following state experience, the MCA extended direct and indirect controls over contract truckers. The ICC would issue operating permits, set minimum rate schedules, and establish rules for hours of service and safety. Other provisions controlled brokers.[58] These controls, then, continued the traditional regulation of common carriers but also focused on the most unstable sector of trucking, the interstate contract and independent truckers. The authority of the federal government would oversee the stablization of the infant industry.

The authority to control, however, was shared for the first time in regulatory history. One of the problems the ATA had faced and not solved during the NRA experiment involved the difficulty of controlling localized businesses from a Washington-based bureaucracy. Under the influence of NARUC, the MCA included an innovation: the joint board. In cases involving operating rights and complaints of a trucker hauling in not more than three states, an official from each would make up a mandatory joint board. At its discretion, the ICC could refer cases involving more than three states to a joint board. Decisions of the boards held the authority of an ICC examiner. Thus, the MCA marked the first time federal powers had been conferred on state officials.[59]

Although Coordinator Eastman had settled for extension of regulation to and cartelization of the trucking industry, he showed little disappointment. In his classic progressive style, he believed that "this legislation is going to have a very beneficial effect on the whole transportation situation, although too much ought not to be expected from it. . . . I think it will help the railroads and also help the bus and truck industries, and it will not eliminate competition in the transportation field. The chief beneficial effect it will have will be in stablizing conditions by preventing demoralizing and destructive competition. It ought to lay the foundation for sound future development in transportation and bring about better cooperation and coordination in that industry."[60]

As we will discover, Eastman's hopes, for the most part, proved unfounded. Certainly trucking, vibrant but disheveled during the early 1930s, would grow more orderly under ICC-sponsored cartelization, but the transportation system as a whole would remain generally confused and ill coordinated until mobilization for war in the early 1940s.

8 The Early Years of Regulation: The ICC and Associationalism

President Roosevelt's signature on the Motor Carrier Act gave the go-ahead to a business-government partnership that would attempt what had to then been impossible, to cartelize trucking. Economic responses, associational activities, and state regulations in the 1920s and the NRA experiment during the first New Deal had failed to stabilize the young and developing industry. Congress, persuaded that the public interest would be served if trucking were stabilized, handed the ICC the authority to oversee cartelization. The MCA, in part, was designed to stem the competitive chaos; in August 1935 the hope for stabilization hinged on the ability of the commission and the industry to make the MCA work.

The magnitude of the task appeared overwhelming. The MCA furnished an outline for a bureaucracy that would control entry into trucking, raise rates to profitable levels, and establish trade rules for the entire interstate industry. Before entry could be controlled, however, decisions had to be made on the tens of thousands of applications to operate that truckers were expected to file under the grandfather clause of the MCA, which allowed common and contract truckers in operation before enactment of the MCA to obtain operating rights from the ICC more easily than those who had not been in the business. Processing those applications, which would establish the initial membership of the industry, raised numerous legal and policy questions, such as defining bona fide operation, dealing with confusion in the new joint board experiment, and distinguishing between common and contract carriers. To stabilize rates required agreement among truckers and regulators, first, on the types of rate structures to use (railway or cost-of-service) and, second, on the levels of the rates. Finally, agreement had to be reached on the trade practices, such as insurance requirements and safety rules. The efforts in these areas before 1935 furnished some guidance, but the regulators and regulated still found themselves exploring uncharted territory, as Joe Eastman explained when he wrote, "I think that our principal difficulties are not due to imperfections in the drafting of the measure, but to inherent difficulties in the subject, many of which could not be discovered in advance of actual experience with motor carriers and many of which involve legal questions of first impression." [1]

In the business-government partnership, the ICC played a dual role as judge and broker. The regulators decided some issues (such as defining different classes of truckers and establishing procedures for applications, complaints, and enforcement) in a quasi-judicial setting in which they interpreted the language of the statute and determined policies that government officials and industry members would follow. Legal precedents guided the commissioners in these matters; the industry members contributed little. The commissioners found, however, that in other areas (such as rate-making and insurance and safety rules) truckers could contribute ideas based upon their experience before federal regulation. Instead of telling the truckers what to do, the ICC encouraged the different factions to come together to iron out their disagreements. In that sense, the commission acted as broker or referee.

Indeed, many of the details of truck regulation materialized through a process that held an uncanny (and ironic) resemblance to Herbert Hoover's concept of the "associative state." The complexity of the industry and its continuing development forced the regulators to look to the truckers for information and ideas. Trucking leaders, building upon the political strength gained during the NRA experience and the legislative battles, used their position to write the trade rules that would stabilize the runaway competition that had plagued trucking since the late 1920s. What distinguished truck regulation from Hoover's pure conception of the associative state, was an authority that would enforce the trade rules; now, the Interstate Commerce Commission furnished that authority.

Yet, the theme that emerges most clearly from the early years of regulation is that neither the regulators nor the regulated fully understood the implications of what they were doing. Thus methods and results included practices that were normally antithetical to American beliefs—discrimination in favor of one group over others and the sanctioning of monopoly practices among businessmen. Such contradictions, however, should have been expected, for the goal of regulation—to stabilize competition—was itself a contradiction.

I

Not surprisingly, the commission tapped Joe Eastman to head the new Division 5 (Division 7 from August to October, 1935), which would oversee administration of the MCA. Reflecting the dual role of judge and broker, the regulators constructed a partly centralized, partly decentralized bureaucracy. Division matters included making policy and adjudicating complaints and application cases. Below the division was the Bureau of Motor Carriers (BMC), which helped to shape and then carry out division policies. Most of the one-on-one contact between regulator and regulated, however, took place in the extensive field force, which consisted of sixteen district offices scattered throughout the U.S. This early bureaucracy hummed with activity; during the first year of regulation, 452 employees in Washington, D.C., and 201 in the field answered, on the average six hundred letters per day.[2]

Eastman appointed one of his protégés, John L. Rogers, to head the BMC. Rogers had joined the commission in 1917, after working for the Southern Railway. While employed with the ICC, the Tennessean earned both a mechanical engineering degree from George Washington University and a law degree at night school. In 1925 the commission made him a special examiner. Meanwhile, Rogers studied accounting in his spare time. When Eastman assumed the post of Federal Coordinator in 1933, Rogers followed as a valuable executive assistant. Now that the Coordinator's job had been extended, Rogers's appointment to the BMC ensured that Eastman's style of regulation would be a guiding force in truck regulation. Congress sustained the estimation of Rogers's colleagues when it approved his nomination as Commissioner in 1937.[3]

Rogers's appointment to the BMC in late summer 1935 reflected Eastman's desire to staff the agency with people familiar with ICC procedures or motor carrier operations or both. In addition to Rogers, early appointments to the BMC included three from within the ICC, four from the state commissions, three from the private sector, one from the Coordinator's office, one from the NRA, and another from the Bureau of Public Roads. Most BMC employees had wide experience in public utility regulation, as either commissioners, staff members, or lawyers. Expertise in traffic management, insurance, and accounting also landed a few jobs. Eastman hoped that these knowledgeable staff members would develop policies quickly and efficiently. They were placed throughout the BMC's various sections: certificates, insurance, traffic, accounts, complaints, finance, safety, research, statistics, legal, enforcement, and administrative. These sections forged links between the division's policy-making and field activities.[4]

An assistant director oversaw the field force. Each of the sixteen district offices included a director, field supervisors, a joint board representative, rate and tariff experts, accounting personnel, and clerical workers. The use of the district offices reflected the commission's desire to educate as well as to control the members of the trucking industry. The ICC reported that the "average motor carrier" was "a small operator; he is not educated as to regulation and does not readily recognize his responsibilities under the law. He requires not only the ordinary regulatory attention, but also education, instruction, cooperation, explanation, adjustment, and detailed individual treatment."[5] The district scheme represented one attempt to meet the peculiar needs of trucking.

The BMC's efforts to capture the trucker's attention and complete the application process faced numerous obstacles. Each supervisor took responsibility for a thousand to fifteen hundred operators; he was to be the ICC representative who made himself readily available to answer questions, to help complete applications, and to explain the mechanics of regulation and the trucker's responsibilities under the law. During the first year of administration, however, he found office space, secretaries, and typewriters in short supply. As late as the fall of 1937, the division expected each supervisor to schedule twenty to twenty-five meetings and to complete at least five applications per day. At the time, only seventy-five supervisors had been hired, nearly 45,000 applications (nearly half the total) remained to be processed, and the deadline of June 1, 1938 was fast approaching.[6]

Paltry appropriations from Congress helped slow disposition of the grandfather applications. Democratic Senator Huey P. Long of Louisiana had single-handedly prevented the lawmakers from enacting a deficiency appropriations bill that had included $1.25 million for administration of the MCA. When congress did appropriate money for the MCA, it pared down the initial request of $3 million to $1.7 million, reflecting continued concern for government austerity during the Depression. The commissioners had failed to convince the law-makers that most of the work and expense of truck regulation would arise during the first few years. The restrictive funding not only slowed the application process but also stifled investigations into safety and labor rules.[7]

The biggest obstacle, of course, was educating the tens of thousands of truckers in the methods of regulation. In addition to the field force, the ICC developed a creative method of communication that spoke directly to the thousands of truckers. During its years of railway regulation, the commission had answered complaints and queries through the mail. This approach seemed inadequate to the task facing the BMC, and in August 1936, the Commission initiated a new regulatory procedure, the "administrative ruling." Questions from industry members and answers from the ICC were now published (and reprinted in industry journals). Although the administrative rulings were not binding and were only tentative pending further ICC action, they nevertheless streamlined and enhanced the BMC's program of educating truckers. The rulings, moreover, signified an alteration in regulatory procedure. Such devices represented "advance advice," which had not been used in the past because regulatory agencies were tied to the routine of awaiting a formal complaint before acting on an issue; apparently, the atomistic structure of trucking forced the change in procedure. The administrative rulings answered questions that ranged from the simple (no, logs are not "agricultural commodities") to more complex issues, such as the status of motor carriers leasing equipment from other carriers.[8]

The BMC, then, became (like the Coordinator's office before it) a beehive of business-government activities. Interested groups—truckers, shippers, labor representatives, manufacturers—used the BMC to air their grievances and to request protection for their interests just as Eastman had envisioned. He had rejected the code process precisely because it could not deal with such a variety of interests in the flexible, yet professional, manner of the BMC. This did not mean that conflict did not arise; indeed, despite the elaborate bureaucracy established, the commissioners faced many difficulties in administering the complex statute.

2

The most pressing job facing the regulators (one that was not completed until 1938) was the disposition of over eighty thousand applications filed under the grandfather clause. Completion of this task was the necessary first step in controlling entry into trucking and thus controlling competition. The commission wished to strike a balance between protecting truckers who had been in business before the MCA was signed and granting overly broad authorities that in effect would create monopolies. Congress, moreover, had demanded that this first step be taken quickly.[9] The vast numbers of truckers, technical problems of definition and problems with the joint board experiment slowed the process.

In October 1935, Commissioner Eastman had warned members of the American Trucking Associations that time would be required to educate members of the industry in the procedure of regulation. Indeed, by early January 1936, the ICC could count only twelve hundred applications on file and, the February 12 deadline was only five weeks away. The ghost of NRA days apparently haunted the application process, for the regulators learned that recalcitrant truckers believed they could avoid commission efforts to control them, as they had those of the NRA. After postponing the filing deadline for one last time (to March 2), the regulators announced a fine of a hundred to five hundred dollars a day for late applications.[10]

The inducement apparently worked. On February 11 and 12, the ICC received twenty-five thousand pieces of mail, and some envelopes included more than one application. Overworked with this deluge, the ICC then faced forty thousand protests of the applications. Generally, the protests challenged the extent of operations (the area covered and commodities hauled) that had been claimed. As predicted, the truckers had applied for as broad authority as possible in hopes of shutting out potential competitors. Thus, the commission had to single out which claims were legitimate and which were not. Division 5, in particular, had to determine what constituted bona fide operations. The regulators focused on past operations; no attention was to be given to future expansion, for the task now was simply to establish the initial members of the industry.[11]

A year after the filing deadline, the division was still debating the issue of bona fide operations. Finally, Eastman untangled the apparent complexity. He noted that the grandfather clause had stipulated that registration under a code of fair competition *could* be used to prove "bona fide" operations, but the stipulation was not binding; further, the clause offered no other test. Eastman pointed out that the regulators could require state certificates and evidence of compliance with state laws as proof, but such had not been "mentioned in committee reports or debates, . . . [leading] to the MCA," and to use them, he believed, would violate the spirit of the clause that required quick disposition. Eastman argued, moreover, that to use compliance with state laws to determine bona fide operations would involve the ICC in judicial proceedings that might be beyond the authority of the commission and would in any event create numerous practical difficulties. Eastman then consulted a dictionary and concluded that the issue was "one of fact rather than law," of "good faith and honest intent." Consequently, the division decided that operating rights should be granted if the applicant had shown good faith in offering the services listed.[12]

The test was applied on a case-by-case basis and some applications furnished more difficulty than others. For example, trucking included a special type of carrier called the irregular-route or call-on-demand hauler. These were usually truckers, like Harry Woods, who held themselves out as carriers to deliver goods wherever and whenever business required. Division 5 established that a mere "holding out" was insufficient to merit a certificate or permit. In more than a few instances, however, business conditions had prevented a trucker from hauling to all points or transporting all commodities listed in his application. The division decided that these operators were not responsible for business trends; if the trucker conducted his operations in a manner consistent with the facts stated in his application, but had not performed services to all points, he would nevertheless be granted authority to continue. This especially helped household goods haulers and oil field suppliers, two types of truckers susceptible to seasonal or erratic business trends.[13]

The joint boards attempted to carry out the general policies on applications that Division 5 had developed. The theory behind the joint board procedure reflected the structure of trucking in the 1930s; since most hauls were local (that is, usually no more than three hundred miles), state regulators could more easily judge the credibility of applications. For example, if a trucker applied to haul hardware products from Chicago to Lexington, Kentucky, regulators in Illinois, Indiana, and Kentucky could determine more easily than an examiner in Washington, D.C., whether the trucker had indeed been hauling hardware products in the area defined. Of course, joint board decisions could be appealed to the commission if the applicant or one of his competitors believed the joint board members had erred. Statistics suggested that the joint board procedure worked well. Out of 825 joint board decisions in 1938, for example, the ICC fully sustained 739, modified 57, and reversed only 29. These numbers, moreover, did not include the special "short form" reports that dealt with straightforward cases and in which the ICC usually concurred.[14]

Yet, the statistics were misleading. In fact, the joint board concept fell victim to the very industry characteristics for which it had been designed. Problems arose in staffing the boards, educating truckers, assigning locations and times for hearings, and dealing with numerous protests from railways and trucking competitors. Many hearings occurred with only the ICC examiner present, for state representatives often failed to show up. Absences resulted from a lack of communication between field force and board members, conflicts in scheduling, and simple neglect. As a gesture of good will toward the inexperienced truckers, examiners scheduled hearings at the convenience of the applicant. This practice, though sound in intent, proved confusing, for the state representatives sometimes found hearings listed back-to-back but in different towns miles apart. Determining how board members would be paid also caused delays, and in at least one case, a state official was caught bribing the applicants. Contrary to the glowing statistics, then, the joint board practice was floundering.

One particular problem undermined the whole experiment. Was a sustained application valid if only the examiner had been present at the hearing or if one of the state members had been absent? The spirit of the MCA maintained that local regulation was in the public interest; yet the absence of state members appeared to violate the law. Of course, final authority always rested with the full commission, and Division 5 made concerted efforts to monitor the process. Eventually, however, the joint boards failed and Congress diluted the practice in the Transportation Act of 1940.[15]

3

The joint board experiment represented only one of several complex issues brought before Division 5. Disputes over contract carriers plagued the regulators from the beginning. They discovered that, in some cases, truckers simply did not know under which category to file;

in others, the applicants knew they were common carriers but tried to pass themselves off as contract haulers. The state regulators had dealt unsuccessfully with these very same problems. The contract carriers were a type of private carrier that could choose their customers on the basis of convenience and profit; common carriers could not.[16] If the regulators allowed an unlimited number of contracts or if they did not restrict the nature of those contracts, then contract haulers would gain a competitive advantage over the more closely controlled common carriers.

In screening these applications, Division 5 noted not only the number but also the character of the contracts. For example, one applicant served at least twenty-four shippers, but only six of these contracts were written; fourteen were verbal agreements, and the remaining four were apparently ad hoc. The list of commodities hauled, however, remained consistent for all the contracts claimed. Therefore, Division 5 decided that the applicant was a common carrier who restricted his hauling to those commodities. In another case, the regulators awarded a permit to a trucker who, under verbal contracts, hauled film and accessories for fourteen theater owners. This case-by-case approach was time consuming for regulators and regulated, but the uniqueness of each case seemed to require it. Such careful attention to detail was intended to prevent one competitor from gaining an unfair advantage over another.[17]

Two cases in particular troubled the division (originally composed of Eastman, Marion M. Caskie, and William E. Lee). One concerned the status of truckers hauling for railways; the other involved the extent to which the regulators could control contract operations. A detailed analysis of these two cases is instructive in understanding not only its complexity but also the essence of truck regulation during the late 1930s. Two of the principals in the cases—the railways and contract carrier truckers—represented potentially formidable competition for the third—common carrier truckers, the very group that had lobbied for federal regulation since 1932. The controversies, moreover, suggested that the Motor Carrier Act was poorly written and that the regulators were "making law," a task supposedly reserved for Congress. Eastman had predicted such problems would arise and was fully prepared to rethink some of the issues as the administrative scheme unfolded.[18] The pragmatic method of ICC regulation, then, continued under the MCA.

The *Scott Brothers* case appeared at first to be a simple one. The firm applied under the MCA for a permit because it held a contract with the Pennsylvania Railroad and Long Island Railroad to perform pickup and delivery service in Jersey City, New Jersey, and in certain portions of New York City. The trucking company used railroad bills of lading and had no direct relation to the railway's shippers. Since Scott Brothers did not hold itself out to the general public, but rather restricted its operations to the two railroads, it appeared to be a prime candidate for a permit.[19]

Complaints filed with the ICC focused on two issues: whether or not Scott Brothers represented contract motor trucking and whether the services described fell under Part I of the Act to Regulate Commerce (the original 1887 statute, with amendments, that controlled railways) or under Part II, (the Motor Carrier Act). Common carrier truckers alleged that Scott Brothers, because it worked for a common carrier (the railroads) was a common carrier itself. That is, as an agent of a common carrier, the firm had to assume the responsibilities of its employer. These truckers wanted Scott Brothers declared a common carrier in order to force the company to file the rates and tariffs under which it operated. At this time, the MCA required full disclosure of rates for common carriers, but not for contract haulers. From the published rates, the common carriers could discover if their suspicions were correct, that Scott Brothers represented a front for the railroads to lower pickup and delivery rates below the cost of service in order to drive local truck competition out of business. A group of western railways, however, complained that the Scott Brothers application was filed under the wrong part of the Act to Regulate Commerce. Citing convenience, the railroads believed that the company's business represented railroad services and therefore was subject to control under Part I.[20]

In June of 1937, Division 5 released a report on the case. Chairman Eastman, in his usual pragmatic style, explained that the application formed a test case that embraced "certain important and difficult questions for statutory construction" in the Motor Carrier Act. Eastman expected the report to be appealed, so he did not bother the full commission with what he believed was an ill-defined case. Indeed, Eastman found himself on the short end of a two-to-one split within the Division.

Commissioners Caskie and Lee wrote the majority opinion that Scott Brothers was a contract motor carrier. To support their decision, the commissioners noted that in previous cases involving railroads and trucks (before enactment of the MCA), the ICC had focused solely on railway services and had expressly avoided authority over truck operations. Scott Brothers clearly represented trucking operations, and therefore, if the regulators were to follow the public interest in creating a sound trucking industry, they must control Scott Brothers under the authority of the MCA. To allow the agent (Scott Brothers) to assume the status of the principal (the railways) would be detrimental to effective control over trucking.[21]

Eastman dissented. He chided his colleagues for distinguishing motor carrier operations from rail services, for to him, they represented one and the same thing in this case. He alleged that the exception included in the MCA's definition of common carriers— "such motor vehicle operations of carriers by rail or water, except to the extent that those are subject to provisions of part I"—had been inserted expressly to avoid "such subtleties of reasoning." Eastman contended that if the majority opinion withstood appeal, then the railways would be subject to both parts of the Act to Regulate Commerce, and this would create a bureaucratic nightmare for the commission and the railroads.

Eastman turned to the contract carrier definition to bolster his position, but instead lapsed into "subtleties of reasoning" himself. He saw in the definition a relation between carrier and shipper, not between carrier and carrier. This was an inference, however, for the term "shipper" did not appear in the contract carrier definition. (Indeed, the railways, given the contract with Scott Brothers, could be viewed as the shipper in this case, thus negating Eastman's distinctions.) Nevertheless, Eastman cited numerous ICC cases in which the commission had decided that the agent assumed the status of the principal; from these, he concluded that Scott Brothers represented, not a contract motor carrier subject to the MCA, but rather a common carrier engaged in railroad services and thus was subject to Part I.[22]

The reasoning behind Caskie and Lee's position on the one hand and Eastman's on the other exposed the problem of regulating competing kinds of transportation and of controlling a young industry still growing and defining itself. The majority's position was straightforward: now that Congress had authorized regulation of trucks, all truck operations should be subject to Part II. The MCA, moreover, expressly directed the regulators to consider trucking separate from railways. Eastman viewed the issues more loosely. Assuming a broad perspective of how the entire MCA might operate in practice, he developed an ingenious, but incorrect, analogy. He equated the Scott Brothers' operations with those of owner-operators, truckers who held agreements with other motor carriers, not railways. These owner-operators represented (and still do today) one of the flexibilities inherent in motor trucking. They often switched from firm to firm, depending on the amount of business available, perhaps working for a produce company during harvest season and then changing to a meat-packer after the crops had been delivered. To require these owner-operators to obtain permits every time they changed firms, Eastman believed, would impose burdens upon them and the ICC that would be detrimental to effective control over trucking. The BMC would either deny the owner-operators authority to operate during the grandfather period or resort to granting sweeping authority to each one. The former procedure penalized the trucker and the latter could demoralize the entire trucking industry, presumably because such operating rights would become extremely valuable and thus susceptible to constant selling and buying.[23]

The *Scott Brothers* case was appealed to the full commission, and in February 1938 the ICC reversed the Division 5 ruling and declared the trucking firm subject to Part I. A bare majority of the commission (six of the eleven commissioners) ruled that the Scott Brothers operations represented only a portion of the complete transportation service from shipper to recipient and that Scott Brothers was an agent for the railroads and thereby assumed the status of the railroads, becoming a common carrier subject to Part I. Eastman had won his points, but he was not content to let the ruling stand without additional comment. He wished, he said,

to express regret that those who dissent from the conclusions that have been reached have seen fit to go beyond the issues by predicting, in so extreme a way, that chaos will reign, accompanied by all manner of inequities and injustices, because of our decision. I do not believe this to be true. On the contrary, I believe that one effect of the decision will be to relieve hundreds of small local operators of burdens in attempting to meet requirements of the [MCA], particularly in securing authority to operate, which they would have found it difficult, if not impossible, to bear. The principles of the decision . . . are likely . . . to extend like relief to many operators not here involved and employed by motor carriers as well as railroads.[24]

Commissioner Rogers (recently promoted from Director of the

BMC) submitted a stinging dissent with which Lee and Caskie concurred. At one point he wrote: "A careful consideration of this problem leads me to the determination that the majority conclusion is unsound in law and chaotic in result. I can see in it nothing except administrative inequality and confusion, unfair and preferential treatment, and destructive competitive methods piled upon the many which already exist. The fact that such results flow from fallacious premises magnifies the reasons which should condemn them."[25] Why did this acrimonious split occur between the principal author of the MCA and the commissioners most responsible for the administration of that act?

The case represented a classic one of loose constructionism versus strict constructionism. Eastman's position and that of five other members reflected a desire for efficiency in administration and concern for the "little man," the owner-operator—legitimate concerns of the regulator, it seems. Yet the argument the majority employed curiously lost sight of one of the central conflicts underlying enactment of truck regulation, that is, competition between railways and trucks. Eastman's analogy of the Scott Brothers operations with those of owner-operators was false, because it confused bureaucratic efficiency with competition between different kinds of transport. Caskie, Lee, and Rogers focused strictly on this issue; to allow such rail-motor combinations as the majority had done seemed to them to violate the central purpose of the regulatory statute.

In hindsight, the commission might have compromised. The regulators could have established one set of procedures for rail-motor operations and another for owner-operators.[26] That they did not expressly do this suggests that they did not comprehend the real relationship between competing carriers or the evolving nature of trucking. The regulators' decision, however, did not reflect a railroad bias *per se*; a careful reading of the opinions suggests that the commissioners were more concerned with bureaucratic efficiency. Yet, in retrospect, the case involved a grandfather application; future applications, after the initial members of the industry had been established, could be decided with more careful attention to intermodal competition. The Transportation Act of 1940 would help clarify the relationship between railways and trucks.[27]

The other major contract carrier case involved competition within the trucking industry. Originating in 1937 from a complaint filed by common carriers in the Midwest, the case became so important that the ICC opened it to include all contract carriers in the industry. As we will learn in the following section, common carriers had overcome numerous obstacles in agreeing on regional rate agreements. Lower rates of contract carriers, however, could undermine these agreements. Therefore, common carriers requested the ICC to investigate the rates that contract haulers were charging. If those rates were below the common carriers', then the rate agreements would have to be altered; if the rates were below the cost of service, then they were illegal under the MCA.[28] The case, *Contracts by Contract Carriers,* reflected the immemorial desire of businessmen to know what their competitors were charging. More important, it reflected one of the major problems facing the regulators: how to ensure, through legal regulatory procedures, that trucking competition was stabilized so that profits could be made.

At first, the ICC followed the associational impulse evident in the early years of regulation and encouraged the two groups to meet informally to negotiate a settlement. In fact, a tentative agreement was reached, but the contract truckers nevertheless petitioned the commission to explain why they should have to reveal information about their businesses. Language in the statute was unclear, if not contradictory, and perhaps the contract haulers could avoid releasing the information through a technicality and thus gain a competitive advantage. Common carriers, of course, had to publish their rates. Thus, the case embraced several important regulatory issues—the authority of the ICC to require the public filing of contracts, the distinction between "minima" rates and "actual charges," and the legality of releasing business information. Most important was whether the MCA had been enacted to protect one form of trucking (common carriers) from competition from another (contract carriers).

In November 1939 the full commission decided that contract truckers had to file copies of contracts with the ICC, that they had to include the actual charges collected, that the information would be open to the public. Further, contract haulers had to supply additional information about their firms on a questionnaire. The regulators had decided that the MCA did indeed protect common carriers from the actions of contract carriers.[29]

The majority used appeals to legal principle, public testimony, and regulatory history to support their contentions. For example, the issue of filing contracts focused on Section 218(a) and Section 220(a) of the statute. Did an option exist to file either minima or actual rates, and if so, did the option rest with the regulators or the regulated? The majority logically decided that minima rates did not meet the requirements of a contract in law, for contracts involved the actual charges to be collected. Section 222(e) prohibited the disclosure of information from contracts if the disclosure amounted to releasing business "trade secrets" to competitors. The regulators scrutinized the language of the section and concluded that it referred to shippers, not to truckers. Since no shipper had protested the publication of contracts at the ICC hearings, the majority concluded that publication could be required. As further justification they wrote, "A basic principle of carrier regulation is that full publicity of a carrier's charges is necessary and desirable in the public interest." Although vague in defining the public interest, the justification was grounded in the history of regulation in the U.S. In the early state sunshine commissions in the last half of the nineteenth century and in Theodore Roosevelt's Bureau of Corporations in the first decade of the twentieth century, public officials released business information in hopes that the publicity would force companies to alter abusive practices. From the original 1887 statute forward, of course, the ICC used the tactic of disclosing charges to discourage rebating between railway and shipper. As for requiring additional information on a questionnaire, the majority pointed to the established ICC practice of initiating investigations without the filing of a formal complaint; the questionnaires would be useful in any future commission investigation into motor carrier operations.[30]

Five of the eleven commissioners dissented in part. Eastman supported the assumption that the Motor Carrier Act protected common carriers from unfair competition, but he believed the requirement to file actual charges exceeded the regulators' authority. To him, minima rates would be sufficient until the filing of a complaint required the release of actual charges. Caskie disagreed with the interpretation of Section 222(e), and Commissioner J.H. Alldridge noted that the assumption that the statute protected common carriers "has some support in reason and in law," but it was too narrow. It neglected the public's interest in contract hauling, and it negated the desires of Congress.[31]

Commissioner Lee (with Claude R. Porter concurring) took issue with the basic assumption that the MCA protected common carriers. He could find in the statute no direct reference to the assumption and concluded that the majority had made common carriers "preferred wards of Congress and ourselves." To the dissenters, the correct policy was equal treatment of both types of trucking that preserved the inherent advantages of each. Similarly, Lee believed that the law did not allow the filing of actual charges or the questionnaire. In a telling conclusion, Lee chastised his fellow commissioners: "Possibly the law is imperfect, and it may be that the theory of contract carrier regulation adopted by the majority would be more effective. However, it is our duty to administer the law as written and not to change it by construction." Lee's admonition notwithstanding, Congress did change the relevant sections in the Transportation Act of 1940. All contract truckers would now file contracts listing actual charges collected and would fill out a questionnaire, which would be open to public inspection.[32]

The proceedings in 1937–40 reflected the pragmatic approach to regulation that the commission had followed since 1887, even if they did suggest that the regulators had made law. A reading of the pertinent clauses, the opposing opinions, testimony from congressional hearings leading to the MCA, and Eastman's correspondence reveals a continual thread of ambiguity toward contract carriers. In fact, just as contract truckers had plagued the state commissions in the late 1920s and early 1930s, they continued to trouble Eastman while he was Coordinator of Transportation. Eastman finally concluded that common carriers should be protected from contract carriers, but these sentiments were not included specifically in the MCA. As Chairman of Division 5, Eastman continued to gather more information and to think about the issues. Final rendering of *Contracts by Contract Carriers*, then, was based upon over a decade of public discussion and investigation. If Eastman and his fellow commissioners had indeed made law, they had done so through an open and solicitous process that Congress found appropriate. (Usually, the ICC followed another procedure in altering statutes. In 1938, for example, the commission petitioned Congress to add sixteen amendments to the MCA, most involving administrative procedure, and the lawmakers made them effective in June.)[33]

4

Defining the industry by means of grandfather applications and distinguishing between common and contract carriers represented the quasi-judicial aspect of truck regulation. Tariff and rate making, however, involved quasi-legislative activities. Since the MCA instructed the ICC to consult the various trucking associations whenever possible and since the truckers knew more about truck rates than did the regulators, the commission left to the truckers the complicated task of creating the cat's cradle of rates. BMC Director Rogers appeared at numerous rate-making meetings to add comments and to provide encouragement, but for the most part, the ICC left the work to internal industry committees.[34] The ICC retained final authority, of course, but the regulators rarely entirely rejected the industry agreements. More often than not, the commission acted to raise the levels of rates. Indeed, the low rate levels masked what, in retrospect, clearly represented collusions of businessmen, with government sanction, that apparently violated the antitrust spirit, if not the law, in the U.S.

The sheer complexity of rate making, however, checked the extent of collusion during the early years of regulation. Once regional committees had been established, agreement had to be reached, first, on the structure of the tariffs, then, on the actual rates. Tariffs represented guides for shippers and truckers; they listed the fixed charges of common carriers for shipments and were usually based upon weight and distance. Contract carriers used schedules. Tariffs were divided usually into two kinds of rates, commodity and class. Commodity rates included freight hauling that involved unusual conditions, such as refrigerated products, out-of-the-way pickups and deliveries, and high-value goods. Class rates embraced a wide variety of goods with similar hauling requirements. Divided into first, second, third, and fourth class designations, class rates signified the value of the goods hauled.

Both commodity and class rates were based on tonnage and distance, but geography often complicated the formulas. For example, the ton-mile rate (per unit cost) of a three-hundred-mile shipment would be less than that for a two-hundred-mile shipment, everything else being equal (weight, fuel costs, driver-time, climatic conditions, driver efficiency, and the like). When everything was not equal, the ton-mile rates would change. A 500-mile shipment from Denver, Colorado, to Salt Lake City, Utah, for example, could cost more per ton-mile than a shipment of equal weight from Denver 260 miles northeast to North Platte, Nebraska. The first would traverse the Rocky Mountains, costing more in fuel and driver time than the second, which covered the relatively flat terrain of the High Plains. The geography thus altered the scale economy of distance. Once the regional committees worked out these matters, they had to meet with other committees to devise interterritorial agreements.[35]

Tariff and rate committees faced a choice. They could start from scratch and devise new classifications based upon the costs of trucking plus a profit, or they could simply modify the established rail classifications to reflect the peculiar characteristics of trucking. Truckers who favored the cost-plus approach argued that new classifications would be simpler to use than the seemingly infinite railway ones, that they would boost the prestige of the young industry, that they would establish trucking as a distinct transport mode, and that all of these benefits would attract shippers. Truckers who supported the rail classifications disagreed. To them, the cost-plus method seemed too awkward, for trucking costs were too complicated to determine accurately. Shippers, moreover, were familiar with the rail methods, might be confused by any new system, and might therefore take their business to the railways. The debate raged into 1936. Apparently, the complexities inherent in the cost-plus approach forced the truckers to accept modified rail schemes.[36] Neither ICC nor railroad pressures influenced the decision; it was based on practical considerations.

In October 1935, the American Trucking Associations took the lead and published a list of five principles that the regional committees should follow. First, if a plan had been accepted already, it should be retained. Second, lacking an agreement, the committees should apply the rail classifications and alter them to reflect motor vehicle characteristics. Third, rate levels should be uniform for competing haulers and based on costs as much as possible. Fourth, the committees should give close attention to regional competitive factors, values of goods hauled, direction of shipments, cubic measurements and weight differentials, and the effect certain rates might have on the increase or decrease in truck tonnage.

In its fifth principle, the ATA strongly endorsed the agency system of publishing tariffs. A mechanism of stability, the agency system was simple in conception. A group of carriers would list their rates with an agency or rate bureau, usually paying monthly dues based on a percentage of gross receipts. The rates, listed in one or two volumes, would be accessible to shippers and carriers alike and thus would simplify the selling and billing of trucking services. A rate bureau, moreover, could more easily monitor industry members who "chiseled" on the agreed-to tariffs and rates.[37]

Despite the ATA's suggestions, the committees found the rate-making process a difficult one to rationalize. Pressure from the ICC-imposed deadline of March 31, 1936, added to the frenzied activity. Almost weekly, *The Traffic World* reported the incorporations of new rate bureaus, many of which overlapped different territories.[38] Delays in staffing the traffic section in the BMC also confused the committees. Before the deadline, however, the ATA submitted to the ICC four general classification schemes and one specifically for household goods carriers. These classifications were to be used in eight territories that generally matched the railway territories—Eastern Trunk Line, Central Freight Association, Southern, Western Trunk Line, Southwestern, Intermountain, North Pacific Coast, South Pacific Coast. Meanwhile, maverick firms published their own tariff classifications and rate levels. Industry members had met the ICC deadline, but the overall results were discouraging. Not only did overlapping rate bureaus and uncooperative firms create confusion, but the rates published also demoralized the industry, for most of them were obviously below the cost of service. In addition (harking back to the early railway competition), many truckers offered rebates and thus were not collecting the charges that they had published.

During the summer of 1936, action toward rate stabilization centered upon the so-called Central Freight territory, which encompassed New York, Pennsylvania, West Virginia, Ohio, Kentucky, Indiana, Illinois, Missouri, Iowa, Wisconsin, and Michigan. This was precisely the area in which early state regulation of trucking had emerged and from which industry animosities in the summer of 1933 had erupted. Once again, Jack L. Keeshin, the innovative and successful, if irascible, common carrier from Chicago, stood at the center of the controversy.[39] Not surprisingly, Keeshin supported the cost-plus approach, although the vast majority of common carriers had agreed to the rail classifications. Keeshin's obstinance attracted such notables as John L. Rogers of the BMC and Ted V. Rodgers, President of the ATA, to the summer discussions. Despite an agreement reached that summer, Keeshin delayed final acceptance of the territorial classifications. His firm had published rates generally lower than those the other truckers had accepted. Two other common carriers had joined Keeshin's protest initially, but their owners were persuaded to join the rate bureau in January 1937. Keeshin finally capitulated in March. In return, he received assurances that a committee would review the classifications and make adjustments that more nearly reflected the peculiar needs and advantages of trucking. Keeshin's acquiescence allowed forward movement on two other obstacles, the rate levels, which were too low and the interterritorial tariffs, which had to be designed.[40]

The common carrier truckers had established the rate bureaus, the classifications, and the rate levels with little direct control from the ICC. The regulators stepped in only when disaffected truckers formally filed complaints. Even then, the ICC interfered with a light touch. For example, in one controversy in the Middle Atlantic states, the commission found that Freight Forwarders, Incorporated, had attempted to leave the Waring tariff bureau for the Lowe tariff bureau because the latter's rate levels were lower and therefore attracted more tonnage. The ICC, in response to complaints from members of the Waring bureau, simply ordered all rates in the territory to be no lower than those found in the Waring tariff; a trucker could belong to any rate bureau he desired, but he had to charge rates at least as high as those in the Waring tariff.[41]

In early August 1938, to cite another example of federal input, the ICC found the rate levels in the Central territory to have created "instability and unsound conditions" and ordered particular rates to be raised. A rather sweeping decision in January of 1940, moreover, attempted to stabilize profit-making rates throughout the Central territory. Division 5 ordered the Central tariff bureau to raise all rates to at least the level of the "key point class rates," key points being major distribution centers used for determining fairly straightforward class rates.[42] The truckers had done most of the work in establishing tariffs and rates; the ICC attempted, through its authority, to ensure that those classifications would not be undermined through below-cost and un-profitable rates. Progress by 1939 was incomplete, but the acceptance of the classifications would make rate adjustments, if not industry collusion, easier in the future. Of course, more tonnage would have helped.

5

Regulation of trucking embraced much more than the direct controls over entry and rates. Indirect decisions, such as standardizing bills of lading, identifying municipal zones in New York City, Chicago and St. Louis, and developing systems of accounting for motor carriers all contributed to the cartelization process.[43] Agreement on insurance requirements and safety rules, and enforcement of all the regulations would solidify cartelization. Once again, the truckers influenced the process of writing regulations. By the end of the 1930s, the industry was on its way to convincing shippers that it was no longer a fly-by-night phenomenon, but rather a group of professional businessmen.

In fact, insurance had been a topic of concern to truckers long before the late 1930s. Large-scale operators in the 1920s had realized that sound insurance policies would enhance the reputation of trucking and attract shippers leery of dealing with independent, inexperienced, and unscrupulous haulers. Investigation and discussion continued during the NRA years, and the MCA included provisions on the subject. Commissioner Eastman admitted that insurance was Greek to him, but the ATA efforts compensated for his lack of knowledge.[44]

Establishing rate limits within the ability of truckers and shippers to pay and certifying truck insurance companies were the two most important issues. ATA insurance committees eventually established minima levels for liability and property damage, but they also allowed shippers to incur extra costs for high-value goods. While the commission decided that truck insurance companies should be incorporated in every state in which their policy holders operated, it did postpone compliance to allow each company to file the required papers. Other problems remained, and to the end of solving those, the ICC, beginning in 1937, sponsored semiannual conferences with representatives of both the trucking and insurance industries.[45]

Safety in operations would also professionalize trucking. Regulators and regulated alike viewed safety as an important part of cartelization; less than one year after the MCA was enacted, the BMC section on safety released its first report. Over twenty organizations and several hundred individuals had contributed information, but the BMC requested more comment on the report itself. The customary pragmatic caution appeared to have additional cause in this subject, for the report represented "the first entry of the federal government into regulation of highway safety" involving vehicle operation. As with so many other firsts in federal control, the proposed rules were "based upon the best practices now existing in many states." The BMC announced a three-pronged approach to safety: "control of driver, control of the vehicle, and the reporting of accidents." The regulators openly admitted that the "safety structure" needed time to develop and modestly proposed a first-year plan centered on driver qualifications, operational rules, parts and accessories, and accident reports.[46]

One year later, the commission's initial safety rules went into effect, but they excluded two sensitive subjects. As of July 1, 1937, drivers had to register with the BMC, prove themselves physically fit, and refrain from driving recklessly or under the influence of alcohol. The rules also forced truckers to maintain proper equipment, which included specific lights and reflectors, adequate braking systems, and safety-glass windshields. When involved in an accident, truckers had to file with the ICC written reports that detailed the circumstances. Through these requirements and their enforcement, it was hoped that trucking accidents could be reduced. The ICC reported that no special field force was available to enforce these rules. Yet seventeen states had adopted all four parts of the plan, and ten others had adopted parts of it. These states furnished enforcement through their state police.

Yet, the two factors that had had so much to do with trucking accidents in the 1930s—driver fatigue and overweight vehicles—were not addressed in these initial regulations. Gypsy truckers, in particular, drove long hours and overstressed their vehicles' capacities, but the peculiar features of trucking labor and conflicts with state police powers delayed consideration of these two issues.[47]

The investigation into hours of service marked one of the early confrontations between the trucking industry and the recently strengthened Teamsters Union, which, as of October 1936, had 313 locals and 200,000 to 300,000 members, most of whom were tied to large-scale firms.[48] Thus, the conflicts focused as much upon economic control as upon safe operations. Union representatives wanted to prevent over-the-road truckers from making local deliveries. Teamsters believed local cartage operations belonged to them by historical right, for since the first decade of this century, they had organized warehousemen and cartage drivers in the cities. The union wanted an eight-hour day, which would restrict the distances over-the-road haulers could cover. The ATA attacked the proposal as too conservative and offered a substitute—sixty-hour weeks and the use of sleeper cabs. (Sleeper cabs allowed one driver to rest on a bunk behind the cab while another drove the vehicle.) Union leaders protested that the ATA program would decrease the number of trucking jobs, still a matter of concern as the Depression wore on toward the 1940s.[49]

The Teamsters lost this early skirmish. Division 5, ignoring the depressed economy, based its rulings on safety considerations alone.[50] Assuming that driving a truck was less tiring than working in a factory, the regulators established liberal rules of operation: effective December 1, 1938, interstate truckers could work ten hours per day before they had to take a mandatory eight-hour rest. The ten-hour rule included loading, driving, and unloading the truck. No trucker could work more than sixty hours in one week, but he could use a co-driver and a sleeper cab. One year later, after additional hearings, the commission made the rules even more lenient. A trucker was now allowed to work fifteen hours per day for a four-day stretch before reaching the sixty-hour limit; he could now work five hours per day loading and unloading the vehicle, in addition to the ten hours' driving. As occurred during the NRA experiment, the peculiar features of trucking dictated liberal labor rules.

In an attempt to enforce these rules, the commission ordered each interstate trucker to maintain a current logbook, or log. These contained pages, each one representing one twenty-four hour period, divided graphlike to indicate the driver's activities, from loading, unloading, and driving, to eating, sleeping, and off-duty time. The effectiveness of the logs, of course, remained moot, for truckers could falsify their entries. A driver could be found in violation of the rules only if he submitted a log that indicated too many hours worked or if a state policeman, during a routine stop, found that the driver's logs were incomplete.[51]

Like the hours-of-work controversy, the one over sizes and weights of vehicles included economic as well as safety considerations. Along with insurance, the issue of uniform vehicle dimensions had been an early concern of industry leaders, for conflicting state laws had frustrated expansion of interstate trucking in the 1920s and early 1930s. The BMC, however, made little headway on the issues. Eastman characterized the problems as "complex and in important respects highly technical." The inquiry dragged on. Congress specifically instructed the ICC to expedite its work in 1940, but geographical and climatic conditions and state politics blocked movement toward uniformity well into the 1980s.[52]

If progress on standardizing weights and sizes was not forthcoming, progress on enforcement of the MCA was. The commissioners realized from the beginning that "vigorous enforcement of the act is essential to its successful administration." Lack of money from Congress impeded initial efforts, but the federal commissioners devised several methods to assure that the truckers would not be able to avoid the ICC as they had the NRA. As of May 7, 1937 all interstate truckers had to display an identification plate that signified that the driver had complied with all regulations pertaining to tariffs and rates and insurance; by 1940, forty states had adopted all or parts of the ICC safety regulations. The state police, then, enforced both state and federal laws, thus reducing the necessity for a large and separate ICC enforcement force. In 1941 the ICC reported: "Enforcement is proceeding satisfactorily. We acknowledge again, as we have before, the continued cooperation of . . . the State governments in this task." However, the ICC continued to complain about the lack of funds for enforcement.[53]

Under the NRA Truck Code, those who filed complaints against competitors had been frustrated by the lack of authority they encountered; with the ICC in control after 1935, complainants usually had their day in court. During the first year of regulation, most of the 2,949 complaints were settled through voluntary compliance agreements. Between November 1, 1936, and November 1, 1937, the commission received, on the average, 302 complaints per month, most of which charged that the defendant was operating without authority or that he was not observing his quoted rates or that he was consolidating with another carrier without authority to do so. Only two out of every three of these complaints were decided quickly. Yet, that the truckers filed the complaints indicates that they had some trust in the ICC's authority. In 1938 the commission's successful prosecution of shippers as accessories to violations indicated that the regulators understood that often shippers were just as responsible for cutting rates as were truckers. In 1940 the commission reported that shippers recently had increased the number of complaints they had filed. Thus, the ICC became for the trucking industry, as it had for railroading, the authoritative agency that could settle the differences of carriers and shippers over rates and charges.[54]

6

The commissioners viewed 1938–39 as a transition year in the regulation of motor carriers. The grandfather applications had been completed (over 93,000 had been processed, although over 42,000 had been denied, dismissed, or withdrawn), and more contact with truckers and improved enforcement had resulted "in better compliance with the law and regulations and [had aided] the stabilization of the motor carrier industry."[55] In addition to the grandfather applications, the agreements on tariffs and rates, and the rules for insurance and safety, one other trend from the early years of regulation indicated that trucking was being stabilized: there existed in 1940 more large firms than in 1935.

Consolidation among truckers had been growing in the late 1920s and early 1930s as truckers attempted to meet competitive pressures. Joe Eastman, moreover, had predicted that regulation would motivate more unifications of motor carriers. He was not wrong. During the first year of regulation, the ICC observed "a marked tendancy [sic] in the industry toward unification," when 122 requests for consolidation were filed. The following year, the commission handled 286 applications. In 1940 the ICC gained authority to prohibit mergers involving twenty or more vehicles if the public's interest would not be served, and in one case, the regulators prohibited a consolidation where there was a "lack of sufficient mutuality of interest" between the carriers proposing the merger. Nonetheless, a report submitted in 1944 by a research group independent of the ICC recognized "the growth, under regulation, of more large and very large motor carriers and the apparent decline and absorption of very small carriers." Thus regulation had quickened the pace of consolidation evident within the industry from its earliest days.[56]

By the early 1940s, then, the truckers had achieved a stability in their business that had eluded them since the first economic and associational responses in the 1920s. Of course, tensions continued. Rate wars between motor carriers, and between them and the railways, still existed, and common carriers and contract carriers still fought each other.[57] Now, however, the ATA and the ICC bureaucracies arbitrated the conflicts. There also existed a new force in the industry— the Teamsters—which would join the array of interests already familiar with the ICC hearing rooms.

In a sense, the story of trucking between the world wars was one of cartelization. Truckers attempted to rationalize the atomistic competition, first, through consolidations of firms and, then, through business associations. Meanwhile, the truckers fell under the shadow of government control as the state commissioners devised regulations to curtail competition with the railways. These controls, plus the intensified competition from independents who evaded the state laws and the decline in freight during the early years of the Depression made the business future for common carrier truckers uncertain. These truckers then led the call for federal help. Although the abortive NRA experiment in self-regulation failed to bring stability, it did produce the politically strong ATA. As a driver easily uncouples his truck from one trailer and hooks up to another, so too did the ATA abandon self-regulation to join Joe Eastman and the ICC in proposing a comprehensive federal regulatory scheme. Together, the truckers and Coordinator Eastman convinced Congress that the interests of trucking paralleled the interests of the public; that the public interest would be served if trucking were stabilized.

Through a mixture of associationalism and quasi-judicial regulatory practices, the truckers and the commission achieved the limited goal of stability by the early 1940s. That the methods used to cartelize the industry included actions contrary to basic American beliefs should not surprise anyone; to achieve stable competition, competition must be curtailed. Given this context of stabilization, protection for common carriers and the rate agreements among truckers, while violating American beliefs against discrimination and collusion, nevertheless had a rational basis.

In its *Annual Report* for 1941, however, the commission noted that the economic environment had changed recently. The war in Europe "had wrought great changes in transportation conditions, . . . the business and revenues of the carriers have mounted almost as a river rises in a spring freshet. While this was a happy change from what had gone before, yet with it have come new questions." Would the cartelized industry that the truckers and the regulators constructed be able to respond to these new questions? Would these new questions involve a redefinition of the public's interest in trucking? Commissioner Clyde B. Aitchison, reflecting the basic pragmatism behind ICC regulation, had concluded earlier, "I think no matter can be said to be established as true until it has stood the test of active and hostile criticism."[58] Only the future would determine if regulation to reduce competitive tensions had also reduced or enhanced the industry's abilities to respond to changing economic conditions.

Conclusions

I

Joe Eastman died in March 1944. His death, which occurred while he was serving as Director of the Office of Defense Transportation, elicited hundreds of eulogies, a reaction usually reserved for war heroes, presidents, and statesmen. Such affection for so undramatic a man reflected the esteem in which so many held the regulator. Although many of the eulogists had clashed with Eastman during his quarter century on the Interstate Commerce Commission, they recognized his fairness and his dedication to public service. Indeed, to his death, Eastman remained an oddity in a town where social and political temptations destroyed careers. The commission consumed his life. There he practiced a profession devoid of scandal and ill-considered actions. Despite his well-known attraction to government ownership of key industries, Joe Eastman embodied the progressive spirit of disinterested policy making.[1]

Eastman's years as a state and federal regulator coincided with the complex convergence of historical forces that shaped the story of trucking.[2] Technologically, the internal combustion engine of the 1890s led to other innovations in tires, brakes, lights, and highway design; these during the 1920s very quickly helped transform the motor truck from a mere replacement for the horse and wagon to an effective competitor of the railroads. Economically, after the First World War had conditioned public acceptance of the truck, the 1920s furnished a fertile environment upon which the trucking revolution quickly expanded its influence; the Depression accented competition between old and new and underscored the atomistic competition among truckers. Meanwhile, politically, the successful experiment in federal controls during the war, although dismantled after hostilities had ceased, affected subsequent business-government relations. Congress in 1920 gave the ICC more authority to manage railway affairs; Secretary of Commerce Herbert Hoover and other government officials encouraged the organization of private trade associations designed to stabilize competition; and the Supreme Court, an institution in transition, gave the go-ahead in many cases to government regulation of private business. At the same time, many state issues were becoming national ones and more private businesses—including the radio, airline, and securities industries—came under federal supervision. Following the then-current trend, interests connected to transportation requested governmental relief from the transportation problem, specifically from trucking competition.

Joe Eastman watched these forces take shape. In 1919 he brought to the ICC a pragmatic approach to regulation, learned under Louis Brandeis and sharpened while Eastman served on the reform-minded Massachusetts commission, that fit well into the continuity of commission policies and procedures. The pragmatic approach, however, covered a plethora of economic and political concerns (shippers and carriers, retailers and wholesalers, legislators and judges, and so on) that made it difficult for Eastman and his fellow commissioners to deal with transportation controversies. For example, according to the Transportation Act of 1920, the regulators were supposed to ensure the financial stability of the railways and to coordinate their systems into an efficient national network. Yet, changes in the market (the appearance of competing transport forms and a much-expanded consumer economy) and the intransigence of railroad executives (in matters such as valuation and rate making) prevented the regulators from fully serving the public interest as Congress had intended in the Transportation Act of 1920. By the early 1930s, the commissioners had not coordinated the railroads, nor had they bolstered the rails' financial security. Absorbed in the detail and controversy of railway regulation, moreover, the federal commissioners—Eastman in particular—recognized only slowly, compared to state regulators, railways, and truckers, the implications of the trucking revolution and how those consequences would alter the public interest. Nevertheless, reflecting the continuing faith in Progressive Era reforms, Congress in 1933 tapped Joe Eastman to be Federal Coordinator of Transportation. His pragmatic style of investigation, consultation, and compromise guided his efforts to rationalize the transportation problem.

In the midst of his work as a public regulator, Eastman underwent a metamorphasis in his thinking on regulation, and it is clear that the Transportation Act of 1920, the regulatory experience of the ICC in the 1920s, and the emerging trucking industry affected his thoughts. Given his belief that "the theory [of private enterprise] is to a very considerable extent fallacious,"[3] Eastman had taken the commission's duty to protect the financial stability of the railways seriously. With the appearance of competing forms of transport, and his penchant for government supervision, Eastman naturally concluded by 1934 that the ICC should monitor the competition to ensure the profitability of firms in every transport industry. To this end, Eastman devised a plan, subject as always to modification in the particulars, through which the commission would coordinate the railroads and trucking firms and barge lines into an efficient transport system in which each business performed the tasks for which its technology was best suited. In this manner, Eastman believed, the public interest in efficient transportation would be served.

What is perhaps most striking in tracing Eastman's change in thinking is the lack of conscious attention he gave to the Depression. Competition between rails and trucks and between truckers appeared natural to Eastman, and although the depressed economy made conditions more uncertain and further motivated truckers to seek help, it did not, for Eastman, present any great aberration in the economic scheme of things. The oversupply of facilities seemed to him to be a natural consequence of uncontrolled enterprise. He responded less to immediate conditions and more to a sense of transport history and its future and his bias toward government supervision of key industries.

Eastman's plan for coordinated controls reflected the apex of progressive thought on transport regulation. Yet, his ideas were modified. In 1935 Congress extended controls only to interstate trucking; it did not accept Eastman's plans to reorganize the ICC and to extend controls over water carriers. Not until 1940 would water carriers be regulated, but again the concept of coordination would be weakly expressed. Obviously, Eastman's reputation and the belief in commission regulation held only so much weight with the American people, represented in this case by Congress, the shippers, and the carriers. Not surprisingly, such a concentration of planning authority as Eastman's plans envisioned was simply unacceptable. The American fear of centralized power (traceable to the seventeenth century) and the lack of a strong constituency behind Eastman's ideas prevented the ideological shift that coordination demanded.[4]

Nevertheless, regulation *was* extended to trucking. And while Eastman had a lot to do with that, other individuals and institutions contributed. For example, Ted Rodgers, first President of the American Trucking Associations, deftly and tirelessly led the diverse trucking population toward cartelization between 1933 and 1935. John Rogers, an Eastman protégé, skillfully established the Bureau of Motor Carriers and then moved on to become a full member of the ICC, where he continued to monitor trucking controls. The irascible Jack Keeshin added a provocative tone to the story. He disagreed often with fellow truckers, but his enthusiasm for the business and his readiness to use competing forms of transport marked his as an innovator in a maverick industry. He led truckers to call for federal controls, and after enactment of the Motor Carrier Act, he forced industry members to consider more carefully how they were to establish tariffs and rates. Others contributed. Henry Kelting, Tom Snyder, Joe Carrington, Carl Ozee, Maurice Tucker, Edward Buhner—all furnished leadership to an atomistic industry, first on the local and state levels, then on the national scene. When forces from within and from without trucking threatened their livelihood, the truckers responded with consolidations, associational activities, and finally with direct policy-making politics. Intuitively, it seemed, these businessmen felt the pulse of economic and political reality and learned quickly how to present their positions before other truckers, as well as judges, lawmakers, and other government officials.

These truckers used institutions to further their self-interests. Through the associations, they not only organized other truckers, but also dealt with policy makers, bureaucrats, and lawmakers in the state commissions and legislatures, before the Supreme Court, within the NRA, the FCT, and the ICC. Consequently, each institution played an important role in the story. The state commissions first identified trucking as a national issue; private truck associations, initially defensive, matured to offer industry services and policy-making powers; the Supreme Court established limits for public control; the NRA forged the state associations into the ATA and revealed that industry self-regulation would not work; the FCT and the ICC gathered information on the transportation problem and designed a regulatory scheme; Congress furnished the legislative authority; and the ICC administered the statute. Throughout the story, the people organized and manipulated the institutions. Some proved more successful than others. Ironically, for example, the state commissioners and the railroad executives (the first to call for regulation of trucks) gained the least from the Motor Carrier Act; the truckers and the ICC, the most.

Louis Galambos has identified several patterns in organization building in the twentieth century: "functional specialization within and between organizations," "the centralization of authority and the development of elaborate managerial hierarchies to coordinate and control our new, large-scale institutions," the use of "power to protect" interests, and the promotion of "technical and organizational innovation in a systematic fashion."[5] The story of trucking fits all of these except the last. The ICC used functional specialization in the form of Division 5, the BMC, the field force, and other subagencies to regulate interstate trucking. The entire MCA reflected an elaborate managerial plan. And the truckers obviously used the ATA; the state commissioners, NARUC; and Eastman, the ICC as sources of power. But the MCA, the ICC, and the ATA produced innovation only within the regulatory apparatus itself—joint boards, field force, administrative rulings, and the like. The application of controls did not tend to stimulate innovation in the trucking industry itself, at least not during the formative years of regulation.

Joe Eastman had worked in the midst of these technological, economic, political, and bureaucratic forces, and even he admitted at times that he was unsure of what it all really meant. In the pragmatic tradition, he was content to await the consequences of the actions and then to act again if necessary. The Second World War and his death in 1944 prevented Eastman from fully testing the Motor Carrier Act of 1935.

2

The trucking industry, then, was regulated rather quickly because of a convergence of historical forces and individual talents. Was any one of these forces more important than the others? Technology quickened the impact of development, but it worked within a fertile economic environment. Technology and economics, moreover, were superimposed upon a background of common law and political control of business. Ideology permeated the story, in the clash between those who opposed government intrusion into the economy, those who preferred industry self-regulation, and those who welcomed federal supervision. Yet, ideology does not seem to be any more or less important than technology. The ICC and state commissions proved to be strong bureaucratic forces, yet they too had to deal with tradition, political infighting, and new institutions (the NRA and ATA, for example); neither maintained total control over events. The people—trucking leaders and public officials—certainly presented a strong force in the movement toward regulation, but again, they played their roles upon a preset, albeit changing, stage of historical forces; they tried to control the forces, but they did not always succeed.

Although the economic structure of trucking (low fixed costs, flexibility, speed, atomistic competition) was not completely laid out in the 1920s and early 1930s, it probably affected the story more than any other force. Historian Thomas K. McCraw has boldly maintained that in the history of regulation in America, *"More than any other single factor, this underlying structure of the particular industry being regulated has defined the context in which regulatory agencies have operated."* [6] In the story of trucking, the underlying structure attracted all the other forces like a magnet. It spurred technological innovation and economic reorganization; it drew out competing ideological and political conflicts basic to American culture; it contributed to the evolution of legal controls over business. Indeed, the forces of technology, economics, ideology, politics, and law were used by individuals to attempt to control the evolving structure of trucking.

The desire to control or to cartelize the structure of trucking appeared early in the emergence of the business; these attempts to control tended to join with and sometimes to curtail the forces that shaped trucking. Controversy arose, not over the goal, but rather over the method of cartelization. In the 1920s the state commissioners wanted to implement the traditional commission form of controls without federal oversight; by the early 1930s truckers favored self-regulation through associational service projects and rate agreements; but by the mid-1930s the ICC strategy of federal regulation (with the innovation of joint boards) won congressional support. That strategy equated the promotion of trucking interests—cartelization—with the promotion of the public interest.

The same forces that brought about regulation continued dominant in its application. Unlike the preregulation era, however, the post-1935 period more clearly reflected the importance of the structure of the industry, for the structure of trucking necessitated alterations in the manner in which transportation competition was controlled. The atomistic aspects (numerous firms spread over forty-eight states) forced the regulators to decentralize administration to effectively deal with controversy. Thus, the commissioners pursued the joint board experiment, established a field force, and instituted the administrative ruling. The joint boards, of course, represented the first time in U.S. history that federal authority was vested in state officials. However, the atomistic structure of trucking demanded that innovation, as the state regulators had foreseen nearly a decade before, and it was the very same structure that ironically led to its failure.

The structure of trucking also led to regulatory strategies that contradicted long-held American values. To control the competition, some truckers were to be protected from others, a violation of beliefs in nondiscriminatory practices. By design and through implementation, moreover, industry members essentially cartelized the industry themselves. Although the ICC regulators decided quasi-judicial issues (who could be a trucker, who was a contract carrier) that limited the membership of the industry, the truckers worked out the quasi-legislative issues that directly (tariff and rate-making) and indirectly (safety and insurance) cartelized trucking. This collusion of businessmen violated American antitrust beliefs, but the ICC commissioners rationalized the strategy on the basis of the structure of the industry. Only the truckers themselves, familiar with local trucking operations, could adequately and quickly establish tariffs and rates. Antitrust fears were muted, however, when competitive pressures, so evident in the days before federal regulation, surfaced again in the rate negotiations; competition resulted in very low rates, which the ICC often raised. Then Congress settled the trust question in the Reed-Bulwinkle Act of 1948, which expressly exempted trucking rate bureaus from antitrust prosecutions.[7]

Whether the structure of trucking became more important during the application of federal controls than it had been before, the ironic fact remains that the economic structure was defined more often through political acts—state controls, associational activities, court decisions, and ICC regulation—than it was through market forces of supply and demand.

3

The Motor Carrier Act was only one of many government intrusions into the economy in the 1930s. Congress placed federal controls over the banking and securities industries and over utility holding companies and labor-management relations, and for the first time, the national government established a social security system.[8] Since the New Deal, political scientists, economists, and historians have attempted to describe what happened, why, and what the consequences have been. Many have theorized that regulation was unnecessary, that it violated basic principles of capitalism, and that it failed to serve the public interest.[9] Two essential problems mar the usefulness of these theories. First, the theories do not always match the actual events. Second, the notion of the public interest in these theories is not the same as that found in the 1930s. This does not mean, however, that the theories are without merit; they can aid in understanding particular twists and turns in the story and, most important, in realizing that the political economy changes over time.[10]

The history of trucking regulation reflects elements of the "public interest," "life cycle," and "capture" theories, but it does not completely coincide with any of them.[11] According to the public interest theory, regulation appears in response to public demands for the government to eliminate inequities or inefficiencies in the market. On the surface, the MCA appears to fit this theory, for Congress stated that it enacted the statute to ensure the public's interest in a stable transportation system. Yet, as we have discovered, the "public" that demanded the MCA consisted for the most part of transportation groups (railways, shippers, and truckers) and government agencies (state regulators and the ICC). Consumers as a distinct group were not consulted or represented in the hearings. Administration of the MCA, moreover, revealed actions contrary to public interest concerns, violating deeply held American convictions about fair and open competition. In short, the public interest in 1935 corresponded with the self-interest of the truckers and the regulators' perception of the public interest.

The story of trucking also fails to fit the life-cycle and capture theories precisely. The life-cycle theory states that early in the administration of a regulatory statute, the regulators respond to heightened legislative interest in business abuses and actively force the members of the industry to comply with the law; as the years wear on, however, and legislative interest wanes, the regulators become less conscientious. Eventually, as the capture theory suggests, the industry members come to control the regulators, making the agency simply a rubber stamp for industry desires. In fact, legislative interest in trucking was not that apparent. During the initial years of federal truck regulation, heightened regulatory activity was noticeable, *despite* small appropriations from Congress. That the truckers welcomed the early controls also contradicts the life-cycle theory. Indeed, in some respects, the truckers "captured" the ICC before enactment of the MCA, for they worked with Eastman in drafting the statute. The truckers and the regulators agreed that the public interest would be served by a cartelized trucking industry; consensus of regulator and regulated guided the early years of federal truck control.

Focus upon only one of these theories, and the story is misleading; combine the theories, and the story becomes more comprehensible. Yet the theories alone do not fully explain or predict the outcome of the narrative. Instead of explaining what happened in the 1930s, the theories have become a part of the story. That is, the theories represent challenges to the chosen strategies pursued during the New Deal and are in effect the "active and hostile criticism" that Commissioner Aitchison expected.[12]

In large measure, the critical theories of the 1960s and 1970s represented a revitalization of market theory. Propounded by members of the so-called Chicago school of economics, market theory directly attacked the regulatory practice of allowing elites (such as the ATA and the federal commissioners) to make management decisions. Market theorists maintained that the consumer should guide business decisions. Using their interpretations of Adam Smith's descriptions of capitalism, the neoclassical economists argued that the removal of government controls would elevate the consumer to a position of influence, which in turn would stimulate more careful attention to efficiency and reduce the bureaucratic costs that regulation imposed on carriers and shippers and consumers.[13] Many members of the Chicago school, however, seem to have skipped lightly over two hundred years of history, for their insistence that elimination of controls would stimulate lower prices and better service ignores that those regulations, for the most part, were enacted precisely to bring about better prices and services. Consumers had not been able to choose. Either monopoly practices raised prices or unfettered competition reduced efficiency and created chaotic marketing practices.

A prominent economist who uses market theory, but who does not subscribe to the Chicago school myopia, is Alfred E. Kahn. Originally trained in the 1930s, Kahn learned first the institutional approach to public policy making that Eastman and other progressives had established. Later in his career, Kahn realized that regulatory decisions were too often based, not on economic costs, but on which interest group was the most effective in presenting its case to the lawmakers. He noted specifically that government regulation tended to divert attention away from marginal costs and toward average costs, thus increasing costs for the regulated and prices for the consumer. Reliance on average costs, Kahn maintained, had created static, lethargic industries unable to adapt easily to changing conditions. Specifically, marginal costs represent the cost of producing one more product (or of not producing one more product). These marginal costs vary according to the demand from consumers. For example, the costs of producing electricity at 2:00 P.M. on a hundred-degree day in July are greater than the costs of producing electricity at 6:00 P.M. on a delightful breezy day in April. Consumers would demand more electricity in the former instance, less in the latter. In transportation, marginal costs involve seasonal variations in demand, less-than-carload lots, and perhaps, backhaul considerations. Kahn believes businesses would be more efficient if they would focus upon marginal costs; consumers, moreover, would pay for only what they used if marginal costs were used as a basis for rate making.[14]

Kahn used his insights into marginal costs and two other theories to analyze the case of trucking in the 1930s. He first described the theory of cartels, which states that an atomistic industry will stabilize itself without government interference, then the theory of "destructive competition," which states that atomistic industries with high fixed costs or low marginal costs and lack of mobility to meet changing conditions tend toward chronic overcapacity. Trucking was atomistic, and it did not have high fixed costs but rather high variable (marginal) costs. The truckers could have sat out low demand periods because their fixed costs were so low, limited essentially to payments on the truck. (In contrast, the railroads had to operate even at a loss in low demand periods to help recover some of their high fixed costs—rolling stock, terminals, track, interest on loans.) Or truckers, with their greater flexibility to find demand, could have sought out business elsewhere. Kahn concluded that the truckers could have survived the 1930s without regulation, for their overcapacity problem was only temporary.[15]

Kahn admits that his theory is unprovable for the past; yet his work illuminates some important aspects about the story of trucking and the subsequent imposition of federal controls. First, Kahn assumes a definition of the public interest that differs from the one used in the 1930s. Kahn emphasizes the consumer's interest in low prices (a reflection of the consumer movement of the 1960s). Eastman, the ICC, and the truckers of the 1930s, however, believed that the public interest would be served better by cartelization that would protect and promote trucking firms, even though, they admitted, such a program would raise prices for the consumer. Second, the very factors that, according to Kahn, should have precluded regulation—numerous firms, high variable costs, and flexibility to meet changing conditions—represented the very factors that common carrier truckers and others cited to argue in favor of regulation. Trucking competition, moveover, represented only part of the transportation problem. Railroading, which reflected the tendency toward overcapacity that Kahn described, and state regulations compounded the transport chaos.

Third, Kahn's emphasis on marginal costs reflects more the growth of economics as a discipline since the 1930s and less a valid tool for understanding the early years of trucking. The costs of trucking, whether fixed, variable, or marginal, simply eluded most truckers and regulators. The cost formula under the NRA did not work; arguments over costs raged throughout the late 1930s as truckers constructed tariffs and rate levels; average costs and the railway tariff schemes were used as expedients toward establishing as quickly as possible a firm basis for the industry; and by 1940 there was still no consensus on what constituted trucking costs. In 1938 the economist James C. Nelson explained the problem: "No doubt, ignorance of costs caused by low business qualifications of the entrepreneurs [in trucking] and the prevailing small-scale operations were factors which have contributed to producing the competitive conditions."[16] In fact, one of the goals of the truck associational movement was to educate truckers in sound management practices and that included attention to costs; the ICC regulatory program continued that educational thrust. Kahn is probably correct in emphasizing marginal costs, but in the 1930s, the majority of truckers did not know what marginal costs were.

4

Contrary to those theorists and critics who argue that regulation in the 1930s generally, and of trucking particularly, perverted the capitalist system, the history and analyses suggest just the opposite—that the story of trucking falls within the general evolution of capitalism in the United States.

A critic of the emerging partnership between truckers and government, Meyer H. Fishbein, quoted Adam Smith to support his contention that the NRA Truck Code in 1933 had been ill advised.

People of the same trade seldom meet together even for merriment and diversion, but the conversation ends in a conspiracy against the public, or on some contrivance to raise prices. It is impossible to prevent such meetings by any law which either could be executed or would be consistent with liberty and justice. But though the law cannot hinder, it ought to do nothing to facilitate such assemblies, much less to render them necessary. A regulation which obliges all those of the same trade in a particular town to enter their names and places in a public register, facilitates such assemblies. It connects individuals who might never otherwise be known to one another, and gives every man of the trade a direction where to find every other man of it.[17]

1776. Alas, the world was very different then. Smith's work, as brilliant as it was for its time, did not foresee the appearance of industrial capitalism, with its large corporations and its major alterations in the market system. The technological revolutions that accompanied industrialism, especially the communications revolution, have rendered Smith's strictures against government sponsorship of business associations a bit quaint, if not unrealistic. More efficient, if not potentially secret, communication methods have forced changes in the political economy; publicity of business actions has been, therefore, a major thrust of government regulation in the twentieth century.

The appearance of industrial capitalism in the nineteenth and twentieth centuries accelerated the coming together of business and government to deal with new problems of the public interest. The emergence of large-scale business resulted in new abuses and new uncertainties. Beginning in the late nineteenth century and carrying over into the twentieth, businessmen and progressive reformers designed institutions to alter the business environment. Motor trucking made its appearance just as business and government underwent the closest partnership experiment in U.S. history to that time; although dismantled after World War I, the basically successful public-private institutions that organized production for the conflict in Europe stayed in the minds of entrepreneurs and public officials alike. While the American traditions against monopoly and business-government collusion tempered business-government relations in the 1920s, they were not strong enough to withstand experiments in associationalism. Businessmen in hundreds of industries, meeting in public and with encouragement from government officials, attempted to reproduce the rationalized economy of the war period but without direct government controls.

At the same time, however, in transportation the trend was toward more direct government regulation of the railways. Not only had transportation been subject to public supervision since medieval times, but the recent war had also exposed transportation as the vital link in the nation's economy. The public interest required a coordinated transport network and that required governmental controls.

Trucking fell into both movements. A business basically individualistic in structure in its infancy, it was consumed in the mania for organization and stability. What separated trucking from other atomistic industries like lumber or bituminous coal,[18] besides its transport nature, was the ability of its leading members to recognize the need for organization to protect their interests from competitors and then to succeed in such an atomistically divided business. Together, these businessmen truckers learned the associational ropes and, later, how to lobby the government for controls beneficial to their industry. In that sense, trucking represents a success story.

That a price was paid for the close partnership between truckers and the government cannot be denied. Certainly the cartel features of truck regulation stifled competition and, perhaps, creativity and innovation. This consequence reflects what political scientists and historians have labeled corporatism. Corporatism involves either businessmen's coopting the public interest as their own or the government's gaining too much authority to plan the economy and so stifling individual initiative.[19] By the early 1940s, truck regulation apparently had stifled the flexibility inherent in trucking.[20]

Yet, another school of political science and history, the so-called pluralists, would argue that those elements of business collusion and centralized planning would not necessarily result in long-term detrimental effects. Pluralists see in the emergence of industrial capitalism a complex democratic structure that precludes long-term control of the economy by any one set of interests. The large institutions of the twentieth century, rather than centralizing elite power, have dispersed that power; economic individualism and democratic competition have survived, the pluralists argue, in the competition between large institutions.[21]

The story of trucking to 1940 appears to fit the pluralist argument more precisely than that of the corporatists. Competition within trucking and between transport industries, which caused chaos in the economic market, was rationalized through democratic give-and-take in the political arena. Although tendencies toward business collusion and government planning were evident by 1940 (along with stifled innovation), those trends did not produce a major perversion of the American political system. The pragmatic tradition, the structure of trucking, and the adversarial nature of business-government relations evident in Congress and in the ICC hearing rooms tended to mitigate any attempts to gain complete control over the process. The attempts of the late 1970s and early 1980s to deregulate trucking may indicate that the system has remained responsive (albeit once again slowly) to changes in the political economy.[22]

Acknowledgments

As this is a history of people and institutions, so too is it a study that received support from people and institutions.

I owe the greatest personal debt to Tom McCraw. He first stimulated my interest in regulatory history in his seminar in business-government relations; then, he furnished a research assistantship from Harvard; and, always, he shared with me his concerns for writing clearly. Lewis Gould and Robert Divine, through their examples as historians and teachers, also supported the completion of this work.

Other historians who commented on various parts of the manuscript-in-progress and thereby helped fashion a better work included Thomas Cogswell, Gilbert Fite, Ellis Hawley, Michael Hogan, Clarence Lasby, Perry Leavell, Albro Martin, Molly Selvin, Robert T. Smith, Michael Stoff, Mark Summers, and Kirk Willis. Naomi Lamareaux and Alan Stone furnished informative and helpful readers' reports, while Mavis Bryant and Katherine Holloway of the University of Tennessee Press appeared with timely support. Judith Bailey enhanced the manuscript with her copyeditor's eye for detail and clarity. Others who contributed academic support included Mansel Blackford, Robert Calvert, Tuffly Ellis, Larry Hill, Will Holmes, Austin Kerr, Robert Kieschnick, Richard Leggett, Layne Moore, and Nancy Rose.

Other friends proved especially supportive: Carla Fraser, Paula Leggett, Julian Martin and Geneva Moore, Mike and Gail Wilson, and Viki Patterson (Kieschnick). Fred Afflerbach graciously shared with me his eighteen-wheeler during three summers of interstate trucking experience and, along with Claude "Mama" Teal, Jim Alexander, and Tony Matisi, helped me become less a gear-jammer than I might have been otherwise.

The silent heroes of the scholarly professions—the archivists—made my research trips more effective. These included John Lancaster and Joanne C. Dougherty of Amherst College; Francis Seeber, Paul McLaughlin, and Sandra Raub of the Franklin D. Roosevelt Library; Betty Gallagher and Cora F. Pedersen of the Herbert Hoover Presidential Library; and Philip Zorich of the University of Oregon. A very special thanks goes to Jerry Hess at the National Archives in Washington, D.C.

Members of my family deserve special commendation. While they might have (silently) questioned my sanity at times, they never wavered in their support.

Grants from the Eleanor Roosevelt Institute and the Herbert Hoover Presidential Library Association facilitated research, as did research funds from the George F. Baker Foundation at the Harvard Graduate School of Business Administration. Typing services at the University of Georgia and the Ohio State University aided immeasurably in the completion of the manuscript.

In timeworn tradition, of course, I remain solely responsible for the contents of this book.

William R. Childs
Ohio State University

Abbreviations

AHFA	American Highway Freight Association
AER	*American Economic Review*
AHR	*American Historical Review*
ATA	American Trucking Associations, Inc.
BellJ	*The Bell Journal of Economics and Management Science*
BHR	*Business History Review*
BMC	Bureau of Motor Carriers
CLR	*California Law Review*
FCT	Federal Coordinator of Transportation
HLR	*Harvard Law Review*
ICC	Interstate Commerce Commission
JAH	*Journal of American History*
JLPUE	*The Journal of Land and Public Utility Economics*
lcl	less-than-carload
MCA	Motor Carrier Act of 1935
Mich. LR	*Michigan Law Review*
Minn. LR	*Minnesota Law Review*
MVHR	*Mississippi Valley Historical Review*
NA	National Archives, Washington, D.C.
NACC	National Automobile Chamber of Commerce
NARUC	National Association of Railroad and Utility Commissioners
NCA	National Code Authority
NRA	National Recovery Administration
RG	Record Group
SCA	State Code Authorities
TTW	*The Traffic World*
TAEA	Transportation Association Executives of America
WSJ	*Wall Street Journal*

Notes

Preface

1. John Steinbeck, *The Grapes of Wrath* (New York: Viking, 1939), 8, 209, 213, 214, 12, 13.

2. For studies of the mixed-economy theme in the nineteenth century, see George Rogers Taylor, *The Transportation Revolution, 1815–1860*, vol. IV: *Economic History of the United States* (New York: Holt, Rinehart, and Winston, 1951), esp. Ch. 16; Carter Goodrich, *Government Promotion of American Canals and Railroads, 1800–1890* (New York: Columbia Univ. Press, 1960), esp. concluding chapter. For a recent study that reflects the mixed-economy concept, see William H. Becker, *The Dynamics of Business-Government Relations: Industry and Exports, 1893–1921* (Chicago: Univ. of Chicago Press, 1982). For an excellent study of business-government relations in the 1930s, see Ellis W. Hawley, *The New Deal and the Problem of Monopoly: A Study in Economic Ambivalence* (Princeton: Princeton Univ. Press, 1966).

3. Thomas K. McCraw, "Regulation in America: A Review Article," *BHR* 49 (Summer 1975), 182. Another way to view the inherent tensions within capitalism is found in Alan Stone, *Economic Regulation and the Public Interest: The Federal Trade Commission in Theory and Practice* (Ithaca, N.Y.: Cornell Univ. Press, 1977), 15.

4. For discussions of the numerous theories of regulation, see McCraw, "Regulation in America," 160–71; Richard A. Posner, "Theories of Economic Regulation," *BellJ* 5 (Autumn 1974), 335–42ff; George J. Stigler, "The Theory of Economic Regulation," *BellJ* 2 (Spring 1971), 3–21; Alfred E. Kahn, *The Economics of Regulation: Principles and Institutions,* vol. II: *Institutional Issues* (New York: John Wiley, 1971), 189, 38, 178ff.

5. Ari Hoogenboom and Olive Hoogenboom, in *A History of the ICC: From Panacea to Palliative* (New York: Norton, 1976), focus on the personalities and qualities of the members of the ICC. A recent

biography of James Landis attempts to tie his personality to the
public policy issues. See Donald A. Ritchie, *James M. Landis: Dean
of the Regulators* (Cambridge, Mass.: Harvard Univ. Press, 1980).
For studies of the changing personality of institutions, see Carl
McFarland, *Judicial Control of the Federal Trade Commission and
The Interstate Commerce Commission, 1920–1930: A Comparative
Study in the Relations of Courts to Administrative Commissions*
(Cambridge, Mass.: Harvard Univ. Press, 1933); G. Cullom Davis,
"The Transformation of the Federal Trade Commission, 1914–1929,"
MVHR 49 (Dec. 1962), 437ff. The recent emphasis on institutional
history has tended to blur traditional periodizations, such as
Progressive Era, New Era, New Deal. See Louis P. Galambos, "The
Emerging Organizational Synthesis in Modern American History,"
BHR 44 (Autumn 1970), 279–90; and his *Competition and
Cooperation: The Emergence of a National Trade Association*
(Baltimore: Johns Hopkins Univ. Press, 1966).

6.   McCraw, "Regulation in America," 181.

Introduction

1.   *Oxford English Dictionary* (Oxford: Clarendon Press, 1970), IX,
      414–15.

2.   John B. Rae, *The American Automobile: A Brief History* (Chicago:
      Univ. of Chicago Press, 1965), 20, 29; and the following articles in
      Scientific American: "Atkinson's Cycle Gas Engine," May 30, 1891,
      p. 339, "A Petroleum Motor Tricycle," Feb. 14, 1891, p. 95, "A
      Gasoline Steam Carriage," May 21, 1892, p. 329, "Electric
      Carriage," Feb. 3, 1894, p. 69, "New Steam Carriage," Mar. 31,
      1894, pp. 200–201.

3.   Rae, *American Automobile,* 6. See also John B. Montville, *Mack*
      (Newfoundland, N.J.: Haessner, 1973), 3–5; the following articles in
      Scientific American: "The Need of Good Country Roads," Apr. 5,
      1890, p. 213,"Road Improvement," Feb. 27, 1892, p. 128, "The
      Doctor and Good Roads," June 18, 1892, p. 393; and William C.
      Hilles, "The Good Roads Movement in the United States:
      1880–1916" (M.A. thesis, Duke Univ., 1958), 131–37. The irony in
      railroad support of good roads did not dawn on rail executives until
      the 1920s. Some saw potential competition from the motor vehicle as
      early as 1916, but the automobile was the focus of their concern, not
      the truck. Indeed, during this period rail executives viewed trucks
      and good highways as conduits to the rail system. Charles L.
      Dearing, *American Highway Policy* (Washington: Brookings
      Institution, 1941), 225–28, and n. 27.

4.   Rae, *American Automobile,* 20, 47–51.

5.   Robert F. Karolevitz, *This Was Trucking: A Pictorial History of the*

First Quarter Century of Commercial Motor Vehicles (Seattle: Superior, 1966), 36–39, 41, 45–47; James J. Flink, *America Adopts the Automobile, 1895–1910* (Cambridge, Mass.: MIT Press, 1970), 89–90.

6.   Rae, *American Automobile,* 38–41.

Chapter 1

1.   H. C. Kelting, "History of Truck Transportation, 1914–1936," MS, Joe C. Carrington Papers, Austin, Tex., copy in author's possession.

2.   For an excellent study of transportation in the nineteenth century, see Taylor, *Transportation Revolution.*

3.   Francis Paul Prucha, *The Sword of the Republic: The U.S. Army on the Frontier, 1783–1846* (London: Collier-Macmillan, 1969), 184, 192.

4.   Karolevitz, *This Was Trucking,* 49–57.

5.   Ibid., 57–61; John J. Pershing, *My Experiences in the World War* (New York: Frederick A. Stokes, 1931), I, 240–41.

6.   Pershing, *My Experiences,* II, 308–309; Karolevitz, *This Was Trucking,* 62–66.

7.   Montville, *Mack,* 61, 69; James Harold Thomas, "Trucking: History and Legend" (Ph.D. diss., Oklahoma State Univ., 1976), 61; George W. Anderson to E.J. Pearson, Nov. 12, 1917, Joseph B. Eastman Papers, Amherst College, Amherst, Mass.

8.   *Automobile Facts and Figures* (New York: Automobile Manufacturers Association, 1940), 5. Rae, *American Automobile,* 87, 96, emphasizes the emergence of oligopoly. Karolevitz, *This Was Trucking,* 114–17; *Ward's 1941 Automotive Year Book* (Detroit: Ward's Reports, 1941), 47; Alfred D. Chandler, Jr., ed., *Giant Enterprise: Ford, General Motors, and the Automobile Industry, Sources and Readings* (New York: Harcourt, Brace, 1964); Chandler, *Strategy and Structure: Chapters in the History of the American Industrial Enterprise* (Cambridge, Mass.: MIT Press, 1962, 1966), Ch. 3 and pp. 370–74.

9.   *Ward's 1941,* 47; Karolevitz, *This Was Trucking,* 81.

10.   Montville, *Mack,* 67–69, 80–82, 96.

11.   Gini Rice, *Relics of the Road,* No. 2: *Keen Kenworth Trucks, 1915–1955* (New York: Hastings House, 1973), 23–27.

12.   Gini Rice, *Relics of the Road,* No. 3: *Impressive International Trucks, 1907–1947* (Lake Oswego, Ore.: Truck Tracks, 1975), 57, 79–85; Harold C. Livesay, *American Made: Men Who Shaped the American Economy* (Boston: Little, Brown and Company, 1979), Ch. 3.

13.   Homer H. Shannon, "The Refrigerator Truck," *TTW*, Aug. 15, 1931,
      pp. 339–40; "Memoirs of John J. Brady, Sr.," *Woods Highway Truck
      Library*, New York Times Oral History Program (Glen Rock, N.J.:
      Microfilming Corp. of America, 1975), 8; Athel F. Denham, *20
      Years' Progress in Commercial Motor Vehicles, 1921–1942*
      (Washington: Military Vehicles Div., Automotive Council for War
      Production, 1942), 186–87.

14.   Denham, *20 Years' Progress*, 102–05, 179–81.

15.   Ibid., 27–34, 208–209; Montville, *Mack*, 87.

16.   Harold G. Moulton, *The American Transportation Problem*
      (Washington: Brookings Institution, 1933), 519.

17.   *Facts and Figures of the Automobile Industry* (New York: NACC,
      1928), 19 (1931), 82–85.

18.   Bennehan Cameron to Woodrow Wilson, June 24, 1916, Wilson [?]
      to Senator J. H. Bankhead, June 28, 1916, Wilson to Frank A.
      Cannon, June 30, 1916, all in Woodrow Wilson Papers, Library of
      Congress; Karolevitz, *This Was Trucking*, 75.

19.   Dearing, *American Highway Policy*, 78–85; Dwight D. Eisenhower,
      At Ease: Stories I Tell to Friends (Garden City, N.Y.: Doubleday,
      1967), 157, 166–67; Frederic L. Paxson, "The Highway Movement,
      1916–1935," *AHR* 51 (Jan. 1946), 245.

20.   Moulton, *Transportation Problem*, 530–38.

21.   John Chynoweth Burnham, "The Gasoline Tax and the Automobile
      Revolution," *MVHR*, 48 (Dec. 1961), 435–55.

22.   Moulton, *Transportation Problem*, 540–41, 552. For a study of
      highway building in America, see Mark H. Rose, *Interstate: Express
      Highway Politics, 1941–1956* (Lawrence: Regents Press of Kansas,
      1979).

23.   Wayne G. Broehl, Jr., *Trucks . . . Trouble . . . and Triumph: The
      Norwalk Truck Line Company* (New York: Prentice-Hall, 1954),
      14–42. This was the first academic study of a trucking firm.

24.   James F. Filgas, *Yellow in Motion: A History of Yellow Freight
      System, Incorporated* (Bloomington: Indiana Univ. School of
      Business, Div. of Research, 1971), 3–7.

25.   "Memoirs of Maurice Tucker," *Woods Truck Library*, 1–7, 11, 13,
      16–17.

26.   "Memoirs of Carl Ozee," *Woods Truck Library*, 1–2, 4–9.

27.   Clippings in Lillie Drennan folder, Carrington Papers.

28.   "Memoirs of Mr. X," *Woods Truck Library*, 1–2, 7–12, 14. See also
      Humbert S. Nelli, *The Business of Crime: Italians and Syndicate
      Crime in the United States* (New York: Oxford Univ. Press, 1976),
      150, 154, 156–57.

29.   D. Philip Locklin, *Economics of Transportation*, 5th ed.

(Homewood, Ill.: Richard D. Irwin, 1960), 639–44; John R. Meyer
et al., *The Economics of Competition in the Transportation
Industries* (Cambridge, Mass.: Harvard Univ. Press, 1959), 88–95;
Harold Barger, *The Transportation Industries, 1889–1946: A Study
of Output, Employment, and Productivity* (New York: National
Bureau of Economic Research, 1951), 240.

30. Kahn, *Economics of Regulation,* II, 182–85; Ben H. Petty, *Truck
Operating Costs* (Bulletin No. 10, Purdue Univ. Engineering
Experiment Station, Feb. 1923), 5, 7, 8–14. Petty noted that the
general lack of accounting procedures also led to many failures in
trucking.

31. L. C. Sorrell, "Changes in Transportation, Production, and
Marketing," *TTW,* Apr. 12, 1930, pp. 982–83; "Motor Bus and
Truck Operation," No. 18300, Apr. 10, 1928, *Interstate Commerce
Commission Reports,* 140 (Washington: U.S. GPO, 1928), 717;
Barger, *Transport Industries,* 241, suggests that the truck responded
well to the "hand-to-mouth buying" trend in the 1920s.

32. Copy from *Chilton Automotive Multi-Guide,* Autumn, 1930, p. 193,
found in National Archives, Record Group 9, NRA, Central Files of
the ATA, Tray 1997, folder 620.

33. "Motor Bus and Truck Operation," 717–18.

34. Lars J. Sandberg, "Truck Selling, Simultaneous Selling, and Delivery
in Wholesale Food Distribution," Division of Research, Business
Research Studies, No. 7 (Cambridge, Mass.: Harvard Univ. Graduate
School of Business Administration, 1934), 1, 4.

35. Moulton, *Transportation Problem,* 597–99.

36. Ibid., 610–13.

37. Ibid., 612–17.

38. Homer H. Shannon, "Fruit and Vegetable Shipments Go to Trucks,"
TTW, Mar. 26, 1932, pp. 681–83; Moulton, *Transportation Problem,*
615–17.

39. Moulton, *Transportation Problem,* 606–608, 599–601.

40. Ibid., 621–35, 645–59; L. Tuffly Ellis, "The Texas Cotton Compress
Industry: A History" (Ph.D. diss., University of Texas, 1964),
328–36; Walter Beck, *The Cotton Truck* (Austin: Texas Motor
Transportation Association, 1932), copy in ATA Central Files, Tray
1997.

41. Moulton, *Transportation Problem,* 578–95.

42. L. C. Sorrell, "Market Effects of Improved Transportation," *TTW,*
Apr. 5, 1930, pp. 911, 914–15; "Changes in Transportation,
Production, and Marketing," *TTW,* Apr. 19, 1930, pp. 1051–52;
"Recent Changes in Transportation, Production and Marketing,"
TTW, May 3, 1930, pp. 1187, 1190–91. Historians are often captive
of their subject. In describing the emergence of trucking in this

chapter, I have emphasized agriculture for the simple reason that most of the material does so. In one of the most comprehensive studies produced during the period, the author stated that, next to agriculture, "The next most numerous group of trucks comprises those engaged in city and suburban distribution." (Moulton, *Transportation Problem,* 578) Since Moulton was concerned mainly with the plight of the railroads and since trucking in retail and wholesale products in the cities and suburbs did not compete with the rails, he ignored trucking in urban areas. Even the articles by Sorrell and Shannon cited above omitted specific references to this aspect of trucking.

43. In *Economics of Transportation,* rev. ed. (New York: Harper, 1959), Marvin L. Fair and Ernest W. Williams, Jr., devised "life cycles" for different modes of transportation. They argue (pp. 39–41) that transportation industries progress through five steps: (1) *experimentation* in modes of power, design of the vehicle and the manner of travel (rail, road), (2) *early extension* where the public accepts the new mode by promoting it and large capital investments occur, (3) *rapid expansion* where larger systems emerge and the field is recognized as a good investment, giving rise to intense competition which gives rise to state restriction, (4) *maturity* results in slower rates of efficiency, and (5) *decadence* where the mode loses traffic to competing agencies, few companies make a profit, and restrictions are relaxed. For trucking, Fair and Williams place the following years into their life cycle motif: (1) 1884–1908, (2) 1908–1938, (3) 1938–1953, (4) 1953–? As the rest of the present study will show, the history of trucking does not fit this model. State regulation increased in the late 1920s and into the 1930s, well before 1938. Further, as the deregulation legislation of 1980 shows, relaxation of restrictions came, not because the industry was hurting for profits, but rather because the energy crisis exposed inefficiencies and because prevailing economic theories supported the lessening of controls.

Chapter 2

1. Albro Martin called my attention to the friction problem. See *Scientific American,* Oct. 5, 1895, and Dec. 28, 1895, for examples of steam vehicles that antedated the railways. See Taylor, *Transportation Revolution,* Ch. 5, for an excellent description and analysis of the rise of railroads in the United States.

2. Locklin, *Economics of Transportation* 129–31, 133, 137; Glenn Porter, *The Rise of Big Business, 1860–1910* (New York: Thomas Crowell, 1973), 31–39. For a modern view of scale economies, see Thomas K. McCraw, "Rethinking the Trust Question," in McCraw, ed., *Regulation in Perspective: Historical Essays* (Cambridge, Mass.: Harvard Univ. Press, 1981), 6–9 and n. 10.

3.   A more detailed analysis will be found in Ch. 5.

4.   Homer H. Shannon, "The Truck, Rail Competitor and Ally," *TTW*,
     Dec. 20, 1930, p. 1563; Thomas Lamont to President Hoover, Nov.
     20, 1931, Presidential Papers, Box 244, Railroads Correspondence,
     1931, Herbert C. Hoover Papers, West Branch, Iowa.

5.   Homer H. Shannon, "Local Cartage Services," *TTW*, Aug. 14, 1937,
     pp. 367–68.

6.   Homer H. Shannon, "The Truck in Terminal Service," *TTW*, May
     24, 1930, pp. 1393–96.

7.   Homer H. Shannon, "Motorization of Railway Express Service,"
     TTW, Mar. 28, 1931, pp. 779–81.

8.   Homer H. Shannon, "Welding Rails and Highways," 2 parts, *TTW*,
     Dec. 19 and 26, 1931, pp. 1347–49, 1395–97. See also "Loaded
     Trucks by Rail," *TTW*, Apr. 9, 1932, p. 785.

9.   Shannon, "Welding Rails and Highways," pt. 1, p. 1348; *Facts and
     Figures of the Automobile Industry* (NACC, 1931), 19.

10. Shannon, "Welding Rails and Highways"; "Loaded Trucks by Rail,"
     785.

11. Untitled article, *TTW*, Jan. 25, 1930, p. 236; "Chicago Terminals
     Corporation," *TTW*, Aug. 15, 1931, p. 341.

12. Stanley H. Smith, "Motor Transport and the Return Load," *TTW*,
     Feb. 22, 1930, pp. 505–506.

13. Homer A. Shannon, "Allied Van Lines, Inc.," *TTW*, Apr. 12, 1930,
     pp. 987–90.

14. Locklin, *Economics of Transportation*, 646; Donald V. Harper,
     Economic Regulation of the Motor Trucking Industry by the States
     (Urbana: Univ. of Illinois Press, 1959), 17–19.

15. "How a Motor Freight Line Operates," *TTW*, Jan. 17, 1931, pp.
     159–62.

16. "Coordination of Motor Transportation: A Report by Leo J. Flynn,
     Attorney-Examiner to the ICC," *Senate Documents*, No. 43, 72nd
     Cong., 1st Sess., Jan. 1932, pp. 36–37; *Facts and Figures of the
     Automobile Industry* (1924), 21 (1931), 37; "Coordinating Highway
     Transportation," *TTW*, Sept. 19, 1931, pp. 615, 618–19.

17. *Senate Hearings on S 2793*, Committee on Interstate Commerce,
     72nd Cong., 1st Sess., 1932, p. 67; *Senate Hearings on S 1629*,
     Committee on Interstate Commerce, 74th Cong., 1st Sess., 1935, p.
     309. For another example of consolidation to meet competition, see
     "Chicago Terminals Corporation," 341.

18. *Sen. Hearings on S 2793*, pp. 66–67.

19. Harper, *Economic Regulation by States*, 10.

20. Ibid., 39. Locklin, *Economics of Transportation*, 645, quotes a
     government study that suggested trucking "epitomizes the classical

model of 'perfect' competition." Kahn, *Economics of Regulation,* II,
172–93, analyzes trucking through the concept of "destructive
competition," and concludes that trucking probably would not have
succumbed to intense competition.

21.   I have found no statistics estimating the number of gypsy truckers
engaged in over-the-road operations in the early 1930s, but according
to National Automobile Chamber of Commerce compilations (based
upon statistics furnished by the U.S. Bureau of Public Roads),
900,304 trucks were on the farm in 1932. From a total of 1,100,000
privately owned trucks, that leaves 199,696 privately owned trucks
not connected to the farm. Some of these were local cartage trucks.
In 1935 the ATA estimated that there were 43,000 local cartage
trucks, some of which were common carriers and other contract
carriers. To be conservative, I subtracted all 43,000 from 199,696 to
arrive at 156,696. The normative evidence in the text provides a
more important basis for analysis of the effect of the gypsy truckers.
Remember that the figure 150,000 is an estimate and that it was
always changing as truckers went bankrupt and exited the business
while others were just entering. For the NACC statistics, see *Sen.
Hearings on S 2793,* p. 67, and for the ATA statistics, see *House
Hearings on HR 5236* and *HR 6061,* Subcommittee of Committee on
Interstate and Foreign Commerce, 74th Cong., 1st Sess., 1935, pp.
30–31.

22.   S. S. Caldwell to Edward F. Loomis, Feb. 1, 1928, in NA, RG 9,
NRA, Edward F. Loomis Files, Tray 2029, folder Douglas Truck
Manuf. Co., Omaha, Neb.; Ben. H. Petty, *Truck Operating Costs,* 5,
7; Shannon, "Fruit and Vegetable Shipments Go to Trucks," *TTW,*
Mar. 26, 1932, p. 682; "Motor Transport," *TTW,* May 3, 1930, p.
1167; "Memoirs of Wilbur Dean," *Woods Truck Library,* 22–26;
Moulton, *Transportation Problem,* pp. 521–22, 609–10.

23.   "Dean Memoirs," 20–21; "Memoirs of Wayne E. Klink, Sr.," *Woods
Truck Library,* 32, 43–44.

24.   "Memoirs of Harry D. Woods," *Woods Truck Library,* 2, 5–6. The
following narrative was constructed from scattered references in these
memoirs, 12, 20–25, 28–29, 33–37, 43, 49–52, 57, 62–63, 71,
73–74, 89–92, 98–99, 121–23, 127, 128–29, 134, 138, 142,
146–47, 154. See also, "Dean Memoirs," 13, 21.

25.   "Woods Memoirs," 71.

26.   Ibid.

27.   *House Hearings on HR 5236, 6061,* p. 54. See "N.Y. to Chicago
Tractor Service," *TTW,* Nov. 7, 1931, p. 1011; "Woods Memoirs,"
61.

28.   *House Hearings on HR 5236, HR 6061,* pp. 40–41, 98–101, 111,
341–42.

29.   Ibid., 100–101, 108–109; *Sen. Hearings on S 1629,* p. 294.

30. William E. Leuchtenburg, *The Perils of Prosperity, 1914–1932* (Chicago: Univ. of Chicago Press, 1958), 245, 259.

31. For a concise listing of the motor truck's advantages, see Edward Loomis, "Railway and Motor Truck Competition," *Motor Transportation* (Austin, Tex.) (Nov. 1931), 16.

32. *Sen. Hearings on S 1629*, p. 295.

33. "New Haven Fights Trucks," *TTW*, July 11, 1931, p. 81; "Meeting Motor Competition," *TTW*, Oct. 11, 1930, p. 901; Joseph B. Eastman to William Hirth, Feb. 3, 1932, JBE Papers. Despite persuasive arguments in favor of increasing federal support of highway construction, President Hoover declined to substantially increase federal monies in that area. See W. P. Holaday to Walter Newton, Nov. 21, 1930, Presidential Papers, Box 172, Highways 1930, Apr.–Dec., Hoover Papers. Indeed, Federal expenditures dropped proportionately from 1920 to 1930. See "Road Building Sets Record for Employment," press release, Sept. 29, 1931, Presidential Papers, Box 172, Highways 1931, Hoover Papers. The Hayden-Cartwright Road Act of June 1934 did authorize expenditures of $522 million for road work, but it also included provisions for matching state funds and for the reduction of emergency highway monies. See "The Hayden-Cartwright Road Act," press release, June 18, 1934, Official File 129, Box 1, Roads & Highways, Jan.–Dec. 1934, Franklin D. Roosevelt Papers, Franklin D. Roosevelt Presidential Library, Hyde Park, N.Y.

34. *House Hearings on HR 5236, HR 6061*, pp. 23–24.

35. Moulton, *Transportation Problem*, 883–86. Moulton included an entire chapter on the thorny issue of truck subsidies, Chapter 25. On government subsidies to the railroads, see Lloyd J. Mercer, "Taxpayers or Investors: Who Paid for the Land-Grant Railroads?" *BHR* 46 (Autumn 1972), 279–94.

36. Henry Adams, *The Education of Henry Adams* (Boston: Massachusetts Historical Society, 1918).

Chapter 3

1. "Report of the Transportation Conference Called by the Chamber of Commerce of the United States," Jan. 1924, pp. 3–19, Box 605, "Address of Secretary Hoover Before the National Conference on Street and Highway Safety at the U.S. Chamber of Commerce Building, Washington, D.C., Monday Morning, Dec. 15, 1924," pp. 1–8, Box 160, both in Commerce Papers, Hoover Papers. The report, "Relations of Highways and Motor Transport to Other Transportation Agencies," Nov. 2, 1923, was one of five committee reports submitted to the Transportation Conference, Box 504, ibid.

2. "Address of Secretary of Commerce Herbert Hoover at the Annual

Meeting of the United States Chamber of Commerce, Cleveland, Ohio, Evening of May 7, 1924," pp. 6, 14, and *passim,* Commerce Papers, Box 84, Hoover Papers. Atomistically structured industries like the bituminous coal industry proved least able to achieve associative cooperation. See Ellis W. Hawley, "Secretary Hoover and the Bituminous Coal Problem, 1921–1928," *BHR* 42 (Autumn 1968), 269.

3. David A. Shannon, *Between the Wars: America, 1919–1941*, 2nd ed. (Boston: Houghton Mifflin, 1979), 49–52. For the story of associationalism in the 1920s, see Robert F. Himmelberg, *The Origins of the National Recovery Administration: Business, Government, and the Trade Association Movement, 1921–1933* (New York: Fordham Univ. Press, 1976); Ellis W. Hawley, untitled essay in J. Joseph Hutchmacher and Warren I. Susman, eds., *Herbert Hoover and the Crisis of American Capitalism* (Cambridge, Mass.: Schenkman, 1973), 3–33; Hawley, "Three Factors of Hooverian Associationalism: Lumber, Aviation, and Movies, 1921–1930," in McCraw, ed., *Regulation in Perspective*, 95–123; Thomas C. Blaisdell, Jr., *The Federal Trade Commission: An Experiment in the Control of Business* (New York: Columbia Univ. Press, 1932); Davis, "The Transformation of the Federal Trade Commission," 437–55.

4. In perusing the Hoover Papers in West Branch, Iowa, I found no direct connection between Hoover and the truck associational movement. Historian Ellis Hawley, who is more familiar with the Hoover Papers, confirmed this conclusion, Hawley to author, July 8, 1980. While researching another topic in the minutes of the Federal Trade Commission for the 1920s and early 1930s, I found no references to the trucking associations.

5. Edward Walter Smykay, "The National Association of Railroad and Utility Commissioners as the Originators and Promoters of Public Policy for Public Utilities" (Ph.D. diss., Univ. of Wisconsin, 1955), 107.

6. Henry Carter Adams to DeFreest, Apr. 23, 1894, Letterbook, Henry Carter Adams Papers, Bentley Historical Library, University of Michigan, Ann Arbor. Smykay, "NARUC," 13, 22–24, 32–36, 42, 46–47; McFarland, *Judicial Control of the FTC and the ICC*, 103–106; *Houston, East and West Texas Railway Company* v. U.S., 234 *U.S.* 342 (1914).

7. Smykay, "NARUC," 333, 338; David E. Lilienthal and Irwin S. Rosenbaum, "Motor Carriers and the State: A Study in Contemporary Public Utility Legislation," *JLPUE* 2 (July, 1926) 3, p. 260. Smykay argues that NARUC's actions were far-sighted rather than self-serving as I suggest.

8. Smykay, "NARUC," 69, 341–42.

9.   See *Proceedings of the 37th Annual Convention of NARUC, 1925* (New York: NARUC, 1926), 313.

10. *Sen. Hearings on S 2793*, pp. 22, 27, 222; "Coordination of Motor Transportation," 113–19. At least one employee of the ICC did believe federal controls were necessary.

11. The distinction between direct and indirect regulation is based somewhat loosely on Alfred Kahn's definitions in *Economics of Regulation*, II, esp. 172 n. 2.

12. "Comparative Analysis of Motor Vehicle Laws of the North Eastern States Prepared for the Interstate Conference Called by the American Legislators Association Pursuant to a Resolution of the Pennsylvania Legislature" (pamphlet of graphs), ATA Central Files, Tray 1997, folder 700.

13. Ibid.

14. W. A. Sutherland to John R. Cowling, Jan. 24, 1935, Sutherland to C. J. Speicher, Jan. 25, 1935, both in ATA Central Files, Tray 1959, folder PMTA, 34; Stephen D. Bryce, Jr., to Henry C. Kelting, May 26, 29, 1930, Loomis Files, Tray 2034, folder Motor Truck Club of Kentucky; Tom Snyder to Kelting, Aug. 26, 1932, Carrington Papers.

15. *Sen. Hearings on S 2793*, pp. 77–78, 231.

16. Gradually, trucking leaders realized that much of their problem with legislation was the result of poor public relations. See, for example, the following articles in *Motor Transportation* (Barker Archives, Univ. of Texas, Austin): "The Public's Notion of the Motor Truck," 3 (Apr. 1930) 1, pp. 9–10; "Beware, Truckmen," 3 (Aug. 1930) 5, p. 13; "Lack of Courtesy May Be Real Secret of Our Troubles," 5 (Apr. 1932) 1, p. 11.

17. Kenneth G. Crawford, *The Pressure Boys: The Inside Story of Lobbying in America* (New York: Julian Messner, 1939), 245, 259–63; *Ohio Truck Journal*, 1 (Mar. 15, 1932) 1, pp. 1–4, Tray 2045, folder Ohio Association of Commercial Haulers, Kelting to Loomis, June 6, 1933, Tray 2034, folder Kentucky Assoc. & Legisl. Data, both in Loomis Files; C. O. Sherrill to General B. H. Markham, Jan. 2, 1934, ATA Central Files, Tray 1965, folder 115.16; "Memoirs of Maurice Tucker," *Woods Truck Library*, 25–34.

18. "Minutes of the Meeting of the Truck Owners Association Held at the Chamber of Commerce, Nov. 28, 1930, Charlotte, N.C.," Loomis Files, Tray 2044, folder N.C.T. Owners Assoc.

19. *Ohio Truck Journal* 1 (Mar. 15, 1932) 1, p. 1, Loomis Files, Tray 2045, folder Ohio Assn. of Commercial Haulers.

20. Roy H. Compton to Loomis, Aug. 15, 1933, ATA Central Files, Tray 1961, folder California.

21. Snyder to E. R. Greenlaw, July 5, 1932, Snyder to Kelting, July 15,

1932, Kelting to Carrington, Aug. 4, 1932, Snyder to Frank E. Kirby, June 19, 1933, all in Carrington Papers.

22. "Report of Eastern Meeting: The Fifth Meeting of Truck Association Executives of America," July 16–17, 1930, pp. 1–41, Loomis Files, Tray 2049, folder Tr. Assn. Execs. of Am.

23. "Report of Detroit Meeting: The Seventh Meeting of Truck Association Executives of America," Jan. 11–13, 1932, *ibid.*; Snyder to Dan R. Lamson, Aug. 22, 1932, Snyder to R. S. Burnett, Aug. 22, 1932, Snyder to Kelting, Aug. 22, 1932, all in Carrington Papers.

24. Caldwell to Loomis, Feb. 1, 1928, Loomis to Caldwell, Feb. 23, 1928, Caldwell to Loomis, Oct. 19, 1931, all in Loomis Files, Tray 2029, folder Douglas Truck Manuf. Co.

25. Loomis to Caldwell, Nov. 29, 1927, *ibid.*; Loomis to H. O. Kemp, Jan. 21, 1932, Loomis Files, Tray 2034, folder Kentucky Assoc. & Legisl. Data.

26. Loomis to T. A. Horrocks, Dec. 15, 1930, Loomis Files, Tray 2038, folder Minn. Truck Assn.; Loomis to J. F. Winchester, Apr. 14, 1931, Loomis Files, Tray 2042, folder Motor Tr. Club of New Jersey; "Report of Field Representative Walton Schmidt, Kansas City, June 7, 1932," Loomis Files, Tray 2039, folder Mo. Assn. & Legisl. Data.

27. Joseph H. Hays to Loomis, Feb. 7, 1931, Tray 2034, folder Iowa Truckers Assn., Loomis to Charles E. Hall, July 14, 1931, Tray 2042, folder Nebr. Motor Transport Assn., Loomis to James V. Yarnell, Nov. 6, 1931, Tray 2036, folder Motor Tr. Owners Assn. of Md., Loomis to Horrocks, Sept. 20, 1932, Tray 2038, folder Minn. Truck Assn., all in Loomis Files.

28. *N.A.C.C. Truck Department Expands*, Motor Truck Assoc. Bulletin, No. 29, Mar. 25, 1930, Tray 2033, folder Ind. Motor Truck Assn., John V. Lawrence to Linwood E. Porter, Dec. 30, 1932, Tray 2036, folder Commercial Motor Vehicle Assn. of Maine, both in Loomis Files.

29. Loomis to Kemp, Jan. 21, 1932, Tray 2034, folder Kentucky Assn. & Legisl. Data, Loomis to Caldwell, Oct. 6, 1930, Tray 2029, folder Douglas Truck Mfg. Co., "Reports of Joint Meeting Between Truck Committee . . . and a Special Committee . . . ," Mar. 15, 1932, Tray 2049, folder Fed. Truck Assns. of Am., Inc., Misc., all ibid.; Snyder to Lamson, Aug. 22, 1932, Snyder to Sutherland, Sept. 1, 1932, both in Carrington Papers.

30. Loomis to Earnest Reeves, Mar. 11, 1931, "Report of Field Representative Walton Schmidt, June 7, 1932, both in Tray 2039, folder Mo. Assn. & Legisl. Data, Loomis Files.

31. Arthur C. Butler to John Osstedal, Jan. 14, 1932 [1933], Loomis Files, Tray 2044, folder N. Dak. Assn. & Legisl. Data.

32. "Bulletin," Regulated Motor Carrier, Inc. of Indiana, Oct. 24, 1932,
     p. 2 and Apr. 17, 1933, p. 4, NA, RG 9, NRA, Central Files of the
     American Highway Freight Association, Tray 1957, folder 112;
     "Bulletin," Certified Motor Carriers of Pennsylvania, n.d., Files,
     Tray 2001, folder 715.31, Compton to Loomis, Aug. 15, 1933, Tray
     1961, folder Calif., both in ATA Central Files.

33. "Report of Field Representative Walton Schmidt, Mar. 26, 1931,"
     Loomis Files, Tray 2039, folder Mo. Assoc. & Legisl. Data. See
     Stuart Simmons to NACC, Aug. 8, 1933, Tray 1947, folder 121,
     Jack L. Keeshin to H. C. Davis, Feb. 18, 1933, Tray 1955, folder
     011, both in AHFA Central Files.

34. William F. Ardern to Sutherland, Nov. 25, 1931, Tray 1955, folder
     013, Roy E. Steller to C. B. Guthrie, July 7, 1932, J. P. Dempsey to
     O. B. Sutton, Jan. 24, 1933, both in Tray 1956, folder 059, *Motor
     Freight* clippings (Jan. and Feb. 1933), Tray 1955, unmarked folder,
     all in AHFA Central Files.

35. Charles E. Cotterill to Malcolm Muir, July 29, 1933, Loomis Files,
     Tray 2041, folder NRA; Cotterill to Keeshin, Jan. 23, 1933, folder
     019.1, Keeshin to P. L. Greenbury, Dec. 27, 1932, folder 021.1,
     both in AHFA Central Files, Tray 1955.

36. Dempsey to Ray Fairbanks, Feb. 3, 1933, Tray 1956, folder 050,
     Keeshin to Joe Preston, Apr. 29, 1933, Tray 1955, folder 020,
     Maurice Connellan to AHFA, May 4, 1933, Tray 1956, folder
     054.1, Dempsey to H. C. Mims, Dec. 16, 1932, Tray 1956, folder
     050, John R. Bingaman to Dempsey, Nov. 28, 1932, Tray 1955,
     folder 013, all in AHFA Central Files.

37. AHFA to members, Jan. 10, 1933, Tray 1956, folder 050, Cotterill
     to Keeshin, Jan. 23, 1933, Tray 1955, folder 019.1, AHFA to
     members, Dec. 22, 1932, Tray 1955, folder 014, all ibid.

38. For a view of another industry, see Hawley, "Hoover and Bituminous
     Coal," 269. For a broad view of how the truck associational
     movement fits the pattern of associationalism in another industry, see
     note 46, Ch. 6.

Chapter 4

1.   See LaRue Brown and Stuart N. Scott, "Regulation of the Contract
     Motor Carrier Under the Constitution," *HLR* 44 (Feb. 1931),
     530–71.

2.   Paul L. Murphy, *The Constitution in Crisis Times, 1918–1969* (New
     York: Harper, 1972), Chs. 2, 3, 4, and 5.

3.   John B. Prizer, "Development of the Regulation of Transportation
     During the Past Seventy-five Years," *I.C.C. Practitioners' Journal* 21
     (Dec. 1953), 192, 193–94. See Gerald L. Turnbull, *Traffic and*

Transport: An Economic History of Pickfords (Boston: George Allen and Unwin, 1979), 91.

4. Felix Frankfurter, *The Commerce Clause* (Chicago: Quadrangle, 1964), 26–27, 34, 50–53.

5. *Munn* v. *Illinois*, 94 U.S. 113 (1887), 124–29, 130–34 . For two contrasting views of Waite's use of common law precedent, see Breck P. McAllister, "Lord Hale and Business Affected with a Public Interest," *HLR* 43 (Mar. 1930), 759–91, wherein Waite is taken to task for arguing from the particular to the general, and Harry N. Scheiber, "The Road to *Munn*: Eminent Domain and the Concept of Public Purpose in the State Courts," *Perspectives in American History*, 5 (1971), 327–402, wherein Scheiber effectively counters that Waite was on firm ground in announcing the "affected with a public interest" doctrine.

6. Frankfurter, *Commerce Clause*, 83.

7. *Munn* v. *Illinois*, 94 U.S. 136–54. See also Stanley I. Kutler, *The Supreme Court and the Constitution: Readings in American Constitutional History* (Boston: Houghton Mifflin, 1969), 225–46.

8. Kutler, *Supreme Court and Constitution*, 251–57. Kutler quotes, p. 251, from *Stone* v. *Farmers' Loan & Trust Co.*, 116 U.S. 307 (1886). *Smyth* v. *Ames*, 169 U.S. 466 (1898).

9. *United States* v. *E. C. Knight Co.*, 156 U.S. 1 (1895). See Kutler, *Supreme Court and Constitution*, 267.

10. See Kutler, *Supreme Court and Constitution*, 271–77, 282–93, 337–43, 347–55.

11. *Wolff Packing Co.* v. *Court of Industrial Relations*, 26 U.S. 522 (1923), in Kutler, *Supreme Court and Constitution*, 357.

12. *Tyson and Brothers—United Theatre Ticket Offices, Inc.* v. *Banton*, 273 U.S. 418 (1927), 455. See also Stanley I. Kutler, "Chief Justice Taft, National Regulation, and the Commerce Power," *JAH* 51 (Mar. 1956) 4, pp. 651–68.

13. *Nebbia* v. *New York*, 291 U.S. 502 (1934); Frankfurter, *Commerce Clause*, 88.

14. *Michigan Public Utilities Commission et al.* v. *Duke*, 266 U.S. 570 (1925), 574–75 . See also Brown and Scott, "Regulation of Contract Carrier," n. 32 and pp. 541–42.

15. *Michigan PUC et al.* v. *Duke*, 266 U.S. 575–78.

16. *Buck* v. *Kuykendall*, 267 U.S. 307 (1925), 313, 315–16.

17. *George W. Bush & Sons* v. *Maloy*, 267 U.S. 317 (1925), 323–25. Research in the Brandeis Papers at the Harvard Law School Library indicated the *Buck* and *Bush* decisions created little reaction in the Court's deliberations. See 27–7, *Buck* v. *Kuykendall*, and 27–8, *Bush* v. *Maloy*.

18. *Bush* v. *Maloy*, 267 U.S. 325–28. For a typical view of McReynolds' abilities, see Henry J. Abraham, *Justices and Presidents: A Political History of Appointments to the Supreme Court* (New York: Oxford Univ. Press, 1974), 166.

19. Karl Stecher, "Proposed Federal Regulation of Interstate Carriers by Motor Vehicle," *Minn. LR* 17 (Dec. 1932), 1; *Hendrick* v. *Maryland*, 235 U.S. 619 (1914).

20. *NARUC Proceedings* (1925), 278–81ff; NARUC to state commissioners, Mar. 26, 1925, Commerce Papers, Box 418, folder NARUC 1922–26, Hoover Papers; Lilienthal and Rosenbaum, "Motor Carriers and the State," 259–62.

21. *Frost, et al.* v. *Railroad Commission of State of California*, 271 U.S. 583 (1926), 591–92, 599, 600–602. See also Brown and Scott, "Regulation of Contract Carrier," 536 n. 17.

22. *Smith* v. *Cahoon*, 283 U.S. 533 (1930).

23. LaRue Brown to R. S. Armstrong, Mar. 29, 1932, Loomis Files, Tray 2034, folder Kentucky Assn. & Legisl. data.

24. Ellis, "Texas Cotton Compress Industry," 328–30, 334–36.

25. *Sproles et al.* v. *Binford*, 286 U.S. 374 (1932), 380–83.

26. *Sproles* v. *Binford*, 286 U.S. 374, 376–79, 383–87.

27. *Sproles* v. *Binford*, 286 U.S. 383–87; Brown to C. E. Childe, June 14, 1932, Loomis Files, Tray 2033, folder Ind. Motor Truck Assn.

28. *Sproles* v. *Binford*, 286 U.S. 388–89.

29. *Sproles* v. *Binford*, 286 U.S. 389–90, 390–91. See Murphy, *Constitution in Crisis*, 115 n. 42. *Nebbia* and *West Coast Hotel* v. *Parish*, 300 U.S. 379 (1937), marked the end of the use of "freedom of contract." Obviously, *Sproles* contributed as well.

30. *Sproles* v. *Binford*, 286 U.S. 393.

31. *Sproles* v. *Binford*, 286 U.S. 391–92, 394.

32. "Two Decisions Spur Rail War on Trucks," *New York Times*, June 26, 1932, IV, 1.

33. William F. Swindler, *Court and Constitution in the 20th Century: The Old Legality, 1889–1932* (New York: Bobbs-Merill, 1969), 319, App. A; Murphy, *Constitution in Crisis*, 45, 104–105.

34. Merlo J. Pusey, *Charles Evans Hughes* (New York: Macmillan, 1952), II, 696–97, 671–79. Research in the Stone and Hughes Papers at the Library of Congress turned up little material on *Sproles*. Michal Belknap to author, Nov. 6, 1980.

35. See V. E. Phelps, "The Right to Regulate Contract Motor Carriers for Hire," *Public Utilities Fortnightly* 10 (Aug. 18, 1932), 202–11, esp. 211, where the author argues that since the rails carried 76 percent of the nation's freight, their position should be protected; otherwise, all of the nation's businesses might suffer.

36. *Stephenson et al.* v. *Binford*, 287 U.S. 251 (1932); Pusey, *Hughes*, 679.

37. *Stephenson* v. *Binford*, 287 U.S. 261, 262–63; J. Byron McCormick, "The Regulation of Motor Transportation," *Calif. LR* 22 (Nov. 1933), 46.

38. Ibid., 265, 266–69.

39. *Stephenson* v. *Binford*, 287 U.S. 269–71, 272.

40. Ibid., 273–76, 276 (Sutherland quoted *Sproles* at 394); Joel Francis Paschal, *Mr. Justice Sutherland: A Man Against the State* (Princeton: Princeton Univ. Press, 1952), 165–66.

41. *Stephenson* v. *Binford*, 287 U.S. 258; McCormick, "The Regulation of Motor Transportation," 50, suggests that the justices may have compromised on the public interest doctrine.

42. *Nebbia* v. *New York*, 291 U.S. 502 (1934), 539–59, 536, 539.

43. Ibid., 536–37.

44. Murphy, *Constitution in Crisis*, 105–107.

45. "Texas Law Disappoints Railroads," *Motor Transport* 6 (May 1933) 2, p. 1.

46. *Wabash, St. Louis, & Pacific Railroad Company* v. *Illinois*, 118 U.S. 557 (1886).

47. Nearly fifty years later the Supreme Court again faced trucks and state regulation of interstate commerce. See "Trucking Dispute May Define State Power over Commerce," *WSJ*, Feb. 17, 1981; "Top Court Bars Iowa Legislation on Truck Size," *WSJ*, Mar. 25, 1981.

Chapter 5

1. Of course, tariff and monetary policies attempted to control the effects of industrialism, but no institutions like the regulatory commission were used. For incisive accounts of railroad regulation, see Lee Benson, *Merchants, Farmers, and Railroads: Railroad Regulation and New York Politics, 1850–1887* (Cambridge, Mass.: Harvard Univ. Press, 1955); George H. Miller, *Railroads and the Granger Laws* (Madison: Univ. of Wisconsin Press, 1971). The Supreme Court forced Congress to act when in 1886 it ruled that state rail laws interfered with interstate commerce, *Wabash* v. *Illinois*, 118 U.S. 557. For a general analysis of business-government relations in this period, see Robert H. Wiebe, *The Search for Order, 1877–1920* (New York: Hill and Wang, 1967).

2. I. L. Sharfman, *The Interstate Commerce Commission: A Study in Administrative Law and Procedure* (New York: Commonwealth Fund, 1931–37), I, pp. 11–32. Sharfman's multivolume study of the ICC remains one of the most complete factual accounts of the

commission's first fifty years. His analysis tends to be overly complimentary of the regulators, and he believes too uncritically in progressive reform, but he also perceptively describes the complex factors involved in public regulation of private management. For a good study of the first ten years of ICC administration, see John H. Churchman, "Federal Regulation of Railroad Rates, 1880–1898" (Ph.D. diss., Wisconsin, 1976).

3.   Sharfman, *ICC*, I, 35–40.

4.   Ibid., 40–52. For political analyses of the Progressive Era, see Lewis L. Gould, *Reform and Regulation: American Politics, 1900–1916* (New York: Wiley & Sons, 1978); Robert H. Wiebe, *Businessmen and Reform: A Study of the Progressive Movement* (Chicago: Quadrangle, 1962).

5.   Sharfman, *ICC*, I, 52–60; *Houston, East and West Texas Railway* v. *U.S.* 234 U.S. 342.

6.   Albro Martin, *Enterprise Denied: The Origins of the Decline of American Railroads, 1897–1917* (New York: Columbia Univ. Press, 1971). Martin lucidly analyzes the problems facing the railways during the Progressive Era and argues that the "archaic progressives" (as he derisively labels the shippers and reformers) prevented the railways from preparing for the strains of an expanding economy.

7.   Sharfman, *ICC*, I, Ch. 4; Martin, *Enterprise Denied*, 354; Kathel Austin Kerr, *American Railroad Politics, 1914–1920* (Pittsburgh: Univ. of Pittsburgh Press, 1968), Chs. 3–5.

8.   Kerr, *Railroad Politics*, 162–66, 213; JBE to the Committee on Interstate Commerce of the United States Senate, July 8, 1919, JBE Papers.

9.   For a concise and illuminating discussion of pragmatism, see Paul K. Conkin, *The New Deal*, 2nd ed. (Arlington Heights, Ill.: AHM, 1975), 10–12.

10.   See JBE to W. H. Chandler, Sept. 11, 1922, JBE Papers.

11.   Sharfman, *ICC*, IV, 371–73, vacillates on this point, admitting such progress was minimal. Nevertheless, he asserts that these activities reflected the purpose of the commission, which was "to maintain a moving balance between private rights and public interests by directing their various manifestations into nationally desirable channels" (p. 375).

12.   McFarland, *Judicial Control of the FTC and the ICC*, 103ff, 168–69.

13.   Martin, *Enterprise Denied*, 159; Kerr, *Railroad Politics*, 162–66, 180, Ch. 7.

14.   Sharfman, *ICC*, I, 196–235, 177–79, 182–95, 235–44. Sharfman's analysis here is a bit muddled, for he attempts to differentiate between normal powers and those attending emergency conditions, when the ICC was not required to consider the maintenance of

competition. In effect, the act empowered the ICC to compel management to follow its directions, whether in times of emergency or not. Of course, the lack of an emergency would (and did) tend to harden the rail executives against ICC intrusion into management functions.

15. Sharfman, *ICC*, I, 132–37, 243, IV, 53–55.

16. Ibid., *ICC*, III-A, 90.

17. Ibid., 93, 6–8, 20–21, 91.

18. Ibid., IV, 53–55, 293–95.

19. Ibid., 296–99; Smykay, "NARUC," 410–18.

20. See George W. Anderson to Editor, *Boston Herald*, Oct. 15, 1918, JBE Papers, for an early view of the dedicated staff; Sharfman, *ICC*, IV, 295–96 n. 30.

21. See Howard L. Bevis, "Procedure in the Interstate Commerce Commission: A Study in Administrative Law," *Univ. of Cincinnati LR* I (May 1927) 3, pp. 241–56. Bevis argued that ICC procedure, based as it was on justice in individual cases, precluded prediction of what the ICC might do, thus deterring business initiative.

22. Sharfman, *ICC*, III-A, Ch. 7, pp. 134–37; JBE to Felix Frankfurter, May 31, 1929, JBE Papers.

23. George W. Anderson to JBE, Oct. 24, 1921, JBE to William Z. Ripley, Apr. 2, 1927, both JBE Papers; Sharfman, *ICC*, III-A, 474–501.

24. Sharfman, *ICC*, I, 227–35, IV, 55 n. 180; Letter to State Commissions, Mar. 26, 1925, Commerce Papers, Box 428, folder NARUC 1922–26, Hoover Papers; Wilbur LaRue, Jr., to Clyde B. Aitchison, Oct. 15, 1925, Box 13, Misc. Corresp., Clyde B. Aitchison Papers, Univ. of Oregon, Eugene, in which LaRue reports that Senator Albert Cummins admitted to him that Congress had been unfair in dumping the Hoch-Smith task upon the ICC.

25. "Statement by Secretary of Commerce Before the Interstate Commerce Commission, Feb. 4, 1932," Commerce Papers, Box 297, folder ICC 1922 Jan., Hoover Papers. Moulton, *Transportation Problem*, 41–47, did not consider the $5.72 billion as misdirected investment in a declining industry and suggested that some operating economies resulted from the investment.

26. *Historical Statistics of the United States* (Washington: GPO, 1975), Pt. 2, pp. 730, 733.

27. Aitchison to Commission, Apr. 23, 1925, Box 8, Vol. 17–18, Aitchison Papers; B.S. Robertson to W.P. Bartel, June 1, 1925, Box 8, Vol. 17–18, Aitchison Papers; JBE to John Esch, May 17, Sept. 1, 1926, both in JBE Papers. In the latter, Eastman, restating his position that the investigation exceeded ICC powers, agreed

nonetheless that the commission should hold a conference with NARUC on the subject. "Motor Bus and Truck Operation," 696–98.

28. "Motor Bus and Truck Operation," 723, 742, 746.

29. "Coordination of Motor Transportation," 1–2 and *passim*, esp. 93–95, 101–102, 113–19; Loomis to Horrocks, Dec. 22, 1930, Loomis Files, Tray 2038, folder Minn. Truck Assn.; Aitchison to C.R. Sherrington, Apr. 21, 1932, Sherrington to Aitchison, May 11, 1932, Box 14, folder Misc. Corresp. 1932–52, Aitchison Papers. See also JBE to James S. Parker, Feb. 18, 1931, JBE Papers.

30. Harry Barnard, *Independent Man: The Life of Senator James Couzens* (New York: Scribner's Sons, 1958), 85–94; *Sen. Hearings on S 2793*, pp. 74–75; JBE to Grenville Clark, Mar. 30, 1932, JBE Papers. Periodic regulatory bills had been submitted since 1926.

31. *Sen. Hearings on S 2793*, pp. 1–19, 22.

32. *Ibid.*, 26–27, 41, 185–96, 205–209, 58–83, 96–97.

33. *Ibid.*, 238–77, 151, 153.

34. JBE to Legislative Committee, Sept. 16, 1932, JBE Papers; Jordan A. Schwartz, *The Interregnum of Despair: Hoover, Congress, and the Depression* (Urbana: Univ. of Illinois Press, 1970), Ch. 5, pp. 106–41.

35. Lamont to Hoover, Nov. 20, 1931, Presidential Papers, Box 244, RRs Corresp., 1931 Nov., Hoover Papers.

36. McCraw, "Regulation in America," 160–62.

37. Leverett S. Lyon and Victor Abramson, *Government and Economic Life: Development and Current Issues of American Public Policy* (Washington: Brookings Institution, 1940), II, 862. For a more positive and intriguing view of regulation, see Victor P. Goldberg, "Regulation and Administered Contracts," *BellJ* 7 (Autumn 1976) 2, pp. 426–45.

Chapter 6

1. See "The Transportation Problem," *TTW*, Dec. 3, 1932, pp. 1063–66. See Hawley, *The New Deal and Monopoly*, esp. 35, 283–84.

2. William E. Leuchtenburg, *Franklin D. Roosevelt and the New Deal, 1932–1940* (New York: Harper and Row, 1963), p. 17, Ch. 3; Conkin, *The New Deal*, Ch. 1.

3. Himmelberg, *Origins of the NRA*, Ch. 1; Michael E. Parrish, *Securities Regulation and the New Deal* (New Haven: Yale Univ. Press, 1970); Blaisdell, *The Federal Trade Commission*.

4. Bernard Bellush, *The Failures of the NRA* (New York: Norton, 1975), 26.

5.   Hawley, *The New Deal and Monopoly*, Ch. 7; Sidney Fine, *The Automobile Under the Blue Eagle: Labor, Management, and the Automobile Manufacturing Code* (Ann Arbor: Univ. of Michigan Press, 1963).

6.   Bingaman to W. H. Brearly, June 30, 1933, Central Files, Tray 1957, folder 111; Cotterill to Muir, July 29, 1933, Loomis Files, Tray 2041, folder NRA; "Highway Freight Association," *TTW*, Nov. 26, 1932, pp. 1039–40.

7.   Telegram, Keeshin to C. A. Courchene, June 21, 1933, AHFA Central Files, Tray 1956, folder 080; Keeshin to Finance Committee, June 21, 1933, Loomis Files, Tray 2038, folder Minn. Truck Assn.

8.   "Truckers Organize for Code," *TTW*, July 15, 1933, p. 101; "Conference of the Highway Transportation Industry, Chicago, Illinois, June 11–12, 1933," Loomis Files, Tray 2023, folder AHFA; "Truck Operators' Code," *TTW*, July 29, 1933, p. 185. The July 11–12 meeting was called after AHFA members stymied progress at an earlier joint conference in late June. Executive Secretary to A. J. Lindsey, July 3, 1933, AHFA Central Files, Tray 1957, folder 111.

9.   Press Release, "Truck Owner Industry Problem Faces NIRA This Week," Aug. 6, 1933, Tray 2049, folder TONECC Hearing, Aug. 10, *NACC Motor Truck Bulletin*, No. M-345, Aug. 14, 1933, Tray 2040, folder NACC (General Bulletin), "Revised Copy of Code . . . File No. 1411/2/08," Federated Truck Associations of America, Aug. 21, 1933, "Proposed Code of Fair Competition for the Carriage of Property for Hire . . . ," AHFA, Aug. 21, 1933, both in Tray 2027, folder 2, all in Loomis Files.

10.   "Truck Operators' Code," *TTW*, Aug. 26, 1933, p. 345; Loomis to Ted V. Ro[d]gers, Aug. 25, 1933, Loomis Files, Tray 2023, folder AHFA; "Brashears Memorandum," n.d., pp. 1–2, ATA Central Files, Tray 1975, folder 300; "Volume A, History of the Trucking Code," NA, RG 9, NRA, Division of Review, Approved Code Histories, 278 Part I, Box 7617, p. 7.

11.   "Highlights in the Life of Ted V. Rodgers, President of the American Trucking Associations, Inc.," Tray 2047, folder Publicity, Mims to Maurice Tucker, Oct. 4, 1933, Tray 2048, folder Officers, Directors, and Committee Members, both in Loomis Files. Apparently Keeshin's abrasive personality led to his loss of power. See Foster Moreton to Rodgers, Oct. 24, 1933, ATA Central Files, Tray 1963, folder 028; "Truck Associations' Merger,", Sept. 23, 1933, pp. 514–15.

12.   Rodgers to Moreton, Sept. 20, 1933, AHFA Central Files, Tray 1955, folder 019.4. Numerous industry members asked the NACC to release Loomis for work with the FTAA in August. See Alfred Reeves to Frank S. Schmidt, Aug. 10, 1933, Loomis Files, Tray 2040, folder NACC (NY). See also "Truckers for Regulation," *TTW*, Jan. 13, 1934, p. 87.

13. Loomis to F. E. Ertsman, Mar. 29, 1934, ATA Central Files, Tray 1960, folder 010.6; Mims to Keeshin, Oct. 4, 1933, Loomis Files, Tray 2048, folder Officers, Directors, and Committee Members; Morris H. Glazer to David L. Topham, Nov. 12, 1934, Tray 1975, folder 300, Nov., J. C. Nelson to 33 operators, Apr. 18, 1935, Tray 2003, folder 800.2, both in ATA Central Files.

14. "Brashears Memorandum," 2–4; "Progress Report of J. E. Murphy, Industrial Advisor Trucking Industry," n.d., pp. 1–4, ATA Central Files, Tray 1979, folder 312.5; Charles Dearing directed the research and writing of the Brookings Institution's study of the transport system in 1941, *American Highway Policy*. The man Dearing replaced was identified as "Mr. Baruch," presumably Bernard Baruch.

15. Loomis to Caldwell, Jan. 29, 1934, Tray 2030, folder Douglas Truck Manuf. Co. Neb., Rodgers to Edward McCready et. al., Feb. 1, 1934, Tray 2046, folder McCready-Rodgers Co., both in Loomis Files.

16. "Brashears Memorandum," 5; Loomis to Sherrill, Jan. 9, 1934, Tray 2048, folder Sherrill, Col. C. O., Rodgers to A. D. Aldrich, Sutherland, Harold S. Shertz, and Brearly, Jan. 26, 1934, Tray 2047, folder Mr. Rodgers (Personal), both in Loomis Files; "History of the Trucking Code," 11–12; Roy B. Thompson to Z. E. Jones, Feb. 16, 1934, ATA Central Files, Tray 1961, folder Calif. 921.4; C. O. Kuester to John L. Wilkinson, Nov. 22, 1933, H. B. Fowler to E. E. Hughes, Nov. 22, 1933, both in Tray 2044, folder NC Tr. Owners Assn., Loomis Files. On another area of dispute, see Thompson to Rodgers, Dec. 1, 1934, NA, RG 9, NRA, National Code Authority for the Trucking Industry, General File, Tray 2021, folder Dec. 1934 R.

17. Rodgers to George O. Griffin, Jan. 4, 1934, Loomis Files, Tray 2043, folder NY State Motor Truck Assn.; "Progress Report of Murphy," 6–7; D.S. Adams to Rodgers, Sept. 22, 1933, Tray 2040, folder South Western Motor Freight Assn., Mo., H.F. Sixtus to Rodgers, Nov. 22, 1933, E. G. Siedle to ATA, Nov. 21, 1933, both in Tray 2042, folder New Jersey, all in Loomis Files; "History of the Trucking Code," 12. See Hawley's *The New Deal and Monopoly* for an excellent analysis of the NRA and the issue of monopoly.

18. "Brashears Memorandum," 5; Shertz to Rodgers, Jan. 26, 1934, Tray 2048, folder Harold S. Shertz, Rodgers to Aldrich et al., Jan. 26, 1934, Tray 2047, folder Mr. Rodgers (Personal), both in Loomis Files; Rodgers to Harry E. Boysen, Feb. 2, 1934, ATA Central Files, Tray 1977, folder 300 Feb.

19. "Approved Code No. 278 of Fair Competition for the Trucking Industry as Approved on February 10, 1934, by President Roosevelt," *Codes of Fair Competition*, Feb. 1–Feb. 16, 1934 (Washington: GPO, 1934), VI, 432–34.

20.   Ibid., 435–50; "History of the Trucking Code," 97.

21.   "Code of Fair Competition for Trucking," 450–53. For a comparison
       of how another industry drafted a code of fair competition, see James
       P. Johnson, "Drafting the NRA Code of Fair Competition for the
       Bituminous Coal Industry," *JAH* 53 (Dec. 1966) 3, pp. 521–41.

22.   "History of the Trucking Code," 13, 39–40.

23.   Rodgers to H. E. Engel, Apr. 17, 1934, Tray 1987, folder 360.24
       Mo., Lawrence to Roger E. Hard, June 26, 1934, Tray 1988, folder
       360.38 RI, "NCA Memorandum No. 61," Sept. 8, 1934, Tray 1971,
       folder 240, all in ATA Central Files.

24.   "History of the Trucking Code," 25; J. R. Turney to Richard J.
       Welch, May 24, 1934, JBE Papers.

25.   "History of the Trucking Code," 26; "Minutes of the Meeting of the
       National Code Authority for the Trucking Industry Held at
       Headquarters, ATA, . . . Mar. 29, 1934," Tray 1980, folder Minutes
       NCA Meetings, Philip Jacobson to National Trucking Code
       Authorities, Mar. 30, 1934, Tray 1986, folder 360.4 Calif.,
       Thompson to E. E. Hughes, Mar. 7, 1934, Tray 1988, folder 360.31
       NY, William A. Randolph to Rodgers, June 23, 1934, Tray 1987,
       folder 360.19 Md., C. S. Morton to Loomis, July 14, 1934, Tray
       1966, folder 415.45 Va., Greenlaw to Rodgers, Feb. 19, 1934, Tray
       1960, folder 021.17 La., ATA Office Memo Morgan to Loomis,
       May 8, 1934, Tray 1961, folder 921.30 NM, Ed. F. Schwartz and
       Engel to Fred O. Nelson, Jr., May 3, 1934, Tray 1987, folder 360.24
       Mo., all in ATA Central Files.

26.   "Memorandum of Delays in the Development of Code and
       Administration Thereafter, Together with Recommendations," n.d.,
       2–4, ATA Central Files, Tray 2002, folder 761; "History of the
       Trucking Code," 16–17, 77–78, 73–75; Lawrence to Robert K.
       Carter, Jan. 24, 1935, ATA Central Files, Tray 1969, folder 221.36.

27.   R. T. Lauderbach to Loomis, Jan. 3, 1935, Tray 1979, folder
       312.11, Robert N. Springfield to Rodgers, June 13, 1934, Tray
       1991, folder 415.10, both in ATA Central Files.

28.   *House Hearings on HR 5236, HR 6061*, pp. 30–31, 264.

29.   "Division 2. Division Executive Memorandum No. 37, Apr. 19,
       1934: Procedure to Be Followed in Handling Complaints," ATA
       Central Files, Tray 1997, folder 600; "History of the Trucking
       Code," 93–94; Loomis to Shertz, Dec. 29, 1934, NCA General File,
       Tray 2021, folder Dec.34S; *ATA Registration Bulletin*, Aug. 6,
       1934, No. 10, ATA Central Files, Tray 1998, folder 710.2.

30.   "History of the Trucking Code," 39–40; "Brashears Memorandum,"
       10; Loomis to Frank S. Gottry, Dec. 1, 1934, NCA General File,
       Tray 2018, folder Dec. 1934 G; Lawrence to W. McNichols, Jan. 9,
       1935, Tray 1990, folder 4.5, E. X. Murphy to Benjamin G. Eyon,
       Feb. 13, 1935, Tray 1974, folder 240–A–37, "Memorandum on the

Effect of Second Report Coordinator of Transportation upon Code of Fair Competition for Trucking Industry and the N.R.A.," n.d., Tray 1977, folder 300, all in ATA Central Files.

31. For letters complaining of lack of enforcement and supporting the concept of rate agreements, see H. E. Howell to Hughes, Feb. 15, 1934, Tray 1967, folder 215, Chester G. Moore to Rodgers, May 3, 1934, Tray 2004, folder 905.12, A. W. Lewis to Rodgers, Oct. 24, 1934, Tray 1958, folder PMTA 1934, Loomis to H. D. Fenske, Dec. 6, 1934, Tray 2004, folder 905, all in ATA Central Files. For letters opposing rate agreements, see Fenske to Rodgers, Nov. 22, 1934, Loomis to Clinton S. Reynolds, Nov. 30, 1934, both in Tray 2004, folder 905, Memo Thomas H. MacDonald (Chief, Bureau of Public Roads) to Pyke Johnson (lobbyist for NACC), June 20, 1934, Tray 2004, folder 905.8, all in ATA Central Files; Judson C. Welliver to Rodgers, June 2, 1934, Loomis Files, Tray 2029, folder #7-Cost Formula.

32. Sol A. Rosenblatt, "Brief on Price-Fixing in Codes of Fair Competition," ATA Central Files, Tray 1967, folder 212.

33. C. F. Jackson to Earl Girard, Aug. 31, 1934, NCA General File, Tray 2018, folder August; Jackson to Claude R. High, Feb. 23, 1935, folder 905.11, Jackson to Kelting, Mar. 4, 1935, folder 905.16, Jackson to Roswell King, Apr. 24, 1935, folder 905.9, all in ATA Central Files, Tray 2004.

34. "History of the Trucking Code," 87; "Cost Formula—Trucking Industry," Division of Review, Box 7616, folder Vol. B; "Report of Meeting of Cost Formula Committee Held in Washington, D.C., April 29 and 30, 1935," Loomis Files, Tray 2029, folder Cost Formula Meeting.

35. T. D. Pratt to Rodgers, Sept. 24, 1934 (with attached unsigned letter of Sept. 13), Tray 1988, folder 360.31 NY, S. J. Cashel to Rodgers, Aug. 13, 1934, Tray 1987, folder 360.24 Mo., Springfield to W. J. Rea, Aug. 26, 1934, Tray 1987, folder 360.34 Miss., Arthur Tabb to Rodgers, Sept. 18, 1934, Tray 1964, folder 063, copy *Journal— Every Evening*, Wilmington, Del., Sept. 19, 1934, Tray 2002, folder 750, Jackson to Lindsey, Nov. 23, 1934, Tray 2005, folder 904.43, all in ATA Central Files; *ATA Registration Bulletin*, Sept. 24, 1934.

36. Snyder to Loomis, Aug. 16, 1930, Snyder to Hays, Nov. 16, 1931, both in Loomis Files, Tray 2049, folder Tr. Assn. Execs. of Am.

37. See H. B. Rubey to Rodgers, Oct. 26, 1934, Joe C. Carrington to Rodgers, Oct. 29, 1934, Gottry to Rodgers, Oct. 30, 1934, "Proceedings First Annual Convention of American Trucking Associations, Inc.," 95–99, all in AHFA Central Files, Tray 1956, folder 053.

38. "First ATA Convention," 3–10.

39. Ibid., 11–67; Claude Moore Fuess, *Joseph B. Eastman: Servant of the People* (New York: Columbia Univ. Press, 1964), 231.

40.   "First ATA Convention," 65, 82.

41.   See Rodgers to R. S. Koonce, Nov. 27, 1934, Tray 1988, folder
       360.32 N.C., Rodgers to Henry English, Dec. 11, 1934, Tray 1978,
       folder 300 Dec., Rodgers to C. F. Carey, Dec. 17, 1934, Tray 1987,
       folder 360.12 Mich., Jackson to W. R. Herfurth, Dec. 19, 1934,
       Tray 2005, folder 905.31, all in ATA Central Files; Lawrence to J.
       K. Orr, Nov. 6, 1934, NCA General File, Tray 2020, folder Nov.;
       Memo Edward S. Brashears to Loomis, Nov. 5, 1934, ATA Central
       Files, Tray 1975, folder 300 Nov.; Loomis to C. P. Clark, Nov. 21,
       1934, NCA General File, Tray 2017, folder Nov. C. With such
       stressful activity, Rodgers became physically weak, and his doctor
       ordered him to curtail his travels. See Rodgers to C. W. Abraham,
       Nov. 12, 1934, ATA Central Files, Tray 1962, folder 025.13.

42.   Loomis to Donald Richberg, Dec. 7, 1934, NCA General File, Tray
       2021, folder Dec. 34R; "List of Matters to Be Handled Before
       Registration Can Commence," Jan. 9, 1935, ATA Central Files, Tray
       1971, folder 240.4.

43.   Excerpts from Minutes of ATA Policy Committee Meeting, Lafayette
       Hotel, Washington, D.C., Jan. 7, 1935, Tray 1960, folder 013.1, J.
       Ninian Beall to John W. Miller, Mar. 1, 1935, Tray 1971, folder
       240.12, both in ATA Central Files; Rodgers to Moore, Mar. 7, 1935,
       NCA General File, Tray 2020, folder March 1935; Jackson to
       National Industrial Recovery Board, May 27, 1935, Loomis Files,
       Tray 2029, folder Cost Formula Revisions.

44.   Hawley, *The New Deal and Monopoly*, 233–34. Curiously, ATA
       lawyers attempted to redraft a code conforming to the *Schecter*
       decision, Lawrence to Reynolds, May 29, 1935, NCA General File,
       Tray 2021, folder May '35.

45.   "History of the Trucking Code," 84–85, 93, 97; "Memorandum from
       Matthews Ard to W. R. McComb, July 10, 1935," NA, RG 9,
       NRA, Consolidated Approved Industry File, Box 5580, folder
       Reports (Ard), pp. 11, 12. See Alfred D. Chandler, *The Visible
       Hand: The Managerial Revolution in American Business*
       (Cambridge, Mass.: Harvard Univ. Press, 1977), Ch. 4, pp. 137–43.
       In several respects, the history of the railroads in the 1860s and
       1870s, which Chandler describes, parallels that of the trucks in
       the 1920s and 1930s. Competition led to rate cutting, which would
       lead to ruination for everyone (eventually); enlightened
       businessmen (Albert Fink for the railways, Snyder and Rodgers for
       the truckers) saw cooperation as the mechanism that would forestall
       ruination; the businessmen therefore worked diligently to devise
       cooperative structures (railway pools, truck associations) to effect
       cooperation; lack of authority to enforce the agreements stymied
       success. The chief difference in the two periods lay in the
       government's absence in the earlier one and its clear presence in the
       latter one.

46. Shertz to James M. Naze, May 15, 1935, ATA Central Files, Tray 1994, folder 415.37; "Memo from Ard," 12. For a very fine analysis of the NRA period in another industry, see Fine, *The Automobile Under the Blue Eagle*. The telescoped nature of the truck associational movement is seen clearly when compared with the development of the textile industry's national trade association. In his case study, *Competition and Cooperation*, Louis P. Galambos suggested that a pattern of development existed for trade associations. The textile industry moved from informal "dinner-club associations" after the Civil War to "service associations" between 1900 and 1925 to "policy-shaping associations" between 1925 and 1937. In this case, the emergence of a business-government partnership took nearly eighty years to complete. In the trucking industry, a similar pattern developed, but within the space of less than fifteen years. The actions of Tom Snyder and the TAEA and Loomis and NACC in the early to late 1920s parallels that of the "dinner-club associations," wherein the executives only made casual contact with one another. With the NACC's concerted push in the late 1920s and early 1930s to organize state associations and to sponsor educational programs, the movement progressed into the service phase. The NRA period, then, saw the emergence of the ATA as not only a service organization, but also as a policy-shaping association. This will be shown more clearly in the following chapter.

Chapter 7

1. For studies of governmental control of the railways during World War I, see Kerr, *Railroad Politics,* and Walker D. Hines, *War History of American Railroads* (New Haven, 1928). Earl Latham, *The Politics of Railroad Coordination, 1933–36* (Cambridge, Mass.: Harvard Univ. Press, 1959), analyzes Eastman's performance as Coordinator in his dealings with the railroads, underplaying Eastman's participation in the Motor Carrier Act.

2. Latham, *Politics of Coordination,* 268–69, argues that Eastman did not exert his authority and power as coordinator to effect railway reorganization and concludes that Eastman was not politically minded enough to bring about the required changes. Yet, Eastman was indeed a political animal; he had to be to get Congress to authorize truck regulation. Moreover, as Eastman never tired of pointing out, the Emergency Transportation Act tied his hands; he could not effect coordination without reducing jobs, and the act forbade plans that reduced the number of railway jobs.

3. Fuess, *Eastman,* 175–77 and *passim.* Fuess's biography is overly sympathetic and should be used carefully.

4. Fuess, *Eastman,* 7, 8–18, 27–30, 33, 34.

5. Ibid., 37–44, 48–55, 61–67. For a scathing analysis of Brandeis's

style, see McCraw, "Rethinking the Trust Question," in McCraw, *Regulation in Perspective.*

6. Fuess, *Eastman,* 67–68, 71–74.

7. Ibid., 75.

8. Ibid.

9. Ibid., 78; JBE to Dwight N. Lewis, Feb. 7, 1920, JBE Papers.

10. Fuess, *Eastman,* 81–84.

11. JBE to Morris L. Cooke, Dec. 19, 1922, JBE to Commission, "Plan of Reorganization," Jan. 3, 1933, all in JBE Papers; Fuess, *Eastman,* 121, 159–63, 245ff, 252–55; *Excess Income of St. Louis & O'Fallon Ry. Co.,* 134 I.C.C. 39 (1927); series of letters, JBE to Louis Brandeis, Mar. 1929, JBE Papers.

12. For examples of Eastman's style of investigation, consultation, and compromise, see Memo to Aitchison, June 22, 1920 (re additional refrigerator cars for the Wenatchee Valley), JBE to George W. Norris, Jan. 23, 1928 (re rate making), Memo to Director of Inquiry, Apr. 16, 1930 (re investigation of forwarding companies), all in JBE Papers. Latham considered Eastman more like a judge, who came to determinations through "consultation, conciliation, and compromise" (*Politics of Coordination,* 267).

13. JBE to Committee on Interstate Commerce of the United States Senate, July 8, 1919, JBE to Mark W. Potter, Jan. 17, 1923, JBE to Clyde King, Sept. 15, 1919, JBE to Frankfurter, January 30, 1933, all in JBE Papers.

14. JBE to R.H. Aishton, Nov. 12, 1930, JBE Papers; "Eastman on Public Ownership," *TTW,* Nov. 14, 1931, p. 1059; JBE to Clyde King, Mar. 3, 1932, JBE to Col. Henry W. Anderson, Aug. 29, 1932, JBE to George W. Anderson, Nov. 9, 1932, all in JBE Papers.

15. Fuess, *Eastman,* 201.

16. JBE to Grenville Clark, Oct. 30, 1931, Memo to Legislative Committee, Dec. 21, 1931, JBE to Sam Rayburn, Dec. 30, 1931, JBE to James Couzens, Apr. 20, 1932, JBE to Anderson, Feb. 16, 1933, all in JBE Papers.

17. "How to Solve the Railroad Problem," *Railway Age,* Jan. 2, 1932, p. 8; "Getting Out of the Depression," *Railway Age,* Apr. 23, 1932, p. 677, 678.

18. "A Defense of the Commission," *Railway Age,* Mar. 26, 1932, p. 513; "Investigating the Railway Situation," *Railway Age,* Jan. 16, 1932, pp. 111–12; "Responsibility for the Railway Situation," *Railway Age,* Jan. 23, 1932, pp. 151–52.

19. "Seven Years of Trucking," *Railway Age,* Feb. 27, 1932, pp. 369–73; "How the Unregulated Trucks Injure Trade," *Railway Age,* Apr. 2, 1932, pp. 327–29; "The Railway Status and Outlook," *Railway Age,* Mar. 2, 1935, p. 322.

20.   For a sample of railway subsidy arguments, see the following articles
      in *Railway Age:* "Straight Thinking Needed on Highway Taxation,"
      July 13, 1935, p. 35; "Railroad Problems Not Complex," June 1,
      1935, pp. 859–60; "Are Highway Transport Tax Opinions Too
      Conservative," Mar. 12, 1932, pp. 527–28. For a sample of the
      truckers' perspective on the subsidy issue, see the following articles
      in *Motor Transportation:* "Trucks Roll Free Is Popular Fallacy" (Feb.
      1931), 7–8, "Transportation from the Trucks' Viewpoint" (May
      1931), 5–6; "Motor Carriers Pay Adequate Taxes" (June 1932),
      11–12. In *The Economics of Competition,* 66–85, John Meyer et al.,
      demonstrate the enormous difficulties involved in determining what
      the truckers should pay for the use of the highways. Different regions
      require different types of roads, depending upon topography and
      climate. Up until 1958, only three studies (in Louisiana, North
      Dakota, and Montana) furnished any useful information. Eastman
      recognized the difficulties as well. In the May 7, 1934, "Report of
      Joseph B. Eastman, Federal Coordinator of Transportation," JBE
      Papers, the Coordinator acknowledged, "The great difficulty in
      answering the question is encountered in the case of the highway
      carriers. It is necessary to arrive at a conclusion as to what portion of
      the highway system is a proper charge against general taxation and
      what portion should be carried by special taxation on the vehicles
      using it; what special taxes these vehicles now pay in addition to a
      fair share of general taxation; and how the special tax burden should
      fairly be divided among the various classes of vehicles." After
      investigation, the Coordinator reported that a "tentative report seems
      to be much more nearly satisfactory to the highway vehicle interests
      than to the railroads." JBE to Couzens, Feb. 19, 1935, JBE Papers.
      Indeed, the subsidy report was not released until 1940, under the
      title, *Public Aids to Transportation.* The report brought sharp debate
      that has not abated even today. See Latham, *Politics of Coordination,*
      215–16.

21.   The following articles appear in *Motor Transportation:* "Railroads
      Complain of Highway Competition" (Jan. 1931), 7, 9; "Motor Truck
      and Bus Transportation" (Aug. 1931), 13; "Depression, Not Trucks,
      Cut Rail Revenues" (Sept. 1932), 7; "General Business Conditions
      Cause of Rail Ills" (Dec. 1932), 8; "Trucks Roll Free Is Popular
      Fallacy," 7–8; "For Protection, Motor Carriers Mobilize" (Feb.
      1932), 9; "Transportation from the Trucks' Viewpoint," 5–6; "Is the
      Real Question Regulation or Un-Regulation?" (Mar. 1931), 9;
      "Railway and Motor Competition" (Nov. 1931), 16, 14; "Here's the
      Real Reason Why Railroads Need Help" (May 1932), 11; "Motor
      Carriers Pay Adequate Taxes," 12. A study of early railway laws
      suggests the charge of unhampered development was correct, but the
      truck apologists failed to note the difference in circumstances
      between the two historical periods. Railways developed more or less
      within a transport vacuum, while trucks tended to supplant existing
      facilities. Politically, moreover, the rails did not initially face power-

jealous state commissioners, as did the truckers. See Miller, *Railroads and the Granger Laws,* 42–48.

22. Conkin, *The New Deal,* 48; Latham, *Politics of Coordination,* 271–73; Fuess, *Eastman,* 198–99, 210. For example of Roosevelt's haphazard approach to transport policies, see George H. Dern to FDR, Dec. 18, 1934, President's Personal File 1820, Speech Material, Box 20, folder Transportation, "Report for a Coordinated Government Transportation Program by the Transportation Committee of the Business Advisory and Planning Council for the Department of Commerce," Official File 3q, Box 19, both in FDR Papers. On Eastman's desire for apolitical administration by an independent agency, see JBE to Hugh S. Johnson, June 25, 1934, JBE Papers. The movement for a DOT grew in the late 1930s. See Henry Morgenthau, Jr., Diary, Book 118, Apr. 5, 1938, pp. 155–58, 161–62, Book 119, Apr. 18, 1938, p. 278, Book 121, Apr. 27, 1938, pp. 136–37, Franklin D. Roosevelt Library, Hyde Park, New York.

23. JBE to John R. McCarl, July 20, 1933, JBE Papers; Latham, *Politics of Coordination,* Chs. 7 and 9.

24. JBE to R. B. Fletcher, Nov. 3, 1933, JBE Papers; "Answers to Questions as Submited by Joseph B. Eastman . . . Nov. 4, 1933, American Trucking Associations, Inc.," J. Howard Pew to JBE, Dec. 1, 1933, Shertz to JBE, Dec. 12, 1933, all in Loomis Files, Tray 2030, folder Fed. Coordinator of Transportation; JBE to Utah California Motor Lines, Jan. 19, 1932, JBE to Fletcher, Feb. 28, 1934, JBE to E. Kent Hubbard, Oct. 7, 1933, all in JBE Papers.

25. JBE to MacDonald, Aug. 2, 1933, JBE to Charles C. Stewart, Jan. 23. 1934, JBE to Charles J. Symington, Mar. 1, 1934, JBE to Kit F. Clardy, Sept. 24, 1933, JBE to Harvey G. Fields, Nov. 10, 1933, JBE to Frank C. Walker, July 24, 1933, all in JBE Papers; JBE to Roy F. Britton, Nov. 16, 1934, ATA Central Files, Tray 1966, folder 13.

26. For examples of conflict between the FCT and the NRA, see "Inconsistent Policies," *TTW,* Sept. 23, 1933, pp. 491–92; JBE to Hugh S. Johnson, June 25, 1934, JBE to L. M. C. Smith, Sept. 22, 1934, JBE Papers.

27. JBE to Henry A. Wallace, Mar. 28, 1934, JBE Papers; Latham, *Politics of Coordination,* 225–28; "Coordinator [sic] Report on Regulation," *TTW,* Mar. 17, 1934, pp. 499, 501–502.

28. "Coordinator [sic] Report on Regulation," 499, 502; Childe to JBE, Apr. 13, 1934, ATA Central Files, Tray 1965, folder 111.6.

29. JBE to Bingaman, Apr. 18, 1934, JBE to Marvin H. McIntyre, May 15, 1934, JBE to William Wolf, Feb. 6, 1935, all in JBE Papers.

30. Memo, H. C. Wilson to Morgan, Aug. 18, 1934, NA, RG 33, Records of Charles S. Morgan, Box 8, Correspondence Re Motor

Carrier Bill; Loomis to Arthur G. McKeever, Dec. 27, 1934, ATA
Central Files, Tray 1988, folder 360.31 N.Y.; Morgan to Robert H.
Dunn, Apr. 30, 1934, JBE to Charles M. Thomas, May 1, 1934,
Morgan to MacDonald, Aug. 25, 1934, Morgan to Keeshin, Oct. 25,
1934, JBE to C. H. Purcell, Nov. 21, 1934, JBE to Loomis, Jan. 28,
1935, all in JBE Papers.

31. See JBE to Keeshin, Nov. 24, 1934, Mar 4 (telegram), May 25, June
10, 1935, all in JBE Papers.

32. JBE to Cotterill, Feb. 5, 1935, "Report of Joseph B. Eastman, FCT,"
[c. Oct. or Nov. 1934], both in JBE Papers; McFarland, *Judicial
Control of the FTC and ICC,* 100–69; Leuchtenburg, *FDR and the
New Deal,* 117.

33. ? to H. A. Hennessy, May 9, 1935, JBE Papers; "Eastman's
Transport Plan," *TTW,* Feb. 2, 1935, pp. 193–203; *Sen. Hearings,
on S 1629,* pp. 50, 44, 44–51, 78, 79.

34. *Sen. Hearings on S 1629,* pp. 80, 82, 83.

35. Ibid., pp. 62–67, 89. Couzens's position has found support among
economists. See Jesse W. Markham, "Market Structure, Business
Conduct, and Innovation," *AER,* 55 (May 1965) 2, pp. 323–32.

36. *Sen. Hearings on S 1629,* pp. 84, 90.

37. Ibid., pp. 104.

38. Ibid., pp. 124–25, 139; JBE to Cotterill, Feb. 5, 1935, JBE Papers.

39. *Sen. Hearings on S 1629,* pp. 241–43, 267–70, 219–24, 265–66,
256–57.

40. Ibid., pp. 238–39.

41. Ibid., pp. 261, 24, 271; JBE to Gilbert Smith, Apr. 7, 1934, JBE
Papers.

42. *Sen. Hearings, on S 1629,* pp. 107, 108. 229. 264.

43. Ibid., pp. 270–71 n. 39.

44. Latham, *Politics of Coordination, passim; Sen. Hearings on S 1629,*
pp. 244, 294.

45. JBE to George Huddleston, Apr. 17, 1935, Memo on Transportation
Legislation (attached to JBE to FDR, Apr. 20, 1935), both in JBE
Papers; Rodgers to Thompson, Apr. 5, 1935, ATA Central Files,
Tray 1979, folder 312.6; Rodgers to John W. Blood, Apr. 18, 1935,
NCA General File, Tray 2016, folder Apr. '35; "Memoirs of Edward
J. Buhner," 268–69, and "Memoirs of Harold S. Shertz," 18, both
Woods Truck Library.

46. Warren H. Wagner, *A Legislative History of the Motor Carrier Act,
1935* (Denton, Md.: Rue, 1935), 98; *Congressional Record,* 74th
Cong. 1st Sess., pp. 5649–70, 5733–37; JBE to Dunn, Apr. 20,
1935, JBE Papers.

47. JBE to Dunn, Apr. 20, 1935, JBE to Rayburn, Apr. 29, 1935, JBE

to FDR, May 27, 1935, all in JBE Papers; "Motor Carrier Legislation," *TTW*, June 29, Apr. 27, May 4, 1935, pp. 1265, 802, 847.

48. Jackson to Walter W. Belson, May 4, 1935, ATA Central Files, Tray 1996, folder 415.48; Rodgers to Harvey C. Freuhauf, May 14, 1935, NCA General File, Tray 2018, folder May 1935; Lawrence to Fred O. Nelson, Jr., May 7, 1935, ATA Central Files, Tray 1979, folder 312.8; Rodgers to Huddleston, May 1, 1935, NCA General File, Tray 2019, folder May 1935; Public Law, No. 255, 74th Cong., Sec. 204 (b), Sec. 202 (a).

49. *House Hearings on HR 5236, HR 6061*, pp. 56, 59, 66–69, 30; JBE to Burton K. Wheeler, Aug. 5, 1935, JBE Papers.

50. "Motor Carrier Legislation," *TTW*, July 20, 1935, p. 110–11. Rodgers to S. J. Drummond, Apr. 9, 1935, Rodgers to Fisher G. Dorsey, Apr. 13, 18, 1935, both in Tray 2018, folder Apr. 1935, Rodgers to William C. Fitzpatrick, May 2, 1935, Tray 2018, folder May 1935, all in NCA General File; "Over the Road Truckers Meet," *TTW*, July 6, 1935, p. 23.

51. JBE to Wheeler, Aug. 5, 1935, JBE Papers; *Congressional Record, 74th Cong., 1st Sess.*, pp. 12279, 12459–60, 12863.

52. "Motor Carrier Legislation," Aug. 17, 1935, p. 291.

53. "Motor Carrier Legislation," *TTW*, July 20, 1935, p. 111; "Transport Legislation," *TTW*, July 15, 1935, p. 1147; Memo, speaker to President, June 6, 1935, OF 173, Transportation, FDR Papers.

54. Fuess, *Eastman* 195–97, 145–55; JBE to FDR, Apr. 20, 1935, JBE Papers.

55. Public Law 255, Sec. 204 (a); *House Hearings on HR 5236, HR 6061*, pp. 423–33; Latham, *Politics of Coordination*, 321 n. 51. For examples of the local squabbles, see the Westbrook Pegler Papers, Box 97, Herbert Hoover Presidential Library, West Branch, Iowa; Sidney Fine, *The Automobile Under the Blue Eagle*.

56. Fuess, *Eastman*, 249; JBE to Marion Caskie, Aug. 8, 1935, JBE Papers.

57. *House Hearings on HR 5236, HR 6061*, pp. 169, Table F, 176; Public Law 255, Sec. 202 (a).

58. Public Law 255, Sec. 204 (a) (1)–(3), 206, 209, 211.

59. Public Law 255, Sec. 205(b). Paul G. Kauper, "Utilization of State Commissioners in the Administration of the Federal Motor Carrier Act," *Mich. LR* 34 (Nov. 1935). Kauper noted that the concept of shared authority was being touted in other public utility industries.

60. "Motor Carrier Bill Passed," *Railway Age,* Aug. 10, 1935, p. 187.

Chapter 8

1. JBE to Aitchison, Mar. 17, 1937, JBE Papers; JBE speech to NARUC in "State Commissioners Meet," *TTW*, Oct. 19, 1935, pp. 644–46.

2. "I.C.C. Reorganization," *TTW*, Oct. 5, 1935, p. 532, "Motor Carrier Regulation," *TTW*, Oct. 12, 1935, p. 595. Since records of the BMC have been destroyed (see "National Archives and Records Service Accession Number History List, WNRC, 10/30/80," in Room 125 at the Washington National Records Center, Suitland, Md.), *The Traffic World*, which kept a close watch on ICC activities in the 1930s, represents a valuable source. 50th Annual Report of the ICC (Washington: GPO, Nov. 1, 1936), 86.

3. "Motor Carrier Regulation," *TTW*, Aug. 17, 1935, 291. For Rogers's influence in the associational activities, see "Truck Rates and Tariffs," *TTW*, Sept. 21, 1935, p. 475; "Truck Rate Developments," *TTW*, June 27, 1936, p. 1243; Alexander Markowitz to JBE, Mar. 7, 1938, JBE Papers.

4. "Selection of Key Men, Bureau of Motor Carriers," Aug. 12, 1935, JBE Papers; "I.C.C. Reorganization," 532; "Motor Carrier Regulation," (Oct. 12, 1935), 595.

5. *50th ICC Report* (1936), 87–94.

6. *51st ICC Report* (1937), 82; JBE to Alexander M. Mahood, Dec. 30, 1937, JBE Papers.

7. "Motor Carrier Regulation," *TTW*, Aug. 31, 1935, pp. 463–65; *49th ICC Report* (1935), 73; *50th ICC Report* (1936), 86–88; *51st ICC Report* (1937), 83–84; *52nd ICC Report*(1938), 93, 100.

8. "Motor Bureau Rulings," *TTW*, Aug. 22, 1936, p. 345, Nov. 14, 1935, p. 964. See Bevis, "Procedure in the ICC," 241–56. For a discussion of advance advice, see Thomas K. McCraw, *Prophets of Regulation* (Cambridge, Mass.: Harvard Univ. Press, 1984), 128–35, 214–15.

9. *51st ICC Report* (1937) 67; Public Law No. 255, Sec. 206(a) and Sec. 209(a).

10. "Truckmen Convene," *TTW*, Oct. 19. 1935, pp. 656–57; "Motor Carrier Tariffs," *TTW*, Jan. 4, 1936, pp. 23–24.

11. "Motor Carrier Applications," *TTW*, Feb. 15, 1936, p. 317; *50th ICC Report* (1936), pp. 70–71.

12. "Substitute Discussion," [c. Jan. 1937], pp. 1–6, JBE Papers.

13. JBE to Div. 5, Sept. 22, 1937, and Jan. 12, 1938, JBE Papers; *Union City Transfer, Common Carrier Applic.*, No. MC 32528 (7235), June 10, 1938; *System Transfer & Storage Co., Common Carrier Applic.*, No. MC 1214 (Su. No. 1) (7203), Mar. 17, 1938; *L. J. Takin, Common Carrier Applic.*, No. MC 22278 (7321), Sept. 9,

1937. While these cases were found in the *Federal Carriers Cases* (Washington: Commerce Clearing House, 1940), I, they may be located easily in any volume of ICC decisions by using the case name, the docket number, or the paragraph number (the numbers within the parentheses).

14. Kauper, "Utilization of State Commissioners," 45; *NARUC Proceedings* (1938), 218.

15. *NARUC Proceedings* (1936), 187, 207–11; *NARUC Proceedings* (1938), 168; *NARUC Proceedings* (1940), 141–42, 155–57, 159; JBE to Milo R. Maltbie, Apr. 21, 1937, JBE to John E. McCullough, May 25, 1938, JBE to Frank Murphy, Dec. 7, 1939, all in JBE Papers; James C. Nelson to *JLPUE* 13 (Feb. 1937), 97–99; Transportation Act of 1940, Public Law No. 785, Sec. 20(d) modifying Sec. 205(b).

16. Phelps, "The Right to Regulate Contract Motor Carriers," 202–203.

17. JBE to Div. 5, June 1, 1937, JBE Papers; *Slagel, Earl W.*, MC 2600, 2 M.C.C. 127 (7087), June 5, 1937; *Application of Arthur C. Barwood for Extension of Operations*, No. MC 72139 (7018), Oct. 26, 1936.

18. JBE to Clyde [Aitchison], Mar. 16, 1937, JBE to Div. 5, May 27, 1937, both JBE Papers.

19. *Scott Bros., Inc., Collection and Delivery Service*, No. MC 2744, (7089.02), June 10, 1937.

20. Ibid. (7089.03).

21. Ibid. (7089.01, .04–.07).

22. Ibid. (7089.08).

23. Ibid.; JBE to Div. 5, Jan. 16, 29, 1937, JBE to Scott, Legal and Enforement Sec., Feb. 25, 1937, all JBE Papers.

24. *Scott Bros., Inc., Collection and Delivery Service*, No. MC 2744 (7180, 7180.13), Feb. 28, 1938.

25. Ibid. (7180.14). For Commissioner Aitchison's view, see Aitchison to JBE, Nov. 24, 1937, Aitchison Papers.

26. The *Scott Bros.* case appears to have altered the U.S. railroads' practice of providing service only from point to point on the line. See "Railroads and Trucks," *TTW*, Sept. 14, 1935, p. 427. Eastman's suggestions for dealing with owner-operators were established in *Dixie Ohio Express Co., Common Carrier Applic.*, 17 M.C.C. 735, explained in *53rd ICC Report* (1939), 106.

27. Attorney General Thurman Arnold echoed the minority on the commission by opposing the change in the Transportation Act of 1940 because he believed it sanctioned monopoly. See Arnold to General Edwin M. Watson, Sept. 5, 1940, OF 173, Box 2, FDR Papers.

28. *In the Matter of Filing of Contracts by Contract Carriers by Motor Vehicle; Ex Parte,* No. MC 9. (7405), Nov. 6, 1939, as modified Feb. 28, 1940.

29. "Contract Carrier Charges," *TTW,* Mar. 13, 1937, p. 561; *Contracts by Contract Carriers* (7405.01, .07, .10, .09).

30. *Contracts by Contract Carriers* (7504.07., .10, .11, .09). See McCraw, *Prophets of Regulation,* Ch. 1; Arthur M. Johnson, "Theodore Roosevelt and the Bureau of Corporations," *MVHR* 45 (1959), 571–73.

31. *Contracts by Contract Carriers* (7405.17, .19, .20); JBE to Div. 5, May 27, 1937, JBE Papers.

32. *Contracts by Contract Carriers,* (7405.18); 1940 Transp. Act, Sec. 23.

33. The assumption that the MCA protected common carriers from the actions of contract carriers had at least one Supreme Court case as a precedent, *Stephenson* v. *Binford,* as Eastman pointed out in JBE to Div. 5, Jan. 16, 1937, p. 4, JBE Papers.

34. "Motor Carrier Regulation" (Aug. 17, 1935); "Truck Rates and Tariffs," 475; "Truck Rates and Developments," 1243; Markowitz to JBE, Mar. 7, 1938, JBE Papers.

35. G. Lloyd Wilson, "Motor Carrier Tariffs and Schedules," *TTW,* Oct. 2, 1937, pp. 744–46; *Central Territory Motor Carrier Rates, Ex Parte,* No. MC 21, Div. 5 (7446) Jan 25, 1940.

36. "Truck Rates and Tariffs"; "State Commissioners Meet," 659; Memoirs of Maurice Tucker, *Woods Truck Library,* 56–57, 93; "Tucker Resigns Chairmanship," *TTW,* Feb. 8, 1936, p. 267

37. "Truck Rates Principles," *TTW,* Oct. 26, 1935, p. 725; Wilson, "Tariffs and Schedules," 744.

38. The following articles appear in *TTW:* "Truck Rate Bureaus," Nov. 2, 1935, pp. 679–70, "Northwest Truck Proposals," Nov. 16, 1935, pp. 859–60, "Motor Truck Regulation," Dec. 14, 1935, p. 1037, "Motor Rate Bureau Conference," Jan. 11, 1936, p. 69, and Jan. 25, 1936, pp. 168–69. Flood conditions across the nation forced the ICC to postpone the filing date to March 31, "Motor Tariff Filing Time," Mar. 28, 1936, p. 590, and "Motor Tariff Organization," p. 591, "Faulty Motor Tariffs," Apr. 18, 1936, p. 735, "Motor Tariff Troubles," May 2, 1936, p. 862, "Truck Tariff Hauling," May 16, 1936, p. 962.

39. Keeshin's business tenacity is reflected in the following *TTW* articles: "Keeshin Rate Policies," July 11, 1936, p. 86, "Keeshin Transcontinental Service," Dec. 21, 1935, p. 1085, "Keeshin-T.W.A. Coordination," Dec. 28, 1935, p. 1123, "Keeshin Corporate Set-up," Aug. 1, 1936, pp. 209–10, "Keeshin Founders Stock Issue," May 8, 1937, pp. 1029–30.

40. The following articles are found in *TTW*: "Uniform Truck Rates," Nov. 21, 1936, p. 1018, "C.F.A. Truck Rates," Jan. 2, 1937, p. 17, "Truck Rate Compromise," Jan. 16, 1937, p. 135, "C.F.A. Truck Rates," Jan. 23, 1937, p. 177, Mar. 6, 1937, p. 1029, July 24, 1937, p. 201, and Oct. 8, 1937, p. 788

41. *Rates over Freight Forwarders, Inc.*, I. & S. No. M-205, *Motor Carrier Rates in Middle Atlantic States, Ex Parte*, No. MC 14, Div.5 (7167), Dec. 30, 1937.

42. *Motor Carrier Rates in Central Territory, Ex Parte*, No. MC 21, Div. 5 (7263), Aug. 3, 1938; *Centr. Terr. Rates* (7446).

43. JBE to Harry D. Snyder, Dec. 18, 1939, JBE Papers, where a report from the Bureau of Traffic, ICC, notes that the ICC did not order the use of uniform bills of lading; G. Lloyd Wilson, "Motor Bills of Lading and Shipping Documents," *TTW*, Oct. 16, 1937, pp. 857–58; "Commercial Trucking Zones," *TTW*, Apr. 17, 1937, p. 837: *52nd ICC Report* (1938), 86–87.

44. "Motor Insurance Hearing," *TTW*, Mar. 14, 1936, pp. 493–94; "Report of Detroit Meeting: The Seventh Meeting of Truck Association Executives of America," Jan. 11–13, 1932, p. 7, Loomis Files, Tray 2049, folder Tr. Assn. Execs. of Am.; J. C. Nelson to Chellis E. Bellew, Jan. 11, 1935, NA, RG 9, NRA, ATA General Correspondence, Tray 2016, folder Jan. 1935B; Nelson to 33 operators, Apr. 18, 1935, ATA Central Files, Tray 2003, folder 800.2; "State Commissioners Meet," 646.

45. G. Lloyd Wilson, "Motor Carrier Liability," *TTW*, Oct. 30, 1937, pp. 975–76; Wilson, "Motor Carrier Insurance and Safety," *TTW*, Nov. 20, 1937, pp. 1165–67; *51st ICC Report* (1937), 73–74; *53rd ICC Report* (1939), 113.

46. "Motor Safety Regulations," *TTW*, July 4, 1936, p. 31.

47. "Motor Safety Regulations," *TTW*, Jan. 9, 1937, p. 78; *51st ICC Report* (1937), 80.

48. "Labor Relations," *TTW*, Dec. 26, 1936, p. 1254.

49. The following articles appear in *TTW*: "Truck Hours of Service," Feb. 13, 1937, pp. 339–40, "Motor Hours of Service," July 17, 1937, pp. 125–26, Aug. 28, 1937, p. 477, Sept. 18, 1937, p. 620, and Oct. 23, 1937, p. 925, "Motor Safety Regulations," Oct. 2, 1937, p. 733.

50. See JBE to William Green, Jan. 7, 1938, JBE Papers.

51. *52nd ICC Report* (1938), 84; *53rd ICC Report* (1939), 117; personal experience of the author as an interstate co-driver June–August, 1981, 1982, and 1984.

52. JBE to Clarence F. Lea, Mar. 15, 1939, JBE to M. C. Claar, Oct. 28, 1940, both in JBE Papers; "Override of State's Curbs on Truck Size Is Voted by Senate," *WSJ*, Feb. 21, 1980; "Trucking Dispute

May Define State Power over Commerce," *WSJ*, Feb. 17, 1981; "Top Court Bars Iowa Legislation on Truck Size," *WSJ*, Mar. 25, 1981.

53. *50th ICC Report* (1936), 8; *51st ICC Report* (1937), 72; *54th ICC Report* (1940), 115; *55th ICC Report* (1941), 104.

54. *50th ICC Report* (1936), 82; *51st ICC Report* (1937), 79; *52nd ICC Report* (1938), 83; *54th ICC Report* (1940), 103.

55. *53rd ICC Report* (1939), 105; *52nd ICC Report* (1938), 88.

56. *50th ICC Report* (1936); 80; *51st ICC Report* (1937), 77; *54th ICC Report* (1940), 110–11, 106; James C. Nelson, Board of Investigation and Research, *Federal Regulatory Restrictions upon Motor and Water Carriers, Senate Documents,* No. 78, 79th Cong., 1st Sess., p. 15. In 1932, there had been 22,000 fleets of trucks with five or more vehicles; in 1941, there existed 24,271 fleets of eight or more vehicles. See *Automobile Facts and Figures* (1941), 23.

57. The following can be found in *TTW*: "Rodgers on Trucking Outlook," Dec. 28, 1940, p. 1596, "Rodgers Warns of Rate Wars," Dec. 7, 1940, 1411, "ATA Convention," Nov. 16, 1940, pp. 125ff, "Highway Transport Unity," Nov. 23, 1940, pp. 1255–56.

58. *55th ICC Report* (1941), 1; Aitchison to L. Ward Bannister, Dec. 30, 1938, Aitchison Papers.

Conclusions

1. Fuess, *Eastman,* 298–344.

2. See Gerald P. Berk, "Approaches to the History of Regulation," in McCraw, *Regulation in Perspective,* 202–20.

3. JBE to Frankfurter, Jan. 30, 1933, JBE Papers.

4. For an incisive analysis of planning in the 1930s, see Otis L. Graham, Jr., *Toward a Planned Society: From Roosevelt to Nixon* (New York: Oxford Univ. Press, 1976), Ch. 1.

5. Louis Galambos, "Technology, Political Economy, and Professionalization: Central Themes of the Organizational Synthesis," *BHR* 57 (Winter 1983), 471–93.

6. McCraw, *Prophets of Regulation,* 305, emphasis in the original.

7. See Kahn, *Economics of Regulation* II, 69 n. 62, and 113 n. 1.

8. Leuchtenburg, *FDR and the New Deal,* 60–61, 156–57, 150–52, 261–63.

9. McCraw, "Regulation in America," 160–80; Paul W. MacAvoy, *The Crisis of the Regulatory Commissions: An Introduction to a Current Issue of Public Policy* (New York: Norton, 1970).

10. For some cautions on the use of theories to explain historical events, see Berk, "Approaches to Regulation," 194–95.

11. See McCraw, "Regulation in America," 160–71; Posner, "Theories of Economic Regulation," 335–42ff; Stigler, "Theory of Economic Regulation," 3–21; Kahn, *Economics of Regulation*, II, 189, 38, 178ff.

12. Aitchison to Bannister, Dec. 30, 1938, Aitchison Papers.

13. The *Bell Journal of Economics and Management Science* is a good source for following the free-market advocates. For one example, see James W. McKie, "Regulation and the Free Market: The Problem of Boundaries," *BellJ* 1 (Spring 1970), 6–26. Most of the Chicago school economists seem to focus solely upon Adam Smith's thoughts and prescriptions in his *An Inquiry into the Nature and Causes of the Wealth of Nations* (1776). What they seem to forget is that the *Wealth* was intended as a sequel to his earlier work, *The Theory of Moral Sentiments* (1759). See E. G. West, *Adam Smith: The Man and His Works* (Indianapolis: Liberty Press, 1976), esp. Ch. 8, where West notes that the "invisible hand" concept is grounded not in economics, but rather in moral theology.

14. McCraw, *Prophets of Regulation*, Ch. 7; Kahn, *Economics of Regulation*, I, 70–75, and Ch. 7, where Kahn analyzes the difficulties and compromises necessary in utilizing marginal costs in rate making. Kahn does not believe that backhaul considerations are important in determining marginal costs.

15. Kahn, *Economics of Regulation*, II, 178–93.

16. James C. Nelson, "Coordination of Transportation by Regulation," *JLPUE* 14 (May 1938), 179, supported the idea of a centralized agency that would coordinate the transport industries to serve the public interest. Only six years later, however, Nelson questioned the advisability of the ICC's tendency to restrict competition in trucking. See Nelson, *Regulatory Restrictions*, iii, 30.

17. Meyer H. Fishbein, "The Trucking Industry and the National Recovery Administration," *Social Forces* 34 (Dec. 1955), 178, quotation from Adam Smith, *Wealth of Nations* (New York: Dutton, 1913), 102.

18. Hawley, "Three Aspects of Hooverian Associationalism," 101–108, and "Hoover and Bituminous Coal," 269.

19. Alan Cawson, "Pluralism, Corporatism, and the Role of the State," *Government and Opposition* 13 (Winter 1978), 178–98; Hawley, "Three Aspects of Hooverian Associationalism," 95 n. 2; Hawley, *The New Deal and Monopoly*, 227, 234, 245–46.

20. Nelson, *Regulatory Restrictions*, iii, 3.

21. Cawson, "Pluralism, Corporatism, and the State," 178–98; "Implications of the Corporate Revolution in Economic Theory," in Adolf A. Berle and Gardiner C. Means, eds., *The Modern Corporation and Private Property* (New York: Harcourt, 1968).

22. For some insights into the issues of deregulation of trucking, see
    Stephen Chapman, "Busting the Trucking Cartel," *New Republic,*
    Sept. 30, 1978, pp. 21, 24–25; "ICC takes a Step Toward
    Eliminating Truckers' Rate Fixing," *WSJ*, Mar. 1, 1979; James J.
    Kilpatrick, "Second Thoughts on Deregulating the Truckers,"
    Houston Chronicle, Mar. 4, 1979.

Bibliography

Notes on the Manuscript Sources

The Joseph B. Eastman Papers, located in the Robert Frost Library, Amherst College, Amherst, Massachusetts, included 169 letterbook volumes consisting of onionskin copies of outgoing correspondence, including private letters, and internal ICC memos, all written by Eastman and his staff. Only a very few incoming letters appear in the over eighty thousand pages. Approximately three volumes pertain to George W. Anderson, the commissioner Eastman replaced in 1919. The material furnished a day-by-day account of Eastman's work and interests from 1919 until his death in 1944. Also available are miscellaneous scrapbooks and materials. The papers are not indexed but are arranged chronologically.

The Clyde B. Aitchison and Charles D. Mahaffie Papers housed at the University of Oregon, Eugene, consist of similar ICC letterbook volumes, but neither is as extensive as the Eastman collection. Numerous numbered pages were missing from the Aitchison volumes, but an index indicates the nature of those missing items. Together with the Henry Carter Adams Letterbooks and the Thomas M. Cooley Papers at the Bentley Historical Library, University of Michigan, Ann Arbor, the ICC Record Group 134 at the National Archives (which covers 1887 to the late 1890s), and the Balthasar H. Meyer Papers at the State Historical Society of Wisconsin, Madison, these three commissioner collections remain the only archival sources for the history of the ICC. The National Archives destroyed most of the correspondence of the first four decades of the twentieth century.

The story of trucking politics could not have been told without the collection of trade association records housed in the National Archives. Presented to the archives by the ATA, the several collections located in

Record Group 9 contain a gold mine of correspondence between industry leaders and between them and government officials from the late 1920s into the summer of 1935. The over fifty-six feet of material, however, is only marginally organized for the historian's convenience.

Research in over thirty files at the Franklin D. Roosevelt Presidential Library, Hyde Park, New York, uncovered duplicates of material found elsewhere and very little else on trucking *per se*. Research in the Commerce and Presidential Papers at the Herbert Clark Hoover Presidential Library, West Branch, Iowa, furnished a few items not found in the National Archives or in the Eastman Papers. The Westbrook Pegler Papers at the Hoover Library contained several files on early union activity in the trucking industry.

The New York Times Oral History Program includes the *Woods Highway Truck Library,* a collection of over twenty interviews with men and women (truck drivers, truck stop operators, executives, and law enforcement officers) involved in the trucking industry during the 1920s and 1930s. The collection, as with all oral histories, must be used carefully. The interviewer, Harry D. Woods, was himself a "gypsy" trucker who was interested in preserving the history of the industry.

The Joe C. Carrington Papers are unavailable to scholars. While working with the Barker Center Archives in Austin, Texas, to obtain the Carrington holdings (which relate to numerous political, business, and philanthropic topics in twentieth century Texas history); I secured from Carrington's secretary several folders of communications pertaining to Carrington's work in truck insurance matters and associational activities. I xeroxed them and returned the originals; meanwhile, Mr. Carrington apparently decided not to present his holdings to the depository.

Manuscript Sources

Adams, Henry Carter, Letterbooks. Bentley Historical Library, University of Michigan, Ann Arbor.

Aitchison, Clyde B., Papers. University of Oregon, Eugene.

Brandeis, Louis Dembitz, Papers. Harvard Law School Library, Boston, Massachusetts.

Brown, LaRue, Papers. Harvard Law School Library, Boston, Massachusetts.

Carrington, Joe C., Papers. Author's Possession.

Cooley, Thomas M., Papers. Bentley Historical Library, University of Michigan, Ann Arbor.

Eastman, Joseph B., Papers. Robert Frost Library, Amherst College, Amherst, Massachusetts.

Hoover, Herbert C., Papers. Herbert Hoover Presidential Library, West Branch, Iowa.

Mahaffie, Charles D., Papers. University of Oregon, Eugene.

Morgenthau, Henry, Jr., Diary. Franklin D. Roosevelt Presidential Library, Hyde Park, New York.

Pegler, Westbrook, Papers. Herbert Hoover Presidential Library, West Branch, Iowa.

Record Group 9, National Recovery Administration, National Archives, Washington, D.C.

> American Highway Freight Association Central Files.
>
> American Trucking Associations, National Code Authority for the Trucking Industry, Central Files.
>
> American Trucking Associations General Correspondence.
>
> Consolidated Approved Industry File.
>
> Division of Review, Approved Code Histories.
>
> Loomis, Edward F., Files maintained by.
>
> National Code Authority for the Trucking Industry General File.
>
> National Code Authority for the Trucking Industry Rate Cases.

Record Group 22, Federal Trade Commission, National Archives, Washington, D.C.

> Minutes, 1920-1933.
>
> Press Clippings, 1919-1933.
>
> Press Notices, 1920-1933.

Record Group 134, Interstate Commerce Commission, National Archives, Washington, D.C.

Roosevelt, Franklin D., Papers. Franklin D. Roosevelt Presidential Library, Hyde Park, New York.

Wilson, Woodrow, Papers. Library of Congress.

Woods Highway Truck Library. New York Times Oral History Program. Glenn Rock, N.J.: Microfilming Corp. of America, 1975.

Published Government Documents

Annual Reports of the ICC. Washington, D.C.: U.S. Government Printing Office.

Congressional Record.

"Coordination of Motor Transportation: A Report by Leo J. Flynn,

Attorney-Examiner to the ICC." *Senate Documents,* No. 43, 72nd
   Cong., 1st Sess., Jan. 1932.
Federal Carrier Cases. Vol. I. Washington, D.C.: Commerce Clearing
   House, 1936–40.
House Hearings on HR 5236 and *HR 6061.* Subcommittee of Committee
   on Interstate and Foreign Commerce, 74th Cong., 1st Sess., 1935.
"Motor Bus and Truck Operation," No. 18300, *Interstate Commerce
   Commission Reports,* 140. Washington, D.C.: U.S. Government Printing
   Office, 1928.
National Association of Railroad and Utility Commissioners *Proceedings.*
   Annual Conventions, 1923–40.
Nelson, James C., Board of Investigation and Research. *Federal Regulatory
   Restrictions upon Motor and Water Carriers. Senate Documents,* No. 78,
   79th Cong., 1st Sess., 1944.
Senate Hearings on S 2793. Committee on Interstate Commerce, 72nd
   Cong., 1st Sess., 1932.
Senate Hearings on S 1629. Committee on Interstate Commerce, 74th
   Cong., 1st Sess., 1935.

Court Cases

Buck v. *Kuykendall,* 267 U.S. 307 (1925).
Bush, George W., and Sons v. *Maloy,* 267 U.S. 317 (1925).
Frost et al. v. *Railroad Commission of State of California,* 271 U.S. 583
   (1926).
Houston, East and West Texas Railway Company v. *United States,* 234
   U.S. 342 (1914).
Michigan Public Utilities Commission et al. v. *Duke,* 266 U.S. 570 (1925).
Munn v. *Illinois,* 94 U.S. 113 (1887).
Nebbia v. *New York,* 291 U.S. 502 (1934).
Sproles et al. v. *Binford,* 286 U.S. 374 (1932).
Stephenson et al. v. *Binford,* 287 U.S. 251 (1932).
Tyson and Brothers—United Theatre Ticket Offices, Inc. v. *Banton,* 273
   U.S. 418 (1927).
Wabash, St. Louis, & Pacific Railroad Company v. *Illinois,* 118 U.S. 557
   (1887).

Dissertations and Theses

Ellis, L. Tuffly. "The Texas Cotton Compress Industry: A History." Ph.D.,
Univ. of Texas, 1964.

Hilles, William C. "The Good Roads Movement in the United States:
1800-1916." M.A., Duke, 1958.

Smykay, Edward Walter. "The National Association of Railroad and Utility
Commissioners as the Originators and Promoters of Public Policy for
Public Utilities." Ph.D., Univ. of Wisconsin, 1955.

Thomas, James Harold. "Trucking: History and Legend." Ph.D., Oklahoma
State Univ., 1976.

Periodicals

Automobile Facts and Figures. New York: Automobile Manufacturers
Association.

New York Times.

Public Roads: A Journal of Highway Research.

Scientific American.

The Traffic World.

Railway Age.

Ward's 1941 Automotive Year Book (Detroit: Ward's Reports, 1941).

Articles

Aitchison, Clyde B. "The Evolution of the Interstate Commerce Act;
1887-1937." *George Washington Univ. LR* 5 (Mar. 1937) 289-403.

Bevis, Howard L. "Procedure in the Interstate Commerce Commission: A
Study in Administrative Law." *Univ. of Cincinnati LR* 1 (May 1927)
241-56.

Bigham, Truman C. "The Transportation Act of 1940." *Southern Economic
Journal* 8 (July 1941) 1–21.

Brown, LaRue, and Stuart N. Scott. "Regulation of the Contract Motor
Carrier Under the Constitution." *HLR* 44 (Feb. 1931) 530-71.

Burnham, John Chynoweth. "The Gasoline Tax and the Automobile
Revolution." *MVHR* 48 (Dec. 1961) 435–55.

Cawson, Alan. "Pluralism, Corporatism, and the Role of the State,"
Government and Opposition 13 (Winter 1978) 178–98.

Craven, Leslie. "Railroads Under Pressure." *The Atlantic* 162 (Dec. 1938)
767–76.

Fishbein, Meyer H. "The Trucking Industry and the National Recovery Administration." *Social Forces* 34 (Dec. 1955) 171–79.

Davis, G. Cullom, "The Transformation of the Federal Trade Commission, 1914–1929," *MVHR* 49 (Dec. 1962) 437ff.

Galambos, Louis P. "The Emerging Organizational Synthesis in Modern American History." *BHR* 44 (Autumn 1970) 279–90.

———. "Technology, Political Economy, and Professionalization: Central Themes of the Organizational Synthesis." *BHR* (Winter 1983) 471–93.

Gavit, Bernard C. "State Highways and Interstate Motor Transportation." *Illinois LR* 21 (Feb. 1927) 559–67.

George, John J. "Public Control of Contract Motor Carriers." *JLPUE* 9 (Aug. 1933) 233–46.

Goldberg, Victor P. "Regulation and Administered Contracts." *BellJ* 7 (Autumn 1976) 426–45.

Hawley, Ellis W. "Herbert Hoover, the Commerce Secretariat, and the Vision of an 'Associative State,' 1921–1928." *JAH* 61 (June 1974) 116–40.

———. "Secretary Hoover and the Bituminous Coal Problem, 1921–1928." *BHR* 42 (Autumn 1968) 253–70.

———. "Three Aspects of Hooverian Associationalism: Lumber, Aviation, and Movies, 1921–1930" In McCraw, ed., *Regulation in Perspective*.

Heath, Milton S. "Motor Transportation in the South." *Southern Economic Journal*. 1 (Aug. 1934) 13–30.

Herbst, Anthony F., and Joseph S. K. Wu, "Some Evidence of Subsidization: The U.S. Trucking Industry, 1900–1920." *Journal of Economic History* 33 (June 1973) 417–33.

Herring, Pendleton E. "Special Interests and the Interstate Commerce Commission, Part I." *American Political Science Review* 27 (Oct. 1933) 758–51.

Kauper, Paul G. "Utilization of State Commissioners in the Administration of the Federal Motor Carrier Act." *Mich. LR* 34 (Nov. 1935) 37–84.

Kelly, H.H. "The Problem of Motor Vehicle Regulation." *Public Roads* 13 (Dec. 1932) 153–68.

Lilienthal, David E., and Irwin S. Rosebaum. "Motor Carriers and the State: A Study in Contemporary Public Utility Legislation." *JLPUE* 2 (July 1926) 257–75.

McAllister, Breck P. "Lord Hale and Business Affected with a Public Interest." *HLR* 43 (March 1930) 759–91.

McCormick, J. Byron. "The Regulation of Motor Transportation." *CLR* 22 (Nov. 1933) 24–47.

McCraw, Thomas K. "Regulation in America: A Review Article." *BHR* 49
    (Summer 1975) 159–83.

McKie, James W. "Regulation and the Free Market: The Problem of
    Boundaries." *BellJ* 1 (Spring 1970) 6–26.

Markham, Jesse W. "Market Structure, Business Conduct, and Innovation."
    AER 55 (May 1965) 323–32.

Nelson, James C. "Coordination of Transportation by Regulation." *JLPUE*
    14 (May 1938) 167–81.

Paxson, Frederic L. "The Highway Movement, 1916–1935." *AHR* 51(Jan.
    1946) 236–53.

Phelps, V. E. "The Right to Regulate Contract Motor Carriers for Hire."
    Public Utilities Fortnightly 10 (Aug. 18, 1932) 202–11.

Posner, Richard A. "Theories of Economic Regulation." *BellJ* 5 (Autumn
    1974) 335–58.

Prizer, John B. "Development of the Regulation of Transportation During
    the Past Seventy-five Years." *I.C.C. Practitioners' Journal* 21 (Dec.
    1953) 190–228.

Scheiber, Harry N. "The Road to *Munn:* Eminent Domain and the Concept
    of Public Purpose in the State Courts." *Perspectives in American History*
    5 (1971) 327–402.

Stecher, Karl. "Proposed Federal Regulation of Interstate Carriers by Motor
    Vehicle." *Minn. LR* 17 (Dec. 1932) 1–16.

Stigler, George. "The Theory of Economic Regulation." *BellJ* 2 (Spring
    1971) 3–21.

Books and Pamphlets

Abraham, Henry J. *Justices and Presidents: A Political History of
    Appointments to the Supreme Court.* New York: Oxford Univ. Press,
    1974.

Barger, Harold. *The Transportation Industries, 1889–1946: A Study of
    Output, Employment, and Productivity.* New York: National Bureau of
    Economic Research, 1951.

Barnard, Harry. *Independent Man: The Life of Senator James Couzens.* New
    York: Scribner's Sons, 1958.

Becker, William H. *The Dynamics of Business-Government Relations:
    Industry and Exports, 1893–1921.* Chicago: Univ. of Chicago Press,
    1982.

Bellush, Bernard. *The Failures of the NRA.* New York: Norton, 1975.

Benson, Lee. *Merchants, Farmers and Railroads: Railroad Regulation and*

New York Politics, 1850–1887. Cambridge, Mass.: Harvard Univ. Press, 1955.

Blaisdell, Thomas C., Jr. *The Federal Trade Commission. An Experiment in the Control of Business*. New York: Columbia Univ. Press, 1932.

Broehl, Wayne G., Jr. *Trucks . . . Trouble . . . Triumph. The Norwalk Truck Line Company*. New York: Prentice-Hall, 1954.

Chandler, Alfred D., Jr., *Giant Enterprise. Ford, General Motors, and the Automobile Industry, Sources and Readings*. New York: Harcourt, Brace, 1964.

————. *Strategy and Structure: Chapters in the History of American Industrial Enterprise*. Cambridge, Mass.: MIT Press, 1966.

————. *The Visible Hand. The Managerial Revolution in American Business* Cambridge, Mass.: Harvard Univ. Press, 1977.

Cochran, Thomas C., and William Miller, *The Age of Enterprise: A Social History of Industrial America*. New York: Harper and Row, 1961.

Conkin, Paul K. *The New Deal*. Arlington Heights, Ill: AHM, 1972.

Crawford, Kenneth G. *The Pressure Boys. The Inside Story of Lobbying in America*. New York: Julian Messner, 1939.

Crumbaker, Calvin. *Transportation and Politics: A Study of Long- and Short-Haul Policies of Congress and the Interstate Commerce Commission*. Eugene: Univ. of Oregon Press, 1949.

Dearing, Charles L. *American Highway Policy*. Washington, D.C.: Brookings Institution, 1941.

Denham, Athel F. *20 Years' Progress in Commercial Motor Vehicles, 1921–1942*. Washington, D.C.: Military Vehicles Division, Automotive Council for War Production, 1942.

Eisenhower, Dwight D. *At Ease: Stories I Tell to Friends*. Garden City, N.Y.: Doubleday, 1967.

Fair, Marvin L., and Ernest W. Williams, Jr. *Economics of Transportation*. Rev. ed. New York: Harper, 1959.

Filgas, James. *Yellow in Motion. A History of Yellow Freight System, Incorporated*. Bloomington: Indiana Univ. School of Bus., Div. of Res., 1971.

Fine, Sidney. *Laissez-Faire and the General Welfare State*. Ann Arbor: Univ. of Mich., 1964.

Frankfurter, Felix. *The Commerce Clause*. Chicago: Quadrangle, 1964.

Fuess, Claude Moore. *Joseph B. Eastman: Servant of the People*. New York: Columbia Univ., 1964.

Galambos, Louis P. *Competition and Cooperation: The Emergence of a*

National Trade Association. Baltimore: Johns Hopkins Univ. Press, 1966.

Goodrich, Carter. *Government Promotion of American Canals and Railroads, 1800–1890.* New York: Columbia Univ. Press, 1960.

Gould, Lewis L. *Reform and Regulation: American Politics, 1900–1916.* New York: Wiley and Sons, 1978.

Harper, Donald V. *Economic Regulation of the Motor Trucking Industry by the States.* Urbana: Univ. of Illinois Press, 1950.

Hawley, Ellis W. *The New Deal and Problem of Monopoly: A Study in Economic Ambivalence.* Princeton: Princeton Univ. Press, 1966.

Hess, John. *The Mobile Society: A History of the Moving and Storage Industry* New York: McGraw-Hill, 1973.

Himmelberg, Robert F. *The Origins of the National Recovery Administration: Business, Government, and the Trade Association Movement, 1921–1933.* New York: Fordham Univ. Press, 1976.

Hoogenboom, Ari, and Olive Hoogenboom. *A History of the ICC: From Panacea to Palliative.* New York: Norton, 1976.

Hutchmacher, J. Joseph, and Warren I. Susman, eds. *Herbert Hoover and the Crisis of American Capitalism.* Cambridge, Mass.: Schenkman, 1973.

Kahn, Alfred E. *The Economics of Regulation: Principles and Institutions.* 2 vols. New York: John Wiley, 1972.

Karolevitz, Robert F. *This Was Trucking: A Pictorial History of the First Quarter Century of Commercial Motor Vehicles.* Seattle: Superior, 1961.

Kerr, Kathel Austin. *American Railroad Politics, 1914–1920.* Pittsburgh: Univ. of Pittsburgh Press, 1965.

Kutler, Stanley I. *The Supreme Court and the Constitution: Readings in American Constitutional History.* Boston: Houghton Mifflin, 1969.

Latham, Earl. *The Politics of Railroad Coordination, 1933–36.* Cambridge, Mass.: Harvard Univ. Press, 1959.

Leuchtenburg, William E. *Franklin Roosevelt and the New Deal, 1932–1940.* New York: Harper and Row, 1963.

———. *The Perils of Prosperity, 1914–1932.* Chicago: Univ. of Chicago Press, 1958.

Lieb, Robert C. *Freight Transportation: A Study of Federal Intermodal Ownership Policy.* (New York: Praeger, 1972).

Livesay, Harold C. *American Made: Men Who Shaped the American Economy.* Boston: Little, Brown, 1979.

Locklin, D. Philip. *Economics of Transportation.* 5th ed. Homewood, Ill.: Richard D. Irwin, 1960.

Lyon, Leverett S., and Victor Abramson. *Government and Economic Life: Development and Current Issues of American Public Policy.* Washington, D.C.: Brookings Institution, 1940.

MacAvoy, Paul W. *The Crisis of the Regulatory Commissions: An Introduction to a Current Issue of Public Policy.* New York: Norton, 1970.

McFarland, Carl. *Judicial Control of the Federal Trade Commission and the Interstate Commerce Commission, 1920–1930: A Comparative Study in the Relations of Courts to Administrative Commissions.* Cambridge, Mass.: Harvard Univ. Press, 1933.

McCraw, Thomas K. *Prophets of Regulation.* Cambridge, Mass.: Harvard Univ. Press, 1984.

———. *TVA and the Power Fight.* New York: Lippincott, 1971.

———. ed. *Regulation in Perspective: Historical Essays.* Cambridge, Mass.: Harvard Univ. Press, 1981.

Martin, Albro. *Enterprise Denied: The Origins of the Decline of American Railroads, 1897–1917.* New York: Columbia Univ. Press, 1971.

Mertins, Herman, Jr. *National Transportation Policy in Transition.* Lexington, Mass.: Heath, 1972.

Meyer, John R., et al. *The Economics of Competition in the Transportation Industries.* Cambridge, Mass.: Harvard Univ. Press, 1959.

Miller, George H. *Railroads and the Granger Laws.* Madison: Univ. of Wisconsin Press, 1971.

Montville, John B. *Mack.* Newfoundland, N.J.: Haessner, 1973.

Moore, Thomas Gale. *Freight Transportation Regulation: Surface Freight and the ICC.* Washington, D.C.: American Enterprise Institute for Policy Research, 1972.

Moulton, Harold G. *The American Transportation Problem.* Washington, D.C.: Brookings Institution, 1933.

Murphy, Paul L. *The Constitution in Crisis Times, 1918–1969.* New York.: Harper, 1972.

Nelli, Humbert S. *The Business of Crime: Italians and Syndicate Crime in the United States.* New York: Oxford Univ. Press, 1976.

Norton, Strong Vincent. *The Motor Truck as an Aid to Business Profits.* Chicago: A. W. Shaw, 1918.

Parrish, Michael E. *Securities Regulation and the New Deal.* New Haven: Yale Univ. Press, 1970.

Paschal, Joel Francis. *Mr. Justice Sutherland: A Man Against the State.* Princeton: Princeton Univ. Press, 1952.

Pershing, John J. *My Experiences in the World War*. 2 vols. New York: Frederick A. Stokes, 1931.

Porter, Glenn. *The Rise of Big Business, 1860–1910*. New York: Thomas Crowell, 1973.

Pusey, Merlo J. *Charles Evans Hughes*. Vol. II New York: Macmillan, 1952.

Rae, John B. *The American Automobile: A Brief History*. Chicago: Univ. of Chicago Press, 1965.

Redford, Emmette S., and Charles B. Hagan. *American Government and the Economy*. New York: Macmillan, 1965.

Rice, Gini. *Relics of the Road*. No. 2. *Keen Kenworth Trucks, 1915–1955*. New York: Hastings, 1973.

———. *Relics of the Road*. No. 3. *Impressive International Trucks, 1907–1947*. Lake Oswego, Ore.: Truck Tracks, 1975.

Ritchie, Donald A. *James M. Landis: Dean of the Regulators*. Cambridge, Mass.: Harvard Univ. Press, 1980.

Rose, Mark H. *Interstate: Highway Politics 1941–1956*. Lawrence: Regents Press of Kansas, 1979.

Sandberg, Lars J. *Truck Selling, Simultaneous Selling, and Delivery in Wholesale Food Distribution*. Division of Research, Business Research Studies, No. 7. Harvard Univ. Graduate School of Business Administration, 1934.

Schwartz, Jordan A. *The Interregnum of Despair: Hoover, Congress, and the Depression*. Urbana: Univ. of Chicago Press, 1970.

Shannon, David A. *Between the Wars: America, 1919–41*. 2nd ed. Boston: Houghton Mifflin, 1979.

Sharfman, I. L. *The Interstate Commerce Commission: A Study in Administrative Law and Procedure*. 4 pts. New York: Commonwealth Fund, 1937.

Stone, Alan. *Economic Regulation and the Public Interest: The Federal Trade Commission in Theory and Practice*. Ithaca, N.Y.: Cornell Univ. Press, 1977.

———. *Regulation and Its Alternatives*. Washington, D.C.: Congressional Quarterly, 1982.

Swindler, William F. *Court and Constitution in the 20th Century: The Old Legality, 1889–1932*. New York: Bobbs-Merrill, 1969.

Taff, Charles A. *Commercial Motor Transportation*. Homewood, Ill.: Richard D. Irwin, 1955.

Taylor, George Rogers. *The Transportation Revolution, 1815–1860*. Vol.

IV: *Economic History of the United States*. New York: Holt, Rinehart, and Winston, 1951.

Turnbull, Gerald L. *Traffic and Transport: An Economic History of Pickfords*. Boston: George Allen and Urwin, 1979.

Wagner, Warren H. *A Legislative History of the Motor Carrier Act, 1935*. Denton, Md.: Rue, 1935.

Watson, Donald S. *Economic Policy: Business and Government*. Boston: Houghton Mifflin, 1967.

Wiebe, Robert H. *Businessmen and Reform: A Study of the Progressive Movement*. Chicago: Quadrangle, 1962.

————. *The Search for Order, 1877–1920*. New York: Hill and Wang, 1967.

Williams, Ernest W., Jr. *The Regulation of Rail-Motor Rate Competition*. New York: Harper, 1958.

Wilson, G. Lloyd. *Motor Freight Transportation and Regulation*. Chicago: The Traffic World, 1937.

Index

Trucking and the Public Interest has been composed on a Mergenthaler Linotron 202 digital phototypesetter in ten point Times Roman with two-point line spacing. The book was designed by Cameron Poulter, composed into type by Typecraft Company, printed offset by Thomson-Shore, Inc., and bound by John H. Dekker & Sons. The paper on which the book is printed carries acid-free characteristics formulated for an effective life of at least three hundred years.

THE UNIVERSITY OF TENNESSEE PRESS : KNOXVILLE